©Copyright 2003 Richard F. Hogue
First Edition published by Richlyn Publishing
May 2003

Editing - Sheri A. VandeRiet
Writing Consultant - Dr. Gerald Grunska
Cover design - Ron Densmer, George Ferguson, Inc., Denver, CO
Copy layout - Benjamin Hogue

Hogue, Richard F.
  We were the third herd : "I left a peaceful small town in Iowa to face firefights and booby traps in Vietnam." / by Richard F. Hogue.
  p. cm.
  Includes bibliographical references and index.
  LCCN: 2002096512
  ISBN 0-9722264-0-0

1. Vietnamese Conflict, 1961-1975—personal narratives, American. 2. Hogue, Richard F. I. Title.

DS559.5H64 2003   959.704'3'092
                         QBI33-1291

Printed in the United States of America

We Were The Third Herd

"I left a peaceful small town in Iowa
to face firefights and booby traps in Vietnam."

By

Richard F. Hogue

Table of Contents

Dedication and Tribute

**Hold your head high when Old Glory you see,
and remember those who fought so we could be free.**

We Were The Third Herd is dedicated to every American who honorably served in the military during the Vietnam conflict, with sincere gratitude to those who were wounded in action and in respectful honor of those who died as a result of service in Vietnam.

Most specifically this book is my tribute to fourteen comrades who served with me in Vietnam and were killed in action. "Men, I know you're in heaven, because you served your time in hell, Vietnam. I am proud to have briefly known you and to have served with you in Vietnam. I will never forget you. Although your family has endured the sorrow of your loss for many years, they should be proud of your honorable and brave service to your country."

In memory of all who have given their lives in defense of the freedom we enjoy, I ask that you honor and respect them for their courageous sacrifice, speak respectfully on their behalf and remember their families in your prayers.

*Let every nation know, whether
it wishes us well or ill, that we
shall pay any price, bear any
burden, meet any hardship,
support any friend, and oppose
any foe to assure the survival
and the success of liberty.*

John Fitzgerald Kennedy

77% of the military personnel killed in Vietnam held the enlisted rank of Sergeant E-5 or below.

Introduction

Although Vietnam was our longest war, a declaration of war was never invoked. Even though we won nearly every significant battle, many Americans believe we lost the war – a first in our history. We battled with sophisticated weaponry, while the enemy used simple weapons like punji pits and booby traps and often fought from camouflaged spider holes and tunnels. Over 58,000 American lives were lost in Vietnam.

The Vietnam War was unique because it lacked the full support of American citizens. There were anti-war demonstrations across the country, the most notable of which was at Kent State University where four students were killed by National Guard troops on May 4, 1970. Although the last American ground combat forces left South Vietnam in 1972, debate continues regarding our involvement, and controversy remains over the full accounting of American prisoners of war and those missing in action.

While historians debate which American war had the greatest impact upon our country, the war in Vietnam obviously had the greatest impact upon my life. *We Were The Third Herd* describes my transition from a peaceful life in a small Iowa town to fighting as an infantryman in Vietnam. I describe my feelings about being drafted into the Army and you will learn how my family and friends were affected when I marched off to war.

Our lives back in the "world" and even our intense infantry training did not prepare us for the experience of walking with a friend one minute and watching him die the next, or losing half our platoon in a matter of minutes. Although the experience of each infantryman who served in Vietnam was different, we share one common sentiment. It changed our lives forever. We saw comrades maimed by booby traps and shed tears for friends who died in our arms. You will meet the men with whom I proudly served and read of the dramatic events I experienced during my tour of duty in Vietnam. We all lost our innocence and many will carry the physical and emotional scars of their combat experience to their graves.

It was emotionally difficult to relive my experiences in Vietnam. I sat at my computer on several occasions with tears in my eyes while I recounted the fond memories of friends who were killed over thirty-three years ago. I thank God for my survival and want to share my story. Every American should know what was asked of young men thrown into combat in Vietnam. *We Were The Third Herd* details the emotional impact of those of us who faced combat in America's most controversial war.

Although I detail some tragic events, this book is not intended to renew painful memories for anyone. Rather, I hope you will feel the sense of pride I have attempted to instill as my tribute to those men and women who honorably served their country during the Vietnam conflict.

The events in *We Were The Third Herd* are described as accurately as possible based upon the recollections of myself and my family, friends and comrades. A few names have been changed to avoid a negative depiction of anyone, and in a few cases, the actual names have simply long been forgotten.

"... to care for him who shall have borne the battle and for his widow and his orphan."

Abraham Lincoln

Acknowledgements

I have many individuals to thank for their valuable assistance provided to enable me to write *We Were The Third Herd*. Several of my fellow comrades helped to recall names, places and events enabling me to accurately piece together our experience in Vietnam. Family members and friends helped me remember many details that surrounded my two years in the Army, and fellow writing associates provided expert advice and contributed time to review my writing and make recommendations. I thank you all for your contributions and assistance, and especially for your friendship.

To my wife Marilyn, thank you for your loving support and allowing me to spend endless hours writing and editing while I ignored you and many other tasks at home.

Without the valuable assistance, encouragement and support from many, *We Were The Third Herd* would not have become a reality.

I am proud of my service in Vietnam and am proud to be the author of *We Were The Third Herd*.

The first American casualties in Vietnam were suffered long before our significant involvement there. Lieutenant Colonel A. Peter Dewey was killed in an ambush in Saigon on September 26, 1945. Two civilian pilots, James McGovern and Wallace Buford were killed, on May 6, 1954, when their plane was struck by enemy fire and crashed, while delivering an artillery piece to a besieged French garrison during the French Indochina War.

Glossary

AFB - Air Force Base.

APC - Armored Personnel Carrier - heavy track-driven vehicle used to transport troops in the battlefield.

AIT - Advanced Infantry Training - nine weeks of training to become an infantryman.

AK (last chapter) - Above the Knee - an amputation above the knee.

AK-47 or **AK** - Russian made rifle used by enemy troops in Vietnam.

ARVN - Army of the Republic of South Vietnam - supported the South Vietnamese cause and supported American troops.

AWOL - Absent Without Leave.

BK - Below the Knee - an amputation below the knee.

CIB - Combat Infantryman Badge

CO - Commanding Officer.

CP - Command Post - The location where the company commander and his staff were located.

CP Group - Men assigned to the company commander or a general referral to the company commander and his staff.

C-4 - White plastic clay-like explosive.

Dustoff - Nickname for medical evacuation helicopter.

E-1, E-2, etc. - The pay grade for enlisted military personnel - E1 is the pay grade for a private, E-5 is the pay grade for a sergeant

FNG - Fucking New Guy - slang term meaning a person who recently arrived in Vietnam.

GI - Government Issue - slang term for military personnel or relating to the military (GI haircut).

Gook - Derogatory slang for Asian - normally used when referring to enemy troops in Vietnam.

H & I - Harassment and Interdiction mortar or artillery fire.

Hard Spot - A short-term defensive position normally consisting of a perimeter of foxholes (no bunkers or other fortifications).

Huey - UH-1 transport and medical evacuation helicopter.

KIA - Killed in Action.

Glossary

Klick - A kilometer - one klick = 1,000 meters or .6 miles.

LAW - Light Anti-Tank Weapon.

LZ - Landing Zone - area designated to land helicopters.

M-16 - American rifle primarily used in Vietnam.

M-60 - American machine gun primarily used in Vietnam.

M-79 - American grenade launcher used in Vietnam.

Medevac - Abbreviated term for Medical Evacuation Helicopter.

MM - Millimeter - referring to size of artillery or mortar rounds.

MOS - Military Occupational Specialty - 11B was Light Weapons Infantryman.

MPC - Military Payment Currency - paper money used in lieu of American dollars.

NCO - Non-commissioned Officer (sergeant, staff sergeant, etc.).

NVA - North Vietnamese Army - enemy troops.

OCS - Officer Candidate School - six month training to become a military officer.

OD - Olive Drab (green) - the color of Army fatigues and most Army vehicles.

OJT - On-the-Job-Training.

PFC - Private First Class - pay grade E-3

PX - Post Exchange - similar to a super department store.

PT - Physical Training (last chapter physical therapy).

RIF - Recognizance in Force - military term meaning a patrol.

RPG - Rocket-Propelled Grenade - enemy B-40 rocket.

R & R - Rest and Relaxation.

RTO - Radio-Telephone Operator - the man who carried the radio and handled radio communications.

VC - Viet Cong - slang for Vietnamese Communist - enemy troops.

3-6 - Radio call sign for the third platoon leader - often became his nickname.

12th Evac - 12th Evacuation Hospital in Cu Chi.

We Were The Third Herd

Chapter 1

The Peaceful Times

Sweat streaked down the side of my face on a stifling afternoon in the remote countryside of South Vietnam. I walked near the middle of a column as the 25 members of my infantry platoon quietly moved through waist high grass, dense brush and lush green hedgerows. The thirty-pound load of ammunition and other gear I carried seemed to weigh a ton. We had been out on a patrol since 8:00 a.m. that morning. There was no breeze and we were all hot and tired.

Suddenly, a loud BOOM erupted in front of me!

One man flew in the air from the force of the initial explosion as the deafening sound of additional explosions and enemy rifle and machine gun fire sent the rest of us diving for cover. I grabbed my rifle with both hands while I tried to determine where the enemy fire was coming from.

We began spraying the area around us with rifle fire, and then BOOM, BOOM. Two enemy hand grenades exploded behind me with a thunderous sound that sent several of us scrambling and left a buddy screaming in pain, blood gushing from his lower left leg that was partially blown into shreds.

He frantically yelled, "Oh God, Doc, help me!"

"Medic!" I yelled, "Doc, get over here!"

I could tell by the looks on their faces, that everyone was scared as hell. And so was I. We were receiving heavy enemy fire and suffering serious casualties. Every man struggled to find cover, wishing he could miraculously dig a hole to seek protection from the barrage of enemy fire while trying to return as much firepower as he could.

"What the hell's going on?" someone yelled.

"We walked into an ambush. Throw some hand grenades into that hedgerow!" I shouted as I pointed to the long eight-foot high hedgerow in front of us.

"Lay down some fire!" I yelled to our machine gun team who began firing hundreds of deadly rounds through the smoking barrel.

I rose above a small mound of dirt that was the only protection I could find, as I fired my M-16 on automatic, quickly emptying the rounds in my ammo magazine into the hedgerow. I couldn't see the enemy troops, but I saw the smoke and flashes from their weapons when they fired from their concealed positions. After I grabbed a hand grenade from my pistol belt, I rose to my knees and threw it with all my might at the hedgerow over 100 feet in front of me. The sound of the nearly constant rifle and machine gun fire and the exploding hand grenades was deafening. Men were yelling, but I couldn't understand most of what they were saying. I knew we were in trouble. We had been hit hard and the enemy was putting up one hell of a fight.

The man next to me rose to his knees to return fire and was immediately struck in the chest by a volley of enemy machine gun fire. His rifle fell from his hands as he collapsed to the ground.

I yelled, "Doc, I need you!"

I watched the man's green fatigue shirt turn red, soaked with blood from gaping wounds in his chest. Doc crawled up and frantically tried to stop the gushing blood by applying a large field dressing. A moment later I stood on my knees to open fire at the hedgerow, and then I felt my own body jump. Everything went dark.

I opened my eyes and saw a dim shadow of light across my bedroom walls. I felt my heart pounding and realized I had awakened from a frightening dream. I was in the Army fighting for my life in Vietnam. I had never had a dream like that before. I rolled on my side and slowly went back to sleep.

I woke up the next morning and walked through the cold morning air from my apartment to my first class of the day on campus three blocks away. It was January 1968. I had begun the final semester of my senior year at Wayne State College, a small college in Wayne, Nebraska. While most guys in college had student deferments exempting us from the draft, we knew that upon graduation the deferments would end. With the war in Vietnam going strong, being drafted was becoming a likely proposition for many of us.

During my four years of college, the Vietnam conflict had escalated to the point where American casualties were approaching over two hundred weekly. Several guys from my hometown had been drafted or joined the service and had survived a tour in Vietnam or were over there at the time. Realizing that guys I had known all my life were being drafted and likely going to Vietnam brought the war a little closer.

A group of us who lived in Sac County, Iowa, received notices in early March 1968 for military physicals. If a man passed, he remained eligible to be drafted. If he didn't pass, he received a 4-F medical deferment exempting him from the draft. Because the physicals were scheduled mid-week, I rode home the night before with twin brothers Dean and Dennis Christiansen. The three of us had grown up in Schaller, a small farming community in northwest Iowa. We had graduated from high school together and were attending college together. We got up early the next morning to catch a bus at Sac City, the county seat, for a two-hour ride to Omaha, Nebraska. When we arrived at the Induction Center in Omaha, we saw our first glimpse of the military style of business.

A sergeant yelled, "All right you guys, get off the bus and get in line – now," as he pointed toward the Induction Center entrance. Many of us looked at each other with puzzled expressions on our faces as we were herded along like farm animals not knowing what to expect next. Once inside, the sergeant barked out directions for us to follow a colored line on the floor that led into a small room.

The physical started with each of us filling a little cup with urine and then continued by us moving through a series of stations to check our physical well being. The physical ended with a large group of guys standing in a line wearing only underwear. As a doctor moved down the line to check for hernias, each man dropped his drawers and coughed while the doctor completed his examination.

Most of us didn't take that day too seriously. The majority of the guys I knew planned to wait it out and take their chances with the draft. Being drafted into the Army meant we only had a two-year tour but it also meant we didn't have our choice of duty assignment. With the Army providing the majority of the infantrymen in Vietnam, we could end up there serving as infantrymen.

During a trip home a couple weeks after we had taken our military physicals, Dean Christiansen and I stopped at the Air Force Reserve Headquarters in Sioux City hoping to join the reserves. If we were in the reserves we wouldn't be drafted; however, reservists still had to worry about their unit being called to active duty and sent to Vietnam. We walked into the headquarters building and told a sergeant we wanted to join the reserves. He smiled and said we could sign up if we wanted, but the waiting list for that unit had several thousand names on it. It would take years to work through that many people. We didn't bother signing our names.

Although the war in Vietnam was on the opposite side of the world, it began to impact me when I started interviewing for jobs prior to graduation. Each year, company recruiters conducted interviews on campus with students anticipating graduation.

One of the first questions the recruiter asked during my first interview was, "What is your draft status?"

I said, "It's 2-S" (student deferment).

The recruiters knew that within a couple months of graduation most of us would lose our student deferment and be drafted. After the recruiter learned my draft status, he politely proceeded through a brief interview and then told me he would hold my résumé and contact me if they had a job opportunity. What he really meant was they didn't want to hire potential draftees. It may not have been fair but that's the way it was. After getting the identical reaction during a second interview and hearing other guys tell the same story, I gave up trying to find a decent job and didn't schedule any more interviews. Some of the guys who planned to be teachers were getting job offers, but even if a man got a teaching job, he was still subject to the draft.

I could have avoided the draft by enlisting in the service but didn't seriously consider that option. Enlisting in the Army required a three-year tour, and the Navy and Air Force required a four-year enlistment. I finally decided I would go back home after graduation, find a job around town and wait to be drafted. It was a disappointing way to end four years of college.

My only consolation was that I wasn't alone. Most every other male who hadn't been in the service or didn't have a physical deferment was facing the same situation. In fact, during the last few weeks of my final college semester, one of my professors came to class and said his Air Force Reserve unit had been called to active duty and was going to Vietnam in two weeks. Ironically, it was the same reserve unit that Dean and I had tried to join.

During the first week of April I took final exams and passed them all. Me, the guy who my high school principal had told my mother was "too fat and too lazy," was going to graduate from college. After everyone learned they had passed their finals, the gang gathered at Little Bill's bar in downtown Wayne to celebrate. After four long years of attending classes, writing term papers and taking exams, it was finally over. Several of us would receive our bachelor's degree the next afternoon.

The following morning I welcomed my parents and two sisters who arrived just before noon for the graduation ceremony, which was held outdoors on campus. It was a pleasant day with bright sunshine and a gentle warm breeze swaying the trees. When my name was read on the afternoon of April 10, 1968, I joyfully walked forward and accepted my college diploma.

The next morning I drove east toward Iowa and arrived home early that afternoon. I talked with my mom for awhile regarding my very uncertain future and then unpacked my car and took my clothes and other belongings upstairs to my room. I laid on my bed and thought about how I had gotten to that point in my life.

I had lived my entire life in Schaller, with my parents Charles and Jean Hogue and two sisters, Marilyn, four years older, and Jan, two years younger. My mother was born on her parent's farm a few miles southwest of town and had spent her entire life in or around Schaller. Mom worked part time at the school cafeteria and gave piano lessons to kids at home. My dad was born and raised in southern Iowa and had moved to Schaller in the late 1930s. He had worked on my granddad's farm, and in 1940 he and Mom were married. My dad later began working for the P. A. G. Seed Corn Company located two miles north of town and had worked there ever since.

Schaller was a small farming community of 850 much like the other little towns that dotted the Midwest. The entire town covered less than a square mile and was surrounded with rich, rolling farmland owned by local farmers. The downtown business district was two blocks long and two blocks wide.

The major industry was the Central and American Popcorn Companies, who processed and distributed "Bango" and "Jolly Time" popcorn worldwide. Schaller had identified itself as the "Popcorn Capital of the World" and held an annual "Pop Corn Days" weekend celebration each July.

Dr. Velma Boston, the only doctor in town, operated a clinic to care for most of the ills and pains of the local citizens. Like most small towns, Schaller didn't have a full-time police department but we had a town marshal who kept watch over the peaceful town at night. Most people rarely locked the doors to their homes and many left their vehicles unlocked and the keys in the ignition.

A big park in the center of town had playground equipment for the kids and a shelter house to use for gatherings. There were four churches in town and two "country" churches near Schaller. Additionally, there was a Veterans of Foreign Wars (VFW) and American Legion Post and several other clubs and organizations that kept people involved in the community.

Although Schaller was a very small town, it had been a great place to grow up. As youngsters, my friends and I spent the summers playing baseball, riding bikes, going on Boy Scout camping trips and, now and then, getting into a little trouble. As teenagers, we enjoyed hunting rabbits, squirrels or pheasants in farmer's groves or fields. Little did I know, during those hunting excursions, that some of us would someday be carrying rifles through the rice paddies and jungles of South Vietnam.

High school sporting events and other school activities dominated the social life for many people around Schaller. Growing up it seemed like I would live with my parents and go to school forever. But when high school graduation day arrived on May 27, 1964, I knew I would finally be moving on.

I worked with my dad at the P. A. G. Seed Corn Company during the summer of 1964. I arrived home one evening during the first week of August and found Mom in the kitchen fixing supper and Dad in the living room reading the Des Moines Register while Walter Cronkite was broadcasting the evening news. Cronkite said the North Vietnamese had attacked U.S. Navy ships earlier that week and Congress had passed a Gulf of Tonkin Resolution giving President Johnson the power to take further action against North Vietnam, including the use of armed forces.

Mom said, "It sounds like they're getting us into another war – hey, supper is ready, you guys."

"Oh, I don't think North Vietnam wants to take us on. They'll back off," I said as Dad and I sat down at the kitchen table. Our conversation soon turned to our day's activities.

In September 1964 I started college at Ellsworth Junior College in

Iowa Falls, Iowa. I finally got off my lazy butt and maintained a respectable grade point average for the first time in my life. I even made the honor roll one semester. Mrs. Briggs, my high school principal, probably fell off her chair when she saw me listed on the Ellsworth Honor Roll in the Schaller Herald, our weekly hometown paper. After our sophomore year at Ellsworth, Dean and Dennis Christiansen and I transferred to Wayne State and had attended college there for the past two years.

Dennis and I had both graduated the previous day with the spring class of 1968, but Dean had to complete one more semester to graduate. Although I was proud about graduating from college, I didn't have a job and I had no idea what the Army had in store for me. For the first time in my life, my future was totally uncertain.

A few days later, I found a job with Roy Zofka who had a small construction business in Schaller. Transitioning from my relatively soft college life to performing hard physical labor was a shock to my body. The worst job was shingling. Working on an asphalt shingled roof on a hot and humid Iowa summer afternoon was miserable. Carrying a bundle of shingles up a ladder to the roof of a two-story house was worth a lot more than the $2 an hour I was paid.

Another good friend, Allen Schwab, came home from college at the end of May. Allen and I had grown up together and were high school classmates. He was attending the University of Northern Iowa and had one more semester to complete before graduating. He worked as a lifeguard at the "Pit," a former gravel pit four miles east of town that had been converted into a swimming area.

One morning during the first week of June, Allen and I drove to the Selective Service Office in Sac City. We gave the lady in the office our names and asked about our options regarding the draft. She had been notified I graduated from college and my draft status had been changed to 1-A, which meant I was eligible to be drafted. Although Allen could have gone back to college that fall to finish his final semester he decided to get the service behind him. We both volunteered for the draft. We would likely receive our draft notices in July. As Allen and I drove back to Schaller, I began preparing myself to accept the possibility of going to Vietnam.

The weekend after I volunteered for the draft I went to Sioux City for Dick Thompsen's wedding. Dick was another of my Wayne State friends. His bride Sheila had been the Homecoming Queen during our senior year. A bachelor party started early Friday evening with most of the Wayne State gang there. College buddy, Verle Hennings arrived a few minutes after I did.

As we shook hands I told Verle I had volunteered for the draft the past week.

He said, "That's nothing. I've been drafted. I'm leaving next week."

It was great being with my college buddies again but it was also sad knowing Uncle Sam was starting to break us up.

During the first week of July, I was home eating lunch when my mother handed me a letter. It was from the draft board. She didn't say anything, but we both knew what it was. Although that letter was probably the most important letter I had ever received, I laid it on the table while I finished my lunch. I finally opened it to see when I had to report. "August 6, 1968." I was to report to Sac City at 8:00 a.m. and board a bus that would take me to the Induction Center in Omaha. It was finally official. I had been drafted. Allen Schwab also received his draft notice that day. We would be joining the Army in one month but had no idea what would happen after that. We drank a few beers that night knowing our fate had been sealed for the next two years.

That spring I had met Jan Griffin, who was two years younger than me and was mid-way through nursing school in Omaha. I called Jan to tell her I had been drafted and invited her to come to Schaller for Pop Corn Days the third weekend of July. She said, "Yes." I always had enjoyed Pop Corn Days, and with Jan joining me, I looked forward to an especially enjoyable weekend. Each year the Chamber of Commerce sponsored the celebration with activities including a parade, carnival rides and special festivities. For many small midwestern towns, those summer celebrations were one of the highlights of the year.

It was soon the third week of July, the week of the Pop Corn Days celebration. Local businesses, churches and civic groups were making floats for the Saturday morning parade. The firemen hosed down Main Street to clean off the dirt and debris and many people were busy preparing for the weekend's activities. The streets of Schaller were relatively quiet most evenings but that week the town was full of cars driving around while people ran errands in preparation for the big celebration. By Friday afternoon, two blocks of Main Street were completely full of concession stands and carnival rides waiting for the crowds to arrive.

Dean and Dennis Christiansen's older sister Marlys and her husband Kenny Kroese lived in Schaller and were having a Pop Corn Day party starting Friday night. My job was to pick up a keg of beer at Abe's Place, the local bar and pool hall, and set it up at their house Friday afternoon. I also had to drive to Carroll, Iowa, thirty miles south of Schaller, to pick up Jan Griffin who was arriving on a bus from Omaha at six o'clock that evening. I picked up the keg at four o'clock and then I drove to Marlys and Kenny's house. No one was there to help, but I somehow managed to get the keg out of the car myself and move it to the back room of their house. As a favor to Kenny, I decided to tap the keg.

I thought I had the tap firmly connected but when I broke the seal on the keg, beer sprayed everywhere. Beer dripped from my arms and my face as I tried to tighten the tap. It seemed to be a losing battle. I gave the tap one more hard turn, cussing to myself. The beer stopped flowing, but it was way too late. Beer was dripping from the ceiling, running down the walls and pooling all over the floor. Marlys was going to kill me for messing up her house before the party even started. I found some rags and a mop and cleaned up the mess as best I could. I didn't stay around until Marlys came home because I had to get cleaned up and head to Carroll to pick up Jan.

After Jan and I greeted with a hug and kiss, I threw her suitcase in the back seat and we headed back to Schaller. I had only seen Jan during a few trips to Omaha that spring and summer, and I looked forward to sharing the weekend with her.

After we arrived back in Schaller, Jan and I walked downtown and found my parents watching the Kiddies Parade where youngsters rode on floats, walked pets or wore costumes in a two-block-long parade. I introduced Jan to Mom and Dad and spent a few minutes talking before we moved on to stroll through the midway of rides and concessions. Jan and I enjoyed a couple of rides and then stopped by the VFW Hall.

The Schaller VFW Post operated a hall and served great steak dinners on Saturday evenings. The place was packed when we walked inside. I introduced Jan to several friends who soon commenced telling Jan exaggerated stories about me. We all had a good laugh about the friendly ribbing the guys were giving me. Like me, some of those guys were facing the draft and trying to make the best of that year's celebration.

Jan and I then moved on to Marlys and Kenny's house where I would surely catch hell for the beer keg incident. Their house was full of people when we arrived and many others were in the back yard. We immediately ran into Marlys.

She didn't even say, "Hi." "What the heck happened with the keg?"

"Well," I said, "There was a little problem with the tap."

"It looked like it." Marlys said.

"Oh, Marlys," I said, "This is Jan Griffin," as I tried to change the subject.

I knew the mess I made probably miffed Marlys, but she was a great lady and tried to take the accident in stride. I was still glad I wasn't there to see her first reaction. Jan and I finally made it to the back yard and saw Dean and Dennis Christiansen and my future fellow draftee Allen and his girlfriend Vicki. I gave Vicki a hug and introduced Jan.

Jan and I helped ourselves to a cold beer from the keg that was flowing perfectly. People were hanging out, playing yard darts, talking and generally enjoying themselves during an evening that was pretty mild by Iowa summer standards. Jan and I left the party after midnight and walked to my folks' house. We kissed goodnight in the hallway. Jan was sharing my sister's room and I went to my room and hit the sack.

Saturday was the big day of the celebration starting with a parade at ten o'clock. Mom yelled, "Hey, you guys, better get up." Both Jans and I got up and enjoyed a glass of milk and freshly made cinnamon rolls before the parade. My mother was famous around town for her cinnamon rolls. When I was a kid, if friends would come by when she had a batch of rolls cooling on the back porch we stopped whatever we were doing to eat a fresh cinnamon roll.

Jan and I walked with my folks a couple blocks and found a shady spot to sit along the parade route amongst the crowd who were sitting on blankets or lawn chairs. The VFW Color Guard called the Hup-Tu Squad led the parade carrying rifles and the American flag. I stood up while the flag passed and a little shiver tingled down my spine as I watched the American flag flow in the breeze. The parade continued for an hour with floats, antique cars and farm equipment, clowns, horses and fire engines.

After spending a relaxing afternoon at home with Mom and Dad we all headed out for the evening. My folks planned to take their lawn chairs downtown to sit and watch the action along the carnival midway and talk with people about whatever came to mind. It wasn't anything too exciting, but they enjoyed it.

Jan and I spent some time walking around the carnival midway and then ended up at Marlys and Kenny's that Saturday night to finish off the weekend celebration. We saw a lot of the same people that evening, which was no surprise. In a small town you expected to see a lot of the same faces.

I woke up on Sunday morning when Mom yelled, "It's time to get ready for church." She expected me to go to church unless I had a good excuse. Staying out late on Saturday night wasn't a good enough excuse. After the church service, Mom fixed one of her great Sunday dinners. My granddad, my mom's father, usually joined us after church on Sunday. He lived in a small house just across the street from us.

After Sunday dinner I drove Jan back to Omaha. It was a big let down when I drove through town and saw that the carnival rides were gone and Main Street was again quiet. The Pop Corn Days weekend that I had long anticipated and thoroughly enjoyed was over. The draft was two days closer.

It was soon Friday, August 2nd. I drove to Omaha and picked up Jan at her dorm just after five o'clock. She signed out for the evening, as we had planned to stay with Paul Alesch, a Wayne State friend.

Paul had a one-bedroom apartment so Jan and I threw some blankets and pillows on his living room floor that night for our bed. After we crawled under the covers, I pulled her body close and we kissed while I moved my left hand under the T-shirt she was wearing and caressed her soft, petite body. I slowly removed her shirt and moved my hands down her bare back and then reached the small firm cheeks of her little behind and pulled her toward me. We both began to breathe heavily and held a long hard kiss as we shared the warmth of our bodies and finally drifted off to sleep in each other's arms.

On Saturday morning we enjoyed a light breakfast with Paul and his girlfriend Jane and then it was time to move on. I had to head back home, as my sister Marilyn and her husband were coming to Schaller that evening.

I drove Jan back to her dorm and shared a good-bye hug and kiss. It wasn't a teary moment but it was sad. I liked Jan. She was the first girl I had considered a "girlfriend" and the Army was breaking us up just as we had started to get to know each other. We held each other tightly for a moment and said nothing. We then shared one final kiss. I told her I would see her in a few months as I waved good-bye and got into my car.

I crossed the Missouri River and headed north on I-29 and thought about the fun Jan and I had shared the past few months and the pleasure of our first night together. I was also frustrated that our casual relationship had been disrupted, thanks to Uncle Sam.

"Damn it," I said to myself and pounded on the steering wheel of my '63 Ford Fairlane.

When I arrived back home my younger sister Jan was there. She talked about going back to college that fall and her long-term plans to be a teacher. I told her to take good care of my Fairlane while I was gone. She planned to drive it at college. I smiled and told her that was her fringe benefit of my getting drafted. My sister Marilyn, her husband Gary and their young son Tim arrived later that afternoon from Sioux City. I hadn't seen them too much that summer except during a fishing trip to Minnesota in June.

After enjoying a delicious supper, I went out for my final night on the town. Although I was looking forward to going out, it meant spending my last few hours with hometown friends and saying good-bye to them. Marlys and Kenny planned a farewell party for Allen and me. Dean and Dennis welcomed me when I walked in. Dennis had accepted a job teaching in Remsen, Iowa, but he and Dean both knew their own farewell party wasn't too far away. I shared a big hug with Allen's girlfriend Vicki while she said with sadness in her voice, "I hate to see you guys go."

Allen and I enjoyed many toasts made in our honor while we talked and laughed with everyone that evening. I also spent many quiet moments saying good-bye to several people and sharing farewell hugs and handshakes with many friends as the evening quickly passed.

The next thing I knew it was time for church. I sat with my sisters, brother-in-law Gary and Dad. Mom had been the organist for years and sat behind the big organ at the front of the Presbyterian Church. I took a moment during the service to give thanks for what I had accomplished during my life and said a little prayer for the Lord to watch over me for the next two years.

After church my family gathered for my farewell dinner. I talked with my granddad and I told him what little I knew regarding my future. It was pretty simple. I was going into the Army, and after that, I had no idea.

My sister Marilyn gave me a hug when she left and said she would be thinking about me.

I smiled and said "Oh sure, thinking about me doing PT (physical training) exercises and drill sergeants yelling at me."

After spending the past two weeks scurrying around trying to see a long list of friends and making final preparations for leaving for the Army, there was finally a brief time of peace and quiet on Sunday evening. All of my friends were elsewhere; my family, except for my sister Jan and my folks, were gone. It was down to hours before I would be boarding the bus for Omaha. The reality of being drafted had arrived.

I went up to my room to pack a few things. We were told not to bring extra clothes. They would issue our olive drab (OD) green Army fatigues soon after we arrived for basic training. I threw my shaving kit and some extra underwear in a little handbag and was ready to go. And money, that was pretty easy for me. I had a few dollars in my pocket and a few dollars in my checking account, but for all practical purposes, I was broke. I had enjoyed myself that summer and spent most of my hard-earned money along the way. But I had no regrets. I knew I wouldn't need much money for a while. The Army would feed me, clothe me and put a roof over my head at no cost.

About nine o'clock Sunday night, August 5, 1968 Allen and I took a final cruise around town. We talked about the past weekend but didn't talk much about what lay ahead for us. The moment of reckoning was almost there and we were both apprehensive about it. We drove around town looking for one last moment of excitement, but there was nothing to be found. Everyone had packed it in for the weekend and was resting up for a new week. The streets of Schaller were quiet. We finally gave it up and went home.

➤ Walter Lee Nutt III was a fellow student at Ellsworth Junior College. He served in the U.S. Army and arrived in Vietnam on March 22, 1969. He was killed in action on April 28, 1969, at the age of twenty-two.

➤ Albert Du Ward Benson was a fellow student at Wayne State College. He served in the U.S. Marine Corps and arrived in Vietnam on March 15, 1969. He was killed in action on July 6, 1969, at the age of twenty-three.

➤ Steven Eugene Backhaus was another fellow student at Wayne State College. He served in the U.S. Marine Corps and arrived in Vietnam on December 11, 1969. He was killed in action only ten days later on December 21, 1969, at the age of twenty-two.

On January 20, 1968, the siege at Marine outpost Khe Sanh began. Two North Vietnamese Army (NVA) Divisions surrounded the outpost and launched fierce attacks until the siege ended on April 8, 1968, when U.S. Marine and Army Air Cavalry troops reached Khe Sanh. 205 Marines had been killed during the siege. However, an estimated 10,000 NVA soldiers were killed. U.S. forces abandoned Khe Sanh in June 1968.

Chapter 2

You're in the Army Now

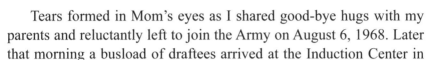

Tears formed in Mom's eyes as I shared good-bye hugs with my parents and reluctantly left to join the Army on August 6, 1968. Later that morning a busload of draftees arrived at the Induction Center in Omaha.

After we got off the bus we were directed inside and proceeded along a series of stations where they gathered more personal information and double-checked our records. Allen and I became separated during the process and I didn't see him the rest of the day. That afternoon I was led into a room filled with about twenty-five other men to take our oath of induction into the United States Army. I raised my right hand and said the following:

"I Richard Hogue, do solemnly swear that I will support and defend the Constitution of the United States against all enemies, foreign and domestic; that I will bear true faith and allegiance to the same; and that I will obey the orders of the President of the United States and the orders of the officers appointed over me, according to regulations and the Uniform Code of Military Justice, so help me God."

We were then asked to take one step forward to ceremonially represent our official Army induction.

Late that afternoon we were taken by bus to Epplie Field in Omaha to board a flight to Seattle, Washington. We would undertake our basic training at Fort Lewis, about forty miles south of Seattle. Most of us inductees enjoyed the flight except for a guy sitting in front of me who barfed in a bag shortly after takeoff.

I asked him, "How do you like the Army so far?" He just laughed.

We arrived at Fort Lewis just before nine o'clock that night and were directed to an old wooden barracks where we each found a bunk for the night. It had been a long day, and I was tired. I crawled under an OD green Army blanket and fell asleep.

At 6:30 the next morning a sergeant came into the barracks and startled everyone by yelling, "Get your butts out of bed! Your civilian life is over!"

We were a pretty raggedy group as we gathered in a formation outside to be marched to breakfast. Most of us still wore the same civilian clothes we had arrived in and slept in. After breakfast we learned we were in an induction holding area where we would complete preliminary activities before being taken to a basic training company.

The forty of us in the barracks would become a platoon during basic training. A platoon was the basic-level Army organizational unit. Three platoons would form our basic training company, the next level in the Army's organizational structure. Normally four or five companies would be organized under a battalion. Above the battalion was a brigade and then an Army division.

One of the first things they did was take us for a free hair cut, Army style. We lined up outside a barbershop with four or five barber chairs in a row inside. When I sat down in a chair the barber wrapped a cover around my neck, and in less than one minute he gave me a total buzz cut, leaving nothing but stubble on my head. Some of us almost didn't recognize each other with our strange new look. We were then issued military clothing including fatigues, dress uniforms, boots and shoes, T-shirts and boxer shorts, socks and hats. After we tried on the clothes to make sure they fit, we were told to leave on a pair of fatigues and boots. We were each given a cardboard box and told to label it with our home address and to place our civilian clothes inside. The boxes were mailed home at the Army's expense.

During my second day at Fort Lewis we were marching past another barracks when someone yelled from a window, "Hey, Hogue!" I looked up and saw Allen Schwab waving at me. I waved back, but couldn't stop to talk. I tracked him down that evening and learned his platoon was waiting to be joined with two other platoons for basic training. Although we had been separated for a couple of days it appeared we might be going through basic training together.

On the third day, we packed our belongings into our OD green Army duffel bag and threw them in the back of a truck. We were then loaded onto buses for a fifteen-minute ride to the basic training company. When we got off our bus all hell broke loose! The drill sergeants were yelling at the top of their lungs.

"Get your ass off that bus!"

"Hurry up and find your duffel bag, trainee!"

16

"Get into formation you lazy maggots!"

Anyone who wasn't hustling caught the wrath of a drill sergeant.

"Get your butt in gear before I kick it between your shoulders."

If we hadn't all been so scared we would have laughed at each other as we scurried around, bumping into one another while we hurried to get into formation. A few minutes later the company commander (commanding officer or CO) walked out from the company headquarters, and we were called to attention as he stopped in front of the platoon formations. The CO held the rank of captain and looked to be in his late twenties. Although we had only been in the Army for three days, we believed that anyone with three or more stripes on their arm was someone to be respected. If we encountered an officer with bars or other insignia on their collar, we had best snap-to and salute. If I had seen an Army officer a week earlier it wouldn't have been significant. But after a few days in the Army we viewed them almost as a god.

One of the first things the CO told us was that we were restricted to the company area. The only exceptions were when we left as a group for training or if we were specifically given authorization to leave. There would be no weekend leave, no trips to the clubs and no women. No women, big deal. I could have counted on one hand the number of women I had seen since I arrived at Fort Lewis. After listening to the CO, each man found his duffel bag and we were guided to our barracks.

The company area primarily consisted of a two-story brick building. Each platoon was assigned a large open bay area on the second floor with bunks lined along each side and a metal wall locker and wooden footlocker for each trainee. On the first floor was a large mess hall, the headquarters area containing the Company Commander's office, the Company Clerk and other offices. There was also an area called the Day Room with a pool table, television and other games we could use only at designated times, which were normally on weekends. Outside, a grass lawn surrounded the building. A gravel-covered area in front of the barracks was where we met to move on to wherever we needed to go. It wasn't much, but it was going to be my home for the next eight weeks.

We unpacked our belongings and were shown how our clothes and other personal items must be stored. Yes, our fatigues and uniforms had to be hung in a certain order and evenly spaced in the wall locker.

Our socks and underwear had to be rolled in a certain manner and placed in a specific location in our footlocker, and other personal items had to be stored in an assigned spot. We all had to do it the exactly the same, and would be subject to inspections for uniformity throughout basic training. What a shock. I was used to picking up my clothes from the floor.

We were issued clean sheets and blankets and shown how to make up our bunks. Wow, my mom had still made my bed when I was home. Unless you were sleeping in your bunk, it had to be made with the corners folded just so and no wrinkles in the OD-green blanket. I soon learned that much of basic training was simply regimentation and uniformity. We spent hours polishing the brass insignias for our uniforms, shining our boots and shoes, shining the tile barracks floor and completing many other tasks to make sure we kept ourselves and the company area "spit and polished."

Allen was in another platoon down the hall from mine, making it easy kept in touch. We didn't talk every day but it was comforting knowing a friend was close by.

During the first few days we received a general orientation about the Army and we also took tests to judge our general aptitude, personality traits and mechanical skills to determine if we could drive a tank or fly a helicopter. For those of us who had a college degree, the tests would also determine our eligibility for Officer Candidate School (OCS) to become an officer. Although several of us had college degrees the majority of the men didn't. In fact, several guys hadn't graduated from high school.

After the first week, we settled into the basic training routine and soon learned about the realities of how the Army determined permanent duty assignments. During the last week of basic training each of us would be given our Military Occupational Specialty (MOS). Some of the men had enlisted for three years and had chosen an MOS. But over half of us were draftees who only had to serve a two-year tour, but we didn't have the opportunity to choose our MOS. Naturally, enlistees rarely choose hazardous infantry duty; however, there was a continual need for infantrymen because of the high casualty rate in Vietnam. Many of us draftees would be assigned to the infantry.

On August 14th, I quietly celebrated my 22nd birthday. For the first time in my life it was just another day. No party, no birthday cake, no gifts, not even a cold beer to celebrate. I did get some birthday cards from Jan Griffin and my family saying, "Enjoy your birthday."

Each of us soon experienced serving on kitchen police (KP) duty. Four trainees were assigned to KP every day to assist the cooks in the mess hall. The cooks used the KP guys mostly for the chores they didn't want to do, like scrubbing out garbage cans, washing dishes, mopping the floor and, of course, peeling potatoes. KP was a long day starting at 5:00 a.m. and continued until the kitchen was cleaned up after the evening meal.

We also shared nightly "fire watch" on rotating one-hour shifts from the time they called lights out at 10:00 p.m. until we got up around six o'clock each morning. It didn't make much sense to me, but one man would roam the barracks for an hour and then wake up the man in the next bunk for his one-hour shift. Obviously a fire could have started somewhere in the barracks, but they were made of brick and concrete. They were practically fire proof except for the contents.

One of the Army's primary basic training objectives was to get us in good physical condition. An hour of physical training (PT) was scheduled nearly every day. We would do a variety of calisthenics, sit-ups, push-ups, jumping jacks, etc., and we would run and run and run. We went on many "double-time" runs that seemed to last forever while we sang cadences like, "I want to be an Airborne Ranger, I want to live a life of danger, Airborne! Ranger!" and on and on. We would run until my boots felt like they weighed a ton and my legs felt almost numb.

The men in my company were of all shapes and sizes. One man was too tall to join the Air Force, but the Army took him. A few guys were even shorter than I (5'6") and several guys were way overweight. After a few weeks there were six or seven guys who still nearly collapsed during the double-time runs or who failed the practice PT test. They were sent to what was called the "Funny Farm" and we never saw them again. The Funny Farm was a temporary assignment where they conducted conditioning drills to get the men into shape so they could ultimately pass the PT test prior to graduation from basic training.

One man who struggled with PT was thirty-six year old Sam Pierce. He had previously been in the Army but had gotten out. He had reenlisted and was going through basic training with the rest of us. Sam really wasn't that old, but compared to the rest of us who were mostly eighteen to twenty-one, Sam was old. We quickly nicknamed him the "old man." Sam smoked and was out of shape. We often had to help him along to finish those torturous double-time runs.

The day we went to the hand grenade range, we learned that a trainee had been killed a short while earlier when a grenade with a defective "short fuse" detonated almost immediately after he threw it. Hand grenades were designed to explode three or four seconds after the handle was released. After an orientation session we formed lines to take our turn throwing a grenade over a three-foot-high concrete wall.

When it was my turn, I walked up to the wall and took a live grenade from the instructor who stood beside me ready to take action in case I dropped it or didn't throw it over the wall. I firmly held the grenade in my left hand chest high. I put my right index finger through the ring attached to the safety pin that held the handle in place and pulled it out. With a tight grip on the grenade I leaned back and threw it over the wall with all of my might. I heard a "ping" and saw the handle fly away from the grenade after I released it. The grenade flew through the air while the instructor and I quickly ducked behind the wall. I felt the ground vibrate slightly as the grenade exploded in front of us. Throwing my first live grenade was quite an experience. Everyone in the company threw a hand grenade that day without a major incident.

Basic training was restricted to eight hours a day. We were up early each morning to eat a hearty breakfast of eggs or pancakes and bacon or sausage, or the good old Army's SOS (slop-on-a-shingle). We also had to make sure the barracks were spick-and-span before we left. Training started about eight o'clock each morning and finished around five o'clock that afternoon. If we had night training we got time off during the day to stay within the eight-hour training restriction. We normally marched to the nearby training sites and would be transported to remote sites by buses, deuce-and-a-halfs (large military transport trucks) or in what we called "cattle cars." The cattle cars were tractor-trailer vehicles with a canvas-covered trailer with long wooden benches along each side. We were packed into those trailers with guys sitting on the benches and the floor.

Saturday was normally a light day with PT or details around the company area in the morning and then time off during the afternoon. Sundays were totally ours with no training. Guys normally spent Sundays writing letters, playing cards or pool in the Day Room or just sleeping. Allen Schwab and I went to church a few times on Sunday and enjoyed a rare hour of personal freedom.

During basic training we held the lowest military rank of Private E-1. We were paid $100 per month in cash on the first day of each month. The only good thing about not making much money was that I didn't need much money. Our meals, our clothes and even the laundry were provided at no cost. We were normally marched to the Post Exchange (PX) once a week to stock up on personal items and snacks we craved, that weren't available in the barracks. If someone got hungry at night he couldn't just go to the mess hall and raid the refrigerator. Midway through basic training, Allen and I decided we would make some money out of that situation.

There was a doughnut shop two blocks from the company area. Because fresh doughnuts weren't served in the mess hall, Allen and I snuck off a few times to the doughnut shop at night. We each brought back a couple dozen fresh doughnuts and sold them for two or three times our cost. In addition to making a few bucks, we enjoyed the challenge of sneaking off the company area without getting caught.

As basic training progressed, we learned to read topographical maps and use a compass to navigate from one point to another. One night we were taken out to navigate through a heavily wooded area to an established destination. We were sent off in pairs with a compass, a map and a flashlight. Navigating at night through the wooded Fort Lewis terrain was difficult because we ran into a tree every few steps, but we ultimately made it to our destination.

Another unique challenge was gas mask training that concluded with a test. It started with our low crawling through an open area without our mask on. Unannounced, they detonated a canister of CS gas. I am not sure what CS gas was, but a small whiff would immediately burn your eyes, nose and throat. A heavy dose of CS gas would choke you and make it nearly impossible to breathe. It might not kill you, but it made you wish you were dead. When I got my first whiff of CS gas I held my breath until I pulled my mask over my face and tightened the rubber straps. I then low-crawled through the cloud of gas while the mask filtered it out.

The weather was pleasant during basic training, not too hot and not much rain. We appreciated nice weather because we spent most of our last two weeks of basic training outside. During week seven we

21

took the firing test with our M-14 rifles. We then completed the PT test that included a low-crawl drill, an obstacle course, parallel bars, one-man carry (where we carried another man about thirty yards) and concluded with a one-mile run. Although I was in good shape, I was far from the fastest or strongest man in the company. But I passed the PT test. That was all that counted.

It was interesting to watch the men as we completed our final testing. Although none of us were too excited about being in the Army, a natural competitive instinct came out in most of us. We strived to score the highest on the rifle range and to complete each PT event as fast as we could, if for nothing else, but a little self-pride. Somehow, the Army actually had us enjoying busting our butts.

Allen and I spent time together talking about alternatives for dealing with our future that included the strong possibility of being assigned to the infantry. Although they offered us the opportunity to re-up for a three-year tour, which would have given us the choice of many non-combat assignments, Allen and I agreed to take our chances and let the Army assign our MOS. I had a college degree and Allen was only one semester away from graduation. Surely the Army would recognize what we had to offer and wouldn't assign us to the infantry. I could have pursued Officer Candidate School, but the only openings were in the infantry and required a four-year tour. I passed on OCS. I also could have become a Warrant Officer and flown helicopters but decided that probably wasn't much safer than being in the infantry.

It was finally the first week of October, the last week of basic training that included a three-day bivouac (camping Army style). We hoped for good weather, because we knew the almost daily autumn rains would soon begin. Bivouac started by navigating through terrain during the first day and simulating taking an enemy position by slowly moving up a hill and overtaking the "enemy." We carried our rifles but of course weren't issued ammunition. At night we established a defensive position and rotated guard duty. The bivouac wasn't as bad as I had expected. They didn't work us too hard during the day, and we got a few hours of sleep at night. Training bivouacs were traditionally concluded with a "forced march" back to the company area. The drill sergeants selected two of the tallest guys with long legs to lead. The intent wasn't to have us run but to walk as fast as we could without taking a break. There were also bragging rights at stake for the CO and drill sergeants for the basic training company that completed the forced march in the shortest time.

On the afternoon of the third day of bivouac we headed down a gravel road in two columns carrying our backpacks and rifles. It was nearly ten miles back to the company area. The first few miles weren't too bad for me but then my 5'6" body and proportionately short legs started to take their toll. I had learned the Army had no sympathy for someone who may not be as big or strong as other men, or if someone wasn't as intelligent and had more difficulty completing a particular training exercise. We were all expected to "suck it up" and somehow do what we were told.

As the march continued the columns spread out. The taller men and those who were in the best condition moved to the front while others slipped behind. I soon realized that several of us "short" guys had fallen behind and jointly cussed that tall son-of-a-gun who led the pack. There were a few men who had stopped to treat blisters or who were completely exhausted as the miles slowly passed. Although I thought I was in pretty good shape, I was becoming as physically exhausted as I had ever been in my life. But I kept forcing one foot in front of the other, determined not to quit. The drill sergeants and company officers moved up and down the columns and gave words of encouragement to those who needed it rather than yelling and cussing as they often had.

One of the drill sergeants, Staff Sergeant Trotten, settled in and chatted with us during the last couple miles of the march. Although the drill sergeants had yelled and cussed at us during most of basic training, we got to know some of them and found their bark normally was louder than their bite. Most of them had good intentions, trying to teach us the order and discipline associated with Army life and to make us follow orders whether we liked them or not.

After a march that I thought would never end, we found a reward waiting for us in the company area: cold beer and soda. I grabbed a can and began drinking the first beer I had seen in eight weeks. I was almost too tired to enjoy it, but it tasted great. We each drank a couple beers while we relaxed and toasted the near completion of basic training. We spent the remainder of the day cleaning up our gear and rifles and then took a long, hot shower. We hadn't had a good night's sleep for three days and after marching nearly ten miles that day, sleep quickly became a priority for everyone.

The next day each platoon was called down to the Day Room to receive our formal orders stating our MOS and when and where to report for our next assignment. The mood was somber.

When I reached a table where the orders were being issued a sergeant pulled my orders and said, "11Bravo, Light Weapons Infantryman. You'll be staying at Fort Lewis for Advanced Infantry Training (AIT)."

He handed me copies of my orders and I turned and walked away feeling a little stunned. Although I knew the majority of draftees would be assigned to the infantry, I had held out some hope I would be one of the few who would be assigned elsewhere. But it wasn't to be. I reluctantly accepted my assignment like dozens of other men did. One of the men in my platoon had been a music teacher and was assigned to an Army band. I should have told the Army I had played the trumpet in my high school band.

I walked down the hall to see Allen. "Infantry," he said as I walked up to him.

I said, "Me, too," while we both shook our heads in disbelief.

We were both staying at Fort Lewis for AIT but Allen was assigned to another company. We both accepted our fate that day and hoped for the best. That afternoon I packed most of my clothes in my duffel bag and went to the Day Room to relax for a while. When I walked in I noticed a banner along the top of a bulletin board that read:

"For those who have fought for it, life has a meaning others will never know."

I read the words twice as though they were meant for me.

The final day of basic training started with a graduation ceremony at a nearby parade ground. Our company and two other basic training companies marched in front of a reviewing stand of Army officers. We then stood in formation and listened to a speech from our battalion commander who said he was proud of us and we would be an important part of the Army's future. He also spent a few moments talking about Vietnam and stated that many of us would be seeing duty there. "Thanks for the good news," I thought.

After the graduation ceremony we marched back to the company area. The men who were flying to other posts for further training grabbed their duffel bags and boarded buses that would take them to the airport in Seattle. We quickly exchanged good-byes as men left and wished each other the best of luck. Although we had been together for only eight weeks, good friendships had been formed. While everyone was happy to be moving on it was also sad. Many of us would never see each other again.

Early that afternoon, those of us who had been assigned to the infantry boarded buses that would take us to our AIT company.

Richard Nixon was elected President on November 5, 1968. He committed to withdrawing troops from Vietnam. During 1968 the U.S. military force level in Vietnam was 536,000. 16,511 Americans were killed in Vietnam that year, making it the worst year for American casualties during the Vietnam War.

Chapter 3

Advanced Infantry Training and NCO School

After a short bus ride, we arrived at our AIT company and were again greeted with drill sergeants yelling at us while we rushed into formation. We were back in an area with wood frame World War II-era buildings. The company area was comprised of three two-story barracks, a one-story headquarters building, a mess hall and a building containing the Day Room. The cool and cloudy weather combined with old and drab surroundings, made for a dismal welcome to AIT.

Many of us who had gone through basic training together at Fort Lewis were assigned to the third platoon along with other men who had just completed basic training at Army posts around the country. Despite being assigned to the infantry and finding our new living quarters old and cramped, there was finally some good news. During a brief orientation we were told we had the rest of the weekend off and we could go off post on future weekends. Finally, some freedom.

However, there was also some bad news. The eight-hour-per-day training restriction no longer applied. If we were out training until midnight, we still had to get up at 6:00 a.m. the following morning. That didn't sound like much fun. We still had rotating KP duty but we wouldn't have fire watch. What was going on? We were in an old wooden barracks that would quickly go up in flames. But no one complained. It sounded like we would need all the sleep we could get.

Before long I joined a stream of guys walking to the nearby Enlisted Club to enjoy our first taste of freedom in eight weeks. We laughed and joked about basic training and the crazy things that happened to us as we enjoyed a cold beer. We also talked about how our outlook on the Army had changed. We no longer thought of officers as gods. And although drill sergeants yelled and cussed at us, most of them were decent men just doing their job. We also knew another piece of our military future was in place. Whether we liked it or not, we were beginning nine weeks of training to become light weapons infantrymen.

I took a few minutes that afternoon to call my old roommate Dennis "Pete" Pederson back at Wayne, Nebraska. I knew it was homecoming weekend at Wayne State and some of the gang would be having a party at Pete's apartment. I talked with some of the guys and told them they would have to party without me. Although it was great to talk with some of my old friends it was discouraging not being with them. I sadly realized I would be missing more good times with those guys, but I also realized I had a new bunch of Army buddies. Rather than getting depressed I made the best of what I had at Fort Lewis and shared the evening with my new friends at the club.

Monday morning rolled around way too soon. We were up at 6:00 a.m. One of the first things they did was issue us M-16 rifles, the rifles used in Vietnam. The M-16 was much lighter than the M-14 rifles we used in basic training and fired a smaller round. However the M-16 round traveled at such an extremely high velocity it caused serious damage when passing through a body, often leaving a huge exit wound. M-16s could fire on semi-automatic or automatic simply by flipping a little lever on the side of the firing chamber. You could empty a twenty-round magazine in two seconds.

Much of AIT was field training that included firing M-16s, M-60 machine guns, M-79 grenade launchers, and again, throwing hand grenades. The M-60 machine gun vibrated your whole body when you fired it. If you didn't firmly brace your body against the recoil, it could spin you around when you fired it standing up. Firing those weapons was fun so long as no one was firing back at us. Physical training continued almost daily and included obstacle courses that were a physical challenge for all of us. We received survival training, continued navigation training across the wooded countryside of Fort Lewis, and went through hours of hand-to-hand combat and bayonet training.

During the month of October the weather got cooler and it started to rain a lot. Although much of our training was conducted outside, nothing was cancelled because of the rain. We began spending many long, cold and miserable days in the rain. We wore ponchos over our field jackets to keep us dry, but after spending a long day out in the cold rain, my whole body felt numb. The rain also created a lot of extra work for us to clean up the mess from the water and mud to keep the barracks presentable for daily inspections. The continued long days in the cold and rain soon resulted in a rash of colds and URI (upper respiratory infection). I felt horrible one morning and went on sick call. The doctor checked me over and said I had URI. He gave me a shot of penicillin in the butt and gave me a day of bed rest. The next day, I felt fine.

We all looked forward to mail call when we returned from each long day of training. A letter from a family member or friend back home provided a few minutes of escape from our controlled Army existence. Although most of us had been away from our families and friends for longer than we had ever been in the past, we didn't have much time to get depressed about our circumstance. Each of us was just one of thousands of men who were enduring the same training across the country. Besides, with forty men crammed into a small barracks, it was difficult to feel too lonely. Most men simply continued on, one day at a time, and tried to make the best of the basically lousy situation we were all in.

I kept in touch with Jan Griffin by letter every few days. I had talked with her during the first week of AIT and told her I had been assigned to the infantry and that my prospects of going to Vietnam had dramatically increased. Although I told her about some of our training, it was nearly impossible for anyone to imagine what it was like unless they were actually there. We were scheduled to complete AIT a week before Christmas, which was great. I would be home on leave over the holidays.

What helped keep us going week after week was knowing we could get away from it all each weekend and experience a little bit of the outside world. I had asked my folks to send some civilian clothes. The weekend after they arrived I joined a group of guys and went to Seattle for a party that a friend of one of the guys was having. Four of us shared a cab and arrived near downtown Seattle not knowing for sure where we were. We started bar hopping and asking directions to the address we were given for the party.

Somewhere along the way I lost everyone else. I wandered around walking into every bar I found, looking for a familiar face. Late that night I finally found one of the guys. We found a cheap hotel for the night and rode on a bus back to Fort Lewis the next morning. None of the guys ever found the party. In fact, a little guy from Alaska got rolled and lost all of his money. After my first experience in Seattle I wasn't too excited about going back. I spent the next few weekends on post going to the club, the post movie theater or just relaxing around the barracks. Sometimes a little peace and quiet was more enjoyable than anything else.

Midway through AIT they again offered infantry OCS to me, and I again passed. I then learned about a four-month Noncommissioned Officer (NCO) Candidate School in Fort Benning, Georgia. Upon graduation I would be promoted to the rank of Sergeant E-5. The NCO School had been established because there was a shortage of infantry NCOs in Vietnam. Rather than promoting a Corporal to replace a NCO who was killed or wounded, the Army decided to provide additional training to those who volunteered for NCO School. New NCOs would be assigned as infantry squad leaders and platoon sergeants in Vietnam.

A recent NCO School graduate was assigned as our platoon sergeant for his on-the-job-training (OJT). Although acknowledging that going to NCO School might increase the likelihood of going to Vietnam, he encouraged me to go because the additional training would better prepare me for combat. He told me I was probably going to Vietnam anyway, so I might as well take advantage of NCO School.

I decided why not. If I was going to Vietnam why not go as sergeant? We had been promoted to Private E-2 after basic training and would be promoted to Private First Class E-3 upon arrival in Vietnam. Although I knew the guys with the stripes on their arms or the brass on their collars really weren't gods, I also knew that rank had its privileges. I volunteered for NCO School.

A few other guys in my platoon also volunteered for NCO School, including the "old man," Sam Pierce. Although Sam reenlisted in the Army, he had volunteered for the infantry. He knew it meant risking his life in Vietnam, but Sam knew it was the fastest way to earn rank. He was willing to take the chance. I didn't have time to see Allen Schwab often but the next time I saw him I told him I had volunteered for NCO School. He was sticking to his decision not to volunteer for anything.

The final weeks of AIT became more intense. One night we were split up in two-man teams to navigate through a wooded area where men identified as the "enemy " would attempt to capture us. My partner and I made it about half way through the area when we heard a noise in front of us. Thinking it might be one of the "enemy" we lay down by a tree. While we lay there a guy snuck up behind us and said,

"You're captured." He grabbed us and took us to a mock POW camp where they yelled at us, put us through an interrogation exercise and then locked us in a cage.

Another exciting night was the "live fire" exercise. We were taken to a fifty-yard long course with barbed wire strung two feet above the ground. It was completely dark when we started to low-crawl under the barbed wire while a group of M-60 machine guns fired over our heads. That was the first time they exposed us to live rounds being fired toward us. Every fifth M-60 round was a tracer that glowed orange as it sped through the air. The glowing tracers raced above my head as hundreds of rounds per minute were fired and explosive charges were detonated around us to simulate mortar and hand grenade explosions. I had no trouble low-crawling below the barbed wire.

We had to pass another PT test and a firing test for both the M-16 rifles and M-60 machine guns. Although we were being trained for the most dangerous job in the world, most of the guys maintained enough personal pride and determination to do the best they could. There were a few slackers, but with the combination of the drill sergeants and instructors cussing them out and the rest of us trainees getting on their case from time to time, most everyone came around. We reluctantly accepted the fact that our lives might later depend upon what we learned during AIT. That in itself provided an incentive for most of us to pay attention and learn everything we could during those nine weeks.

Unfortunately, the weather got even colder and wetter in December. I was getting to the point I didn't care what was in store for me next. All I wanted to do was to get out of that lousy weather and head home for the holidays. It was finally the last week of AIT, and we headed out for another bivouac. It began raining during the first afternoon while we played war games in the muddy countryside. That evening we arrived at a site with bunkers built in a circular perimeter, which we thought would protect us from the rain. However, the bunkers were partially underground and almost useless because water was leaking inside. "Son-of-a-bitch," was the general response when the men looked inside the bunkers.

They relaxed the rules and let us start bonfires to help dry out our clothes and warm up a little. We took turns putting our feet next to the fire in an effort to dry our boots and warm our feet. To make things worse, the rain turned to snow. I knew it rained in Vietnam but I also knew it didn't snow. Water continued to leak inside the bunkers making for a long and miserable night. Our soggy sleeping bags provided little warmth. Several guys were hauled off to sick call the next morning. Although bivouac should have given us time to practice our infantry skills, with the lousy weather we didn't gain much useful experience. We were mostly focused on trying to stay warm and dry and didn't give a damn about much else.

The weather finally cleared up on the third day and warmed up enough to help us slowly dry out. Just like basic training, AIT bivouac concluded with a forced march. Again two of the tallest men in the company led the columns when we headed down another gravel road carrying our backpacks and rifles anticipating another grueling march. A group of us short guys eventually formed toward the rear of the two columns and we laughed because most of us had been in the same spot during basic training. Although I was dead tired, I trudged on and proudly held my head high when I walked into the company area. The "old man," Sam Pierce, was one of the last men to finish with one man on each side helping him when he entered the company area. Sam reached out and grabbed a cold beer that someone handed to him while he sat on the ground looking like he was about to die.

Those of us who volunteered for NCO School knew we would spend the next four months at Fort Benning, GA. The few men who volunteered for OCS would spend the next six months in training and graduate as Second Lieutenants. But for most of the men it was again time to learn what the Army had in store for them. We anticipated the majority would be sent to Vietnam.

I didn't have a lot of opportunity to watch television or read the newspaper accounts of what was going on in Vietnam. I knew peace talks between the United States and North Vietnam had commenced that past summer, and newly elected President Nixon had committed to a withdrawal of American troops. But I also knew hundreds of GIs were being killed and wounded every week and they were still sending men to Vietnam every day. That told me the end of the war was still a long way off.

Each of us knew we could easily become a casualty in Vietnam, but we didn't talk about it often. I think most of the men tried to be macho and not expose their personal fears about what they might face. During AIT the drill sergeants yelled at us if we did something wrong and said things like, "If you screw up like that in 'Nam, Charlie will kill you," or "You better pay attention, you dumb shit, or you'll die in Vietnam."

Although we had became numb to the yelling and name calling, we also knew we were being trained for the most hazardous duty in the world. Most of the AIT drill sergeants had served as infantrymen in Vietnam, and they shared stories of men being killed or wounded because they made a foolish mistake. Their yelling and cussing was their way of getting our attention and trying to help us survive our tour in combat.

When the day of reckoning arrived, the majority of the guys who weren't going to OCS or NCO School received orders for Vietnam, just as everyone had expected. A couple of men in our platoon received orders for Korea, but everyone else was on their way to Vietnam after the holidays. Although going to Vietnam wasn't how anyone wanted to begin the new year, most of the men looked forward to spending time with family and friends rather than dwelling on what would happen in January.

It was Thursday, December 12, 1968. After graduation the following day, I had three weeks of leave. We packed all of our personal belongings into our duffel bags except our Class-A uniforms, which we would wear for graduation and while we traveled. Anything that didn't fit into a guy's duffel bag was offered to someone else or left behind. The priority was getting away from Fort Lewis, Washington.

After I packed my belongings I walked over to Allen Schwab's company to see what his orders were.

I walked up to his bunk, and without my asking, he said, "I'm going to 'Nam."

We chuckled, thinking our strategy of volunteering for the draft and not reenlisting to get our choice of an MOS was working out pretty well. We were both in the infantry. Allen was headed for Vietnam in three weeks, and I was likely only a few months behind him. We had plane reservations to fly back to Omaha together. We agreed to meet by my barracks after graduation and grab a cab to the airport.

After we cleaned up our barracks that Thursday afternoon, most of the men headed to the club for some rest and relaxation during our final night of AIT. I had been with some of those men since our bus ride from the Induction Center in Omaha and I had formed good friendships. This would be our last night together and might be the last time some of us would ever see each other. We enjoyed recalling the screw-ups some of us had made and could finally laugh when we recounted the grueling PT, spending hours training in the rain, the snow during bivouac and the forced marches. We again talked about the drill sergeants, some who were decent men and others who were just plain assholes. A couple trainees had gone AWOL along the way and we never saw them again. And, there were a couple of guys who were just plain jerks that we hoped never to see again.

I was happy to have AIT behind me, but it was again sad because many brief but good friendships were ending. I exchanged addresses with a few men and vowed to keep in touch, knowing that would be easier said than done. Several of us ended the night walking back to the barracks laughing and singing cadences like, "If I go to Vietnam, I will kill Charlie Cong. If someday I may die, tell my family not to cry. Take my body and bring it home, cover my coffin with the flag. When they lower me in the ground, give the flag to my mom."

The next morning we proudly walked outside the barracks in our green Class-A uniforms and acknowledged we all looked a little more handsome since we had been allowed to grow our hair a little longer. As Private E-2s, we wore one bright, yellow stripe on each arm and proudly wore the shiny brass crossed-rifle insignia with a light blue plastic trim signifying we were infantrymen. I had endured some of the most grueling training the Army offered including the greatest physical demands of my life, but had passed every challenge they gave me. I felt proud of my accomplishments, but I was thankful that AIT didn't go on forever.

Graduation day was cool and cloudy, but it wasn't raining for a change. Again, we paraded in front of a reviewing stand and then listened while a senior officer gave us a short speech. After we marched back to the barracks we all quickly shared hugs and handshakes with our buddies and then hustled to get away from Fort Lewis and forget about the Army for a few weeks.

I grabbed my duffel bag and walked outside the barracks to wait for Allen. When he arrived we jumped in a cab with a couple other guys. I smiled and breathed a sigh of relief when we passed through the front gate of Fort Lewis and headed toward Seattle. That was one of the happier days of my life. Because Allen and I couldn't get a flight to Omaha on Friday, we settled into a hotel room near the airport that afternoon and watched television, something we hadn't often done during the past four months.

Allen and I boarded the plane along with many other GIs (government issue) and took off on schedule at 8:30 Saturday morning. The plane stopped at the gate in Omaha and Allen and I made our way up the walkway into the terminal a few minutes later. The terminal was packed, but we soon found our families. I greeted Mom and Dad, my sister Jan and girlfriend Jan and began an enjoyable threes weeks on leave.

I shared the holidays with my family and friends in the familiar surroundings I had grown so accustomed to before I was drafted. And yes, Mom spoiled me by making my bed every morning. Unfortunately, those three weeks passed all too quickly. I also knew I probably wouldn't be spending the 1969 holiday season at home. I anticipated going to Vietnam sometime in July to begin my one-year tour of duty.

It was soon Saturday morning, January 4, 1969. I planned to go to Omaha that afternoon to see my girlfriend Jan before I left Sunday morning. Allen was also leaving that weekend for Fort Lewis and then on to Vietnam. I stopped by Allen's house to say good-bye. We both tried to ignore the possibility we might not see each other again as we shared a difficult farewell with a hug and handshake.

During the two-hour drive to Omaha Mom told me she was already worrying about me going to Vietnam. I told my folks not to worry; I was just leaving for more training. But that was mostly wasted breath. They were going to worry until I was out of the Army.

After arriving at Jan's dorm, I shared farewell hugs with my parents. Jan had borrowed a friend's car and we drove to Paul and Jane Alesch's new apartment where we planned to spend the night. Paul had married his girlfriend Jane that past September.

Later that night Jan and I settled in together on a sofa bed. After spending the past four months sleeping by myself in an Army bunk or on the ground, it was great snuggling with Jan and "playing around" under the covers until we finally fell asleep. If only that night could have lasted forever.

Sunday morning Jan and I drove across town to Epplie Field. The airport was filled with GIs, many headed for Vietnam. I saw several men huddled with their family and friends, sharing their last few precious minutes together. Although I wasn't going to Vietnam I wasn't happy about leaving again. I told Jan not to worry about me. I would be working my butt off, but I didn't anticipate anyone shooting at me.

After they announced my flight I gave Jan a hug and kiss and said, "Good-bye, good-looking, I'll keep in touch."

When we lifted off, I felt truly alone. There were other GIs on board but I didn't recognize any of them. I settled in for a quiet flight to Atlanta and then transferred to a flight to Columbus, Georgia. Fort Benning was just a few miles southeast of Columbus.

It was dark when I arrived at Fort Benning and settled into another wooden barracks in the NCO School company area. The next morning the full realization of my new surroundings hit me. The condition of those barracks made the AIT barracks at Fort Lewis appear like castles. The buildings at our NCO company must have been pre-World War II. Paint was pealing from the wooden siding and the barracks had coal-fired furnaces and hot water heaters.

Those buildings hadn't been used for years, but had been reopened when a NCO School training site was needed. It was about the most depressing site I had seen on an Army post. I again thought, "What have I done to myself?" The inside of the barracks had wooden support beams, the walls were just rough painted lumber and two rows of Army bunks ran down near the middle of the barracks. We each had a desk and chair in addition to a wall locker and footlocker. We again had fire watch, which finally made sense. One of the most important duties while on fire watch was to keep the fires in the furnace and hot water heater burning by throwing in a scoop or two of coal every hour. The hot water heater went out a few times, which meant we skipped showers and shaved with cold water. We also found that whenever we blew our nose it turned our handkerchief black from the coal dust in the air.

The training was formally named Noncommissioned Officer Candidate Course but was referred to as just "NCO School." We also learned the school was jokingly referred to as "shake'n bake" school after the Shake'n Bake coating for fried chicken. We were promoted to the rank of Corporal E-4 upon our arrival and would be promoted to Sergeant E-5 upon graduation. There were some who thought graduates didn't deserve being promoted to the rank of Sergeant with less than a year in the Army and no combat experience. Most infantrymen would have to spend most of their tour in Vietnam before they were promoted to Sergeant. We expected to be called a "shake'n bake" for a while. But that was the least of my concerns. From what I had been told, NCO School would make basic and AIT seem like grade school.

We were normally up at the crack of dawn for chow and off to training by 8:00 a.m. The classroom training covered many of the same subjects we had in AIT but went into much more detail. We would have to pass both written and practical tests on every subject. If you didn't maintain passing scores, you would be "washed out" and normally sent to Vietnam as a corporal. Physical training was a big part of NCO School. In addition to the double-time runs and the normal exercises, we went through obstacle courses like I had never seen before. We would have to roll over a log suspended six feet high, jump ditches filled with water, climb rope ladders, and crawl over ten-foot-high wooden walls and more. I was in the best shape of my life, but those obstacle courses were tough. I was pushed to my physical limit many times, but I never gave up. The guy who designed those courses had no sympathy for us short guys.

Although the training was more difficult, some of it continued to be fun. I rode in a UH-1 (Huey) helicopter during a simulated combat mission and rode in an Armored Personnel Carrier (APC) that even went on a lake. Yes, those things floated. I fired a Light Anti-Tank Weapon (LAW) for the first time. The LAW was an OD green tube three inches in diameter containing a rocket designed to penetrate a tank. The tube expanded to be three feet long and you fired it from your shoulder. We each took a turn shooting at old tanks. I don't remember if I hit a tank or just blew a big hole in the ground. We also learned to call in a "fire mission" for artillery and mortar fire. It was quite an experience to have rounds exploding a few hundred yards away with a loud KABOOM while we watched from the protection of a bunker.

NCO School concluded with a week-long bivouac. Fortunately it was early April and the weather in Georgia was mild. We were each given blank M-16 rounds and each platoon was issued an M-60 machine gun with blank ammunition to use in mock firefights. An enemy compound would be identified on a map. We would have to find the enemy position and then move by squads of eight to ten men while encountering simulated enemy fire. We would tactically move and return the fire until we had taken the position or had been wiped out ourselves. Instructors served as referees to judge if men or groups of men were considered to be "killed in action" (KIA) in order to determine which side won.

There were also trip-wired booby traps (actually small explosives or trip flares) to watch for. If someone tripped a simulated booby trap, they were considered KIA for the remainder of that exercise. The training instructors also used smoke grenades and other small explosives to simulate mortar rounds to make the environment as close to combat action as they could. Each night we established a perimeter and pulled guard duty. We also rotated setting up ambushes and simulated opening fire when "enemy" troops passed by.

By the end of the week we were dirty and tired and ready to get back to our rickety old barracks. However, there was one more forced march ahead of us. I kept up with the pack for the first several miles, but then gradually slipped back and finished near the middle of the pack. The "old man," Sam Pierce, was again in my company and had continued to suffer through the even more strenuous physical demands of NCO School. We encouraged him while he struggled to finish the forced march by saying things like, "Come on, you old fart, you can make it."

That twelve-mile forced march ended much differently than we expected. We weren't back at our company area, and there wasn't any cold beer. Instead, we stopped near a lake to complete a "confidence" course built over a corner of the lake. We were to climb a twenty-five-foot wooden pole that was set at the edge of the lake. We would then walk over the water along a twenty-foot long plank that was attached to another pole set in the lake. The plank was one foot wide and had two steps in the middle. At the far end of the plank was a rope leading back to another edge of the lake. We would crawl along the rope for twelve feet to a little sign that said "Rangers." At that point we would hang from the rope with our hands and drop, feet first twenty-five feet into the water, yelling "Ranger!"

We weren't forced to complete the course but were encouraged to run the course just to prove we could. Half of the guys had completed the course and were standing nearby dripping wet when I started climbing the pole. That was the easy part. I then stood up and began walking along the plank. I concentrated on the plank and not the water far below while I held my arms out to keep my balance. When I reached the steps I slowly took two steps up and back down and then, carefully took the final steps to the end of the plank. Whew! It wasn't as bad as it looked from the ground.

I then grabbed the rope connected to the pole at the far end of the plank with my hands, crossed my legs up over the rope and pulled myself away headfirst. I was doing fine dangling twenty-five feet above the water. I kept a firm grip on the rope and pulled myself along until I reached the Ranger sign. I released my legs and hung from the rope by my hands for a couple seconds. I looked skyward, released my hands and shouted "Ranger!" It seemed to take forever to descend, but finally, I splashed feet-first into the cold water. I took a couple of strokes to a ladder and climbed out of the water. A cheer from the rest of the company greeted each of us when we reached the top of the ladder.

It was a cloudy and cool afternoon, but none of us noticed. We all felt so much adrenalin by the time we hit the water, no one complained about being cold. I walked away from the lake with a smile on my face and gathered with my fellow platoon members. We congratulated each other while we stood together in our soaking wet fatigues.

During the last couple of days of NCO School everyone was in great spirits. We had made it through four months of intense military training and were looking forward to a bit of a breather. After graduation we would be assigned to an AIT Company for two months of on-the-job-training (OJT) before receiving our final orders, likely for Vietnam. I was going back to Fort Lewis for my OJT.

Seven men were designated as honor graduates for earning the highest test scores and were promoted to the rank of Staff Sergeant E-6. One of the honor graduates was the "old man," Sam Pierce. I congratulated Sam the next time I saw him and told him there were many days I thought he would never make it. Sam planned to make the Army his career and was willing to suffer through a few months of training. I told Sam I hoped to survive my two years and get out. We shook hands and shared a "good luck" with each other.

The big event before graduation was to have our sergeant stripes sewn on our fatigues and the uniforms that many of us had tailored so we would look fit and trim. On graduation day we each proudly wore our khaki uniforms with our three yellow sergeant stripes on each sleeve. Sergeant E-5 wasn't a high rank; in fact it was the lowest NCO rank, sometimes referred to as "buck sergeant." But I was proud of what I had accomplished and was happy to finally have a little status as I continued through my first year in the Army. The graduation was like the previous ceremonies except we were each given a diploma that read:

United States Army Infantry School

Be it known that
Sergeant Richard F. Hogue
has successfully completed the
Infantry Noncommissioned Officer Candidate
Course at this institution and that in testimony
thereof he is awarded this Diploma Given at
Fort Benning, Georgia, on this the
15th day of April, nineteen hundred
and sixty-nine.

John M. Wright, Jr.
Major General, U. S. Army
Commandant

After graduation I quickly shook hands with several friends and said good-bye while I scurried through the barracks to grab my duffel bag. Four of us threw our bags in the trunk of a taxi and headed out the gate of Fort Benning. When we hit the airport we shook hands and went our separate ways to catch our planes. I arrived in Seattle around three o'clock that afternoon and caught a shuttle bus to Fort Lewis. I soon found the AIT Company that consisted of another group of World War II style buildings. I checked in at the headquarters building and was again assigned to the third platoon. Thus far every assignment had been in the third platoon.

The barracks was empty when I walked up to my second-floor private room and dropped my duffel bag on the bed. I thought, "Hey, this isn't too bad for Army life." Six of us new shake'n bakes were assigned to the AIT Company, including John Jarvis who had been in my platoon during NCO School. It was nice to have a familiar face around to start my OJT. Later that afternoon we exercised our new status and went to the NCO club, which was a big step up in the military world for the six of us.

Two NCOs were assigned to manage each AIT platoon composed of a group of men fresh out of basic training. Those trainees would be undergoing the same infantry training I had gone through the previous fall at Fort Lewis. However, this time I would be giving out some of the orders and watching and supervising while those men worked their butts off for nine weeks. We were expected to assist with some of the training, conduct most of the PT drills, keep the trainees in line and discipline them when necessary. Permanently assigned to the company were three drill sergeants, a first sergeant and a captain, serving as Commanding Officer. Two second lieutenants, who were recent OCS graduates, were also going through OJT before their probable assignment to Vietnam. The permanent staff went home in the evenings unless there was night training, leaving the company in our hands each night. The trainees would be graduating from basic training that Saturday morning and arriving for their AIT that afternoon.

When the trainees arrived we exercised our newfound authority by yelling at them until they finally got into platoon formation for an initial briefing. Those guys had just graduated from basic training and were still scared of anyone who had three stripes or more on their arm. They didn't know the six of us NCOs had just sewn the stripes on our uniforms a few days earlier. For the majority of my nine month Army career I had been yelled at and been given orders by someone else. It was a strange but nice feeling to be the one giving orders to someone else for a change.

I had learned Dean Christiansen had been drafted and was in basic training at Fort Lewis. The first Sunday after I arrived there, I borrowed a car from one of the NCOs and found Dean's basic training company, not far from my former basic training company. When I walked through the company area to find Dean I almost laughed when the trainees stepped aside when they saw the stripes on my uniform.

Dean and I walked to a parking lot and had a serious talk about what was happening with each of us. Dean had re-upped for another year because he didn't want any part of the infantry in Vietnam. He smiled and said he would let me tell him all about it. Dean was moving on in a week for his advanced training to be a supply technician. We hoped to see each other on leave that July. While I drove back across the post, I thought about our conversation. It was the most serious conversation we had ever shared. The Army had given us both a much different perspective on our lives and our futures.

During OJT we were up early each morning to make sure our platoon got to the mess hall for breakfast, had the barracks cleaned and were ready to move out for training on schedule. It was like baby-sitting forty guys for nine weeks. Some trainees refused to wear a watch and were always late. Also, a few trainees normally caught hell from the first sergeant when they failed an inspection for not being clean-shaven or not having their boots shined. The rules weren't difficult, but most of the men had never been subjected to so much discipline and rules governing most everything they did. It took more than eight weeks of basic training for some men to adjust to Army life.

Part of our job as NCOs was to set a good example for the trainees. We were expected be clean-shaven and wear clean and starched fatigues and shiny boots. I had learned to spit-shine my boots in basic training using a cotton ball and water. During NCO school I also learned a light coat of Glow Coat floor wax made the toes of my boots even shiner.

One night midway through OJT, some men on the first floor of our barracks started a pillow fight after lights out. I yelled at them to knock it off, but they continued. I was tired and after a few more minutes I was mad. I ran down stairs, turned on the lights and told the trainees that if they had so damn much energy, we would get up early and go for a run. The trainees knew I was pissed. They all climbed in their bunks without saying a word. I woke the entire platoon up at five o'clock the next morning and led them on a thirty-minute double time run before breakfast. There were no more late-night pillow fights in the third platoon.

Just as I had anticipated, OJT was undemanding duty. We had to get up early but didn't have to directly participate in much of the training. We spent a lot of time just watching over the trainees while they went through training exercises. We rotated leading the PT drills and double-time runs to get the guys in shape for their PT test. I was in the best shape of my life and could lead a double-time run almost forever without getting tired.

Fortunately, the early summer days at Fort Lewis were normally sunny and mild with only an occasional rain shower. Two of the NCOs had cars that we used to cruise around post during our weekends off or to drive into Tacoma for a change of pace and act like civilians. However, everyone knew we were in the service because of our GI haircuts.

In early June I received a letter from Larry Dolish, one of the Wayne State gang, saying he and his fiancée Cheryl wanted me to be in their wedding on June 28th. I called Larry and said I would just make it. I planned to fly into Omaha on the 27th to start my leave.

I had received a couple of letters from Allen Schwab during NCO School. He was serving in the northern highlands of South Vietnam. I also got a letter from Allen in late June saying he had been home on emergency leave to get married because his girlfriend Vicki was due to have a baby in September. I wrote Allen back to say congratulations. I also jokingly told him that was good planning to miss a couple of weeks of combat duty.

With OJT quickly winding down, I would soon learn if I was going to Vietnam. The trainees had been advised about NCO School, and I encouraged those who I felt would make good NCOs to go. Now and then a trainee would call one of us a shake'n bake in a derogatory manner and would find himself pulling an unpleasant detail for his comment. However, as the weeks passed, a mutual respect developed between most of the trainees and us new NCOs and between the drill sergeants and new NCOs. We often ignored ranks and just talked man to man. The trainees and we shake'n bakes knew that nearly all of us were headed for Vietnam. We were just trying to work together to prepare ourselves for that eventuality.

Our OJT concluded with the traditional AIT bivouac. While on bivouac we assisted the trainees on assault and tactic exercises and led them on simulated ambushes. It was interesting to see how they reacted to the simulated combat exercises designed to create new and challenging experiences for them. One night I took a group of trainees out to set up an ambush along a trail. An "enemy" patrol was to come by, and we would ambush them. By the time the patrol walked by most of the trainees had fallen asleep. If it had been the real thing, they all could have been killed.

It was finally the last day of bivouac. We guided the trainees through their final drills and then started one more forced march, with us NCOs expected to set an example for the trainees. I pushed on as hard as I ever had on a forced march, encouraging the laggers to keep up and not give up until they reached the company area. I tried not to show my true fatigue when I walked into our company area. But I was beat. The trainees enjoyed the beer that awaited them, and I joined them in celebration of completing their AIT.

The next day the trainees and we new NCOs picked up our orders. After the rest of the men in the third platoon received their orders, I stepped up to receive mine. My orders read as I anticipated, "Vietnam." I was given two weeks leave and was to report back to Fort Lewis on Sunday, July 12, 1969. All of us new NCOs and nearly every trainee received orders for Vietnam. I wasn't looking forward to going, but it was finally a relief to know for sure.

When the trainees finished their details around the barracks, they were given the rest of the day off. The men in my platoon wanted me to join them at a nearby club. I bought the first round of beer for some of them and relaxed for a while before returning to the barracks to hit the sack. It was almost dark when I was awakened by a group of trainees who barged into my room, pulled me out of bed, and carried me outside and around the barracks with me wearing only a pair of boxer shorts. They laughed and cheered as they carried the old sarge around the barracks. I let them have their fun and then crawled back into bed and fell asleep, ignoring the noise they were making.

Friday, June 27th was graduation day for the trainees. Our next assignment would be the real thing with real ammunition and men being wounded and killed. I stood with my platoon during the graduation ceremony listening closely to the speaker, hoping to hear some words of wisdom or advice to take with me to Vietnam. Unfortunately, it was the same old, "be proud and brave soldiers" with an expression of his best wishes as we moved on.

After we marched back to the company area the trainees were dismissed. Many of the men in the third platoon took a minute to share a good-bye with me while they grabbed their duffel bags and ran to catch a ride to the airport. They had enjoyed having me as one of their platoon sergeants and wished me well in Vietnam. Several of us shared a taxi ride to the airport in Seattle. I checked in my OD-green duffel bag and moved on to the gate to board my flight to Omaha. It was great to be going home for two weeks as my final fling before going to Vietnam.

159 men graduated with me from NCO School Class No. 27-69. The following members of that class were killed in action in Vietnam.

Name	Age	Date Killed in Action
SSG Samuel H. Pierce, Jr.*	37	August 16, 1969
SSG David P. Henry	19	September 25, 1969
SGT John H. Wilson	19	November 3, 1969
SGT Norris R. Borgman	21	January 6, 1970
SGT Charles M. Shumpert	21	February 11, 1970
SGT James A. Barnes	21	February 16, 1970
SSG Calvin W. Kolb	20	March 14, 1970
and Tactical NCO		
SSG Kenneth R. Kroehler	25	January 21, 1970

* Samuel H. Pierce, Jr. was the "old man" who went through training with me. He arrived in Vietnam on August 4, 1969. Sam's dream of making the Army his career ended when he was killed in action 12 days later. Sam, thank you for your loyal and fearless service to your country.

An infantryman in Vietnam had an approximate 50% chance of either being wounded or killed in action. Infantrymen sustained 80% of the U.S. Army casualties in Vietnam.

We Were The Third Herd

Chapter 4

Home on Leave

I found a pillow and slept most of the flight. I awoke when the pilot announced that we were starting our descent into Omaha. I excitedly walked into the terminal and Jan greeted me with open arms and a smile. We shared a long kiss while I put my arms around her and held her tight. Getting away from the Army again felt great. Jan knew I was going to Vietnam because I had called her after receiving my orders. But I put that in the back of my mind and looked forward to spending time with Jan plus my family and friends. I planned to stay in Omaha until Sunday when my folks would drive down to pick me up and we would drive back to Schaller.

That evening I joined many of my Wayne State friends for Larry Dolish's bachelor party. One of the first questions someone asked was, "Are you going to Vietnam?" A brief silence interrupted the celebration after I said, "Yes." That night was like the good old days, sharing fun and laughter with my college buddies. For those few hours I forgot about what awaited me on the other side of the world.

Larry and Cheryl had a big wedding with all of the trimmings, followed by a reception at a private hall. It was an afternoon I wanted to last forever as I danced with Jan and talked and laughed with good friends. But I reluctantly made the rounds saying good-bye as Jan and I prepared to leave. It had been an enjoyable day, but it ended way too quickly.

Jan and I went to Paul and Jane Alesch's apartment and hit the sack early that night. I snuggled near her and enjoyed the warmth and comfort of her firm little body next to me all night long.

My folks arrived in Omaha about noon that Sunday. While driving home I told my folks about my fairly pleasant past two months at Fort Lewis. We talked a little about my going to Vietnam, but I didn't share any details concerning humping through the rice paddies and jungles carrying an M-16 and hand grenades, or that enemy soldiers would be trying to kill me.

During my first week of leave I slept in every morning and then cruised around town and talked with people. A lot of men who had been in the service knew what it meant when I told them I was in the infantry and going to Vietnam. It was comforting to hear them express their concerns when they learned that another one of the local guys was marching off to war. Having spent nearly a year in the Army I understood the special camaraderie shared among the veterans in Schaller. Some of them already had sons or relatives in Vietnam and hated to see more of us going over there.

In years past there were normally several guys around town during summer evenings, but it was strangely much quieter that summer. There were over a dozen men from around Schaller who were in the service, and several were in Vietnam. In a big city no one would have missed them except their families and a few friends. But in a town of only 850 people, the entire town missed every man who was gone. I spent a couple of nights with one of my buddies, John McDonough. John had a medical deferment from the draft and hated seeing his buddies going to Vietnam. We didn't do anything special. We just enjoyed some time together while I was home on leave.

I had talked with Dean Christiansen's parents and learned that he would be home on leave starting on July 11th or 12th. My orders required me to be at Fort Lewis on Sunday, July 13th. Additionally, Pop Corn Days were the weekend of July 18th and 19th. I had a dilemma.

After spending the July 4th weekend in Omaha with Jan and some of the Wayne State gang, I decided to stay home another week. I knew that lots of men were reporting in late for Vietnam and I heard that they weren't getting busted, which normally meant losing one rank. I called the Debarkation Center at Fort Lewis and told a clerk I had a family emergency and that I wouldn't report there until July 21st. The clerk said, "OK," and told me I could deal with it when I got there without saying anything about what might happen. I told my folks that I had called Fort Lewis and it was OK for me to stay one more week. They didn't question me. They were happy to have me home for another week.

After eating dinner with my folks on Friday, July 11th, I told them that I was going to Dean's welcome-home party at his sister's house. Like I had heard so many times before, Mom said, "Don't stay out too late."

A crowd of people was gathered when I walked into Marlys and Kenny's house. When I found Dean we shared handshakes and a hug. I then asked him where he was going. He said, "'Nam," with a serious look on his face. I then told Dean I should be reporting back to Fort Lewis that Sunday, but I was staying home another week to spend time with him. "That means you'll be AWOL," Dean said with a surprised expression on his face. I said, "Yeah, but I don't care. What are they going to do? Send me to Vietnam?" We both laughed.

We had gone to grade school, high school and college together. Now we were going to Vietnam together. It was hard to believe. Dean's twin brother Dennis wasn't at the party. He had been drafted in June and was in basic training at Fort Leonard Wood, Missouri.

On Sunday morning, the morning I should have left for Fort Lewis, I heard Mom say, "You better get up for church." I wanted to roll over and go back to sleep but I crawled out of bed knowing Mom and Dad wanted me to join them in church since it was my last Sunday at home. I had attended church a few times at Fort Lewis and Fort Benning and felt a sense of comfort in those little Army chapels, singing hymns and listening to the chaplain's sermon. An hour in church on some Sunday mornings helped me deal with being far away from family and friends and my unknown future in the world of combat.

I spent the remainder of that Sunday with my family who had gathered for another farewell. My sister Jan had been home from college again that summer, and I had seen her almost every day while on leave. My sister Marilyn, her husband Gary and their son Tim were there, along with my granddad. Mom fixed another one of her great Sunday noon meals that I especially enjoyed. Not only had I been living on Army chow for most of the past year, I would be eating a lot of C-rations in the not-too-distant future.

Naturally, they all hated to see me go to Vietnam, especially as an infantryman. I didn't go into too much detail about what I expected to be doing, but they all knew that it possibly meant that I could be killed. I shared a good-bye hug with my sister Marilyn and my little nephew Tim when she and her husband Gary left. It was the most difficult good-bye that I had ever shared with my sister.

During the next few days Dean and I enjoyed our time together without anyone telling us what to do. I also stopped by Allen Schwab's parents' house and read a recent letter from him. He complained about the monsoon rains and getting soaked nearly every day. His mom told me about Allen's quick trip home to get married in June and said it was more difficult for him to leave the second time after he knew what it was really like in Vietnam.

Almost before I realized, Pop Corn Day weekend arrived. My leave was almost over. I would leave late Saturday afternoon July 19th for Omaha as my first step toward Vietnam. I soon stopped counting the days I had left and started counting the hours.

That Friday night Schaller was again bustling with activities and filled with people as the weekend celebration began. Dean and I both put Vietnam in the back of our minds as we enjoyed a few more hours together at a farewell party that I wanted never to end. Guys and girls that I had gone to school with and other friends from around town stopped by during the evening to say hi, and then later good-bye.

I thanked Marlys and Kenny for the great party before I left late that night. Marlys said they would have an even bigger party when I got home next year. I turned and waved one final good-bye as I walked up the street to my parent's house.

On Saturday morning I had a couple of Mom's cinnamon rolls with milk for breakfast. I wanted to take a year's supply of those rolls with me. They would have been as much of a hit in Vietnam as they were around Schaller. I then walked with my folks and sat with them to watch the parade. Mom and Dad obviously weren't enjoying the Pop Corn Day weekend. Their thoughts were on my leaving for Vietnam and not much else.

After lunch I packed a khaki Army uniform, my shaving kit and a few personal items in my duffel bag and was soon ready to leave. I would be issued new jungle fatigues and boots and most everything else I would need when I arrived at Fort Lewis. I had talked with Jan Griffin during the week and had arranged for us to spend one more night with Paul and Jane on Saturday night in Omaha.

After I had packed my duffel bag, I wanted to say a final good-bye to a few people. I told my folks I would be back home in an hour or so to head for Omaha. I stopped by Dean's house. He was scheduled to follow me to Vietnam in a week, but it was unlikely we would see each other.

Dean and I told each other to be careful and looked forward to a celebration homecoming in a year. I shared a solemn hug with Dean and his parents on their front porch and then quietly walked away. We had enjoyed a great week together. It was well worth any problems I might encounter later.

I then looked for John McDonough. He wanted to have a shot of whiskey together as our farewell. I found John relaxing in the VFW Hall along with many other people. I walked up to him and said it was time for that farewell drink.

John ordered two shots of whiskey. We stood side by side and solemnly toasted each other. We both shook our heads a little and chuckled as the whiskey burned on the way down. It was a special moment, but definitely not one of our happier times. I shook John's hand and said, "I have to get out of here." It was ironic, making a final stop to say good-bye to friends in the VFW Hall, which represented men who had gone off to war before me. I quickly said good-bye and shook hands with several people on my way out the door.

My folks and sister Jan were patiently waiting for me when I arrived back home. Jan wasn't going to ride to Omaha with us. I gave her a long hug and she said, "Be careful, and write me."

In a shaky voice I said, "Yeah, I will," and gave her a little smile. Driving away from our house that day was one of the hardest things I had ever done. Although leaving for the Army a year earlier was difficult, this day was completely different. I didn't necessarily think I would be killed in Vietnam, but I knew my life as I had known it for twenty-two years would never be the same. Friends and family had been saying, "Be careful over there," and "Take care of yourself," which I planned to do. But I also knew my welfare might be determined by events that were totally out of my control.

While I drove the few blocks to the edge of town, I desperately wanted to reach out and grab something or someone to take with me as part of my past. I was leaving that peaceful little world in northwest Iowa and going to a strange place where men were being killed every day. I didn't want to go, but I had accepted my assignment and was fulfilling my military duty to serve in Vietnam.

Although I had stretched my leave to three weeks, it seemed like it had passed in an instant. The 120 miles from Schaller to Omaha flew by. The next thing I knew we were crossing the Missouri River into Omaha. It was as though the clock was double-timing during my last few hours of leave. Jan spent a few minutes talking with my parents after we arrived at her dorm, and then it was time to say good-bye to them. Mom made it quick as she put her arms around me to share a hug as tears formed in her eyes. She said a quiet, "Good-bye, I love you."

I shook my dad's hand while he said, "Don't try to be a hero."

I smiled and said in a quivering voice, "I won't. Good-bye." I had tears in my eyes and couldn't say anything else. I was going off to war, and we all had to accept it. I stood with my arm around Jan until my parents drove out of sight.

The one thought that helped keep me going during that last week of leave was spending my last night with Jan. I threw my duffel bag in the back seat of Jan's car and we went out for a casual dinner. My last few days back in Schaller had been fun but also depressing. But I found that my mood changed after I arrived in Omaha. I somehow had released my sad emotions about leaving home and was ready to spend a last enjoyable evening with Jan.

After dinner we drove to Paul and Jane's apartment. I hadn't made plans to see any of the rest of the gang that night. I just wanted to spend time with Jan. I talked with Paul and Jane and shared my thoughts about going to Vietnam. Fortunately for Paul, his Army reserve unit hadn't been called to active duty. But he knew that being in the infantry was the most hazardous duty in Vietnam. Like everyone else I had spoken with while I had been on leave, Paul and Jane, and of course Jan, could only wish me their best.

Jan and I made up the hide-a-bed and crawled in together to share my last night on leave. We talked for a few minutes and then embraced with a long kiss. Our passions rose as I pulled her beautiful, warm body close while we kissed and caressed each other in the darkness. Our bodies were ready to unite in the heat of passion when Jan hesitated and said, "Let's not let it happen like this."

We weren't madly in love with each other, and to make love because I was going to Vietnam wasn't the way she wanted it to happen. Making love because I was going to Vietnam certainly seemed like a perfectly good reason to me, but I respected her wishes. I held her close until I fell asleep.

The next thing I knew, Jane said, "Hogie, it's time to get up." It was 7:30 Sunday morning, July 20, 1969. Although the flight to Seattle was one that I would have willingly missed, I knew I had to get to Fort Lewis before the Army came looking for me. I put on my Army uniform for the first time in three weeks. I gave Jane a hug and shook Paul's hand while saying good-bye to the last of the Wayne State gang. It was difficult to walk out of their apartment that morning leaving more friends behind. Jan was my only remaining connection with home, family and friends. In a couple of hours I would be leaving her too. All of the conversations, the parties, the good-bye handshakes and the hugs and kisses, were a memory. I was facing the biggest unknown of my life and the greatest danger that anyone could ever imagine. What would it be like in Vietnam?

I was flying military standby, but was told there were plenty of seats available for the flight when I checked in. Jan and I shared a Coke while we waited for my 10:10 a.m. flight to Seattle. I told her it normally took a couple days to work through the Debarkation Center and be scheduled for a flight to South Vietnam. Although I had openly told her what I would be doing, I'm not sure if Jan truly understood. A year earlier, I wouldn't have understood either.

When they announced the boarding for my flight, I stood up, put my arms around Jan, and told her I would miss her. "Be careful. I'll be thinking about you," Jan said before we shared a final, long hug and kiss. I quietly said, "Good-bye."

I turned and walked toward the walkway. I looked back with tears in my eyes and forced a smile. We waved at each other one last time. I then turned and walked down the walkway and onto the plane.

My final tie with the world that I had known for twenty-two years was broken. I sat down in my seat on the plane and stared out the window, not concentrating on anything. I tried to think about something other than the fact I was leaving for Vietnam. That moment, as I looked through my watery eyes was the saddest and loneliest moment of my life. Shortly after take off I settled into my seat and fell asleep.

In May 1969 U.S. forces located a series of enemy bunkers atop Hill 937 in the Highlands of South Vietnam. For over a week, four infantry battalions attacked the hill. On May 20, 1969, they reached the summit, only to find the bunkers empty. During the battle for "Hamburger Hill" 56 Americans were killed, while nearly 700 NVA troops were killed. U.S. forces occupied Hamburger Hill for only two days and then abandoned it, as the hill was deemed to have no tactical value.

Chapter 5

Welcome to Vietnam

I was half awake when the pilot announced our descent into Seattle. In a few minutes we were on the ground. The terminal was a madhouse filled with GIs headed for Fort Lewis. After I found my duffel bag among the dozens of identical OD-green duffel bags, I headed outside, and climbed aboard a military shuttle bus waiting to take guys to the Debarkation Center at Fort Lewis.

After we pulled into the center we were told to check in to record our arrival. Everyone was pretty quiet as we moved inside a wooden building to check in. I'm sure most of those men were just like me – going through a little withdrawal after enjoying themselves on leave.

My moment of reckoning was about to arrive; however, it was again hurry up and wait. I had learned that standing in line was just a part of Army life. It must have been their way of training us to be patient. I finally moved to a desk and handed my orders that listed my scheduled reporting date, July 13th, to a sergeant. I would soon find out if I was in serious trouble.

He recorded some information and then said, "You're a week late reporting back from leave."

I said, "Yes, I know." I thought: "OK, here it comes."

He took a rubber stamp and planted in big letters on the reverse side of my orders, "REPORTED LATE."

I asked, "What does that mean?"

"They'll deal with it when you get to Vietnam," he replicd.

I said OK and quickly took my orders and moved on. Was that it? Not even a butt-chewing from a first sergeant. Well, that was fine with me. But what would happen when I arrived in Vietnam? I wasn't home free yet.

After we finished reporting in, we were told to claim a bunk in a nearby barracks. We would start processing through the center Monday morning. After throwing my duffel bag on a bunk I found the mess hall. I hadn't eaten anything except for a little breakfast in

Omaha and wanted something to eat, even if it was Army food.

The next morning I joined several hundred men, and a few women, to begin the processing activities. We were given a final medical check to be sure we had all of our shots and were clear to go from a medical standpoint. We were then issued jungle fatigues, jungle boots and a bush hat. We normally wore an OD-green baseball-style cap during the past year of training, but in Vietnam, most GIs wore casual-looking bush hats with a floppy brim all around. I would be issued more gear once I was assigned to a unit in Vietnam. I spent much of the day standing in one line after another processing through each checkpoint. After I completed all of the required actions, I would be scheduled for a flight to Vietnam.

Late that afternoon I went to the little club and sat down with a couple other men who had been making the rounds with me during the day. Those guys were also draftees and were in the infantry. We shared our thoughts concerning what was ahead for us in Vietnam while I relaxed and drank a couple of beers with them. I then ate my last stateside dinner at the mess hall at the Debarkation Center.

That evening I walked past the bulletin board where they posted the flight assignments, but I didn't see my name listed on any of the flights leaving early the next morning. I thought I would run into someone I knew along the way but I hadn't seen a familiar face all day long. When I thought about it, I realized most of the men I had trained with probably reported in when they were supposed to a week earlier and were already in Vietnam.

I didn't sleep well during my last night on American soil. I wasn't afraid of going to Vietnam, but the anticipation of the unknown was always in the back of my mind. I woke up early to shave and take a shower in relative peace while most of the guys were still sleeping. When I started shaving I thought, "Now I can start growing a mustache." I had wanted to grow a mustache, but I wasn't allowed to while I was in training during the past year. I didn't shave my upper lip that morning and started growing what turned out to be a brown bushy mustache I wore from then on.

After I dressed, I went directly to the bulletin board and found my name listed under Flight 218; scheduled departure time: 10:30 a.m., July 22, 1969. In three hours I would be leaving the United States for the first time in my life, headed for South Vietnam. Although I knew it was real and not a dream, it was still somewhat unbelievable that I would soon be facing combat.

When I walked into the terminal shortly before nine o'clock that morning, it was filled with GIs, each carrying an OD-green duffel bag. The terminal was an old warehouse type building with a concrete floor and large painted signs indicating check-in points for each flight. I stood in line while each man in front of me checked in and was given a boarding pass. Men, and again a few women, were sitting or lying all over the terminal, quietly awaiting their flight.

One more time, I stood in line to call home. I told Mom I was leaving for Vietnam in less than an hour, and got a quiet, "OK," for a response. I asked her to call Jan Griffin that night to tell her I was leaving. I told Mom I would write when I had a permanent address for her to send mail.

At ten o'clock we began boarding a civilian plane chartered by the military. Shortly after 10:30 we taxied down the runway and quickly rose into the sky over Washington State, heading for the blue Pacific Ocean. Our first stop was Honolulu, Hawaii about five hours later. After landing we deplaned and walked around the Honolulu terminal during our layover. I don't know if anyone had made a run for it in the past, but it certainly was tempting with palm trees swaying in the breeze. An hour later we were off to Guam, a small U.S.-held island in the Pacific halfway between Hawaii and Vietnam. After another one-hour layover in a small Air Force terminal, we were off to South Vietnam.

It was dark, and we were approximately halfway into the flight out of Guam. Suddenly the plane dropped and I felt my buckled seat belt tug hard on my waist. Guys who didn't have their seat belts fastened flew in the air, many of them actually hit the ceiling of the cabin. The sudden drop was immediately followed by a loud "thud." The plane shuddered and then leveled off and smoothly continued on.

A few passengers had bumps and bruises, but no one was seriously injured. The pilot later announced we encountered an air pocket and fell a couple hundred feet in a second until we finally caught air again. We all looked at each other and shook our heads in amazement. We hadn't even reached Vietnam and almost went down in a plane crash!

After a five-hour flight, we neared Cam Ranh Bay, on the eastern coast of South Vietnam. I couldn't see much when we descended into

57

Cam Ranh. There were almost no lights visible from the air, except a few lights near the runway, when we landed. After we deplaned and found our duffel bags, we gathered in a formation. A sergeant told us that most of us would complete more in-processing there and then be shipped off to one of the Army Divisions scattered throughout South Vietnam for a permanent assignment. The sergeant tried to march us to a barracks, but most of us didn't attempt to stay in step with the cadence he was calling. What could he do? Send us to Vietnam? I looked off in the distance as I walked and saw three strings of red tracers flowing from the sky toward the nearby countryside. It was a C-130 gunship firing 6,000 rounds a minute from each of the three Gatling guns (mini-guns) mounted on one side of the plane. When they fired, it literally looked like it was raining bullets. Those planes were nicknamed "Puff the Magic Dragon." If you were their target, "puff" – you were a goner. I had arrived at the war.

Wars and resistance against foreign powers had dominated Vietnam's history for more than 1,000 years. The French had battled communist forces for years after World War II with little success. The 1954 Geneva Accord established a settlement whereby a Demilitarized Zone was created between North and South Vietnam. Unfortunately, the Geneva Accord did not bring peace. North Vietnam was governed by a communist regime and received Soviet and Chinese support. U.S.-backed South Vietnam continued to fight the spread of communism into the South. The United States initially supported South Vietnam with money and supplies and then provided military advisors. However, as the fighting escalated, American military forces gradually assumed an active combat role. America's involvement reached a peak in 1968, when 536,000 U.S. military personnel served in South Vietnam. That number had been reduced by approximately 50,000 when I arrived in July 1969.

I then noticed a strange odor in the air. It didn't smell like an Iowa barnyard, it was more like the unpleasant combination of odors near a garbage dump. I asked the sergeant who had led us to the barracks what that odor was. He said, "It's just what this place smells like."

The next day I processed into Vietnam. They called it processing "in country." A clerk took my orders with the big "Reported Late" stamped on the backside. I quietly waited and again worried about what might happen. I had been AWOL for a week and deserved to get busted. The clerk annotated my arrival and then noticed the stamp on the back.

He looked at me and said, "You reported in late, huh?"

"Yeah," I said, "I stayed an extra week to spend time with a buddy who is on his way over here."

"Well," the clerk said, "Don't worry about that. You're in Vietnam. That's enough punishment in itself."

He told me my name would appear on the bulletin board outside when my permanent orders were ready in a day or two. I told the clerk thanks and quickly walked away before he changed his mind. After I checked in there wasn't anything else I had to do until I received my permanent assignment. Some of the guys were given clean-up details around the area, but for the most part we just hung out until we were notified to ship out.

Cam Ranh was a military base camp built near Cam Ranh Bay on the South China Sea 200 miles northeast of Saigon, the Capital of South Vietnam. Cam Rahn had a natural harbor that was developed into one of the largest seaports in South Vietnam to supply American forces. During the 1960s the United States built numerous military base camps all over South Vietnam. Many of the base camps were built near small towns and had the same name as the nearby town. The American base camps were well fortified and had restricted access by Vietnamese civilians.

Everything appeared peaceful around Cam Ranh. I hadn't been issued a weapon and I would only occasionally see someone carrying a rifle. Surprisingly, I felt pretty safe. But there was one depressing sight for us new arrivals. While we were processing in country, there were also hundreds of men who had completed their one-year tour who were processing out of South Vietnam. Some of those men noticed our new jungle fatigues and shiny-toed jungle boots and knew we had just arrived. They laughed and told us how sorry we soon would be about being there. "Watch out for Charlie," they jokingly said. "Charlie" or "Charlie Cong" was slang for the Viet Cong (enemy) troops.

I could see peaceful hills in the distance covered with thick green vegetation. But that was also where I had seen the gunship firing its mini-guns the past night. It wasn't as friendly as it appeared out there. I also noticed little plumes of smoke around the base camp and learned the smoke was from burning trash and human waste in steel barrels. No wonder the place had an unpleasant smell.

On July 24th my permanent orders were issued. I was assigned to the Army's 25th Infantry Division. Early that afternoon I boarded a camouflage-painted propeller-driven C-123 airplane that would take several of us to Cu Chi, the 25th Division Headquarters Base Camp.

Shortly after I found a seat on a row of webbed benches inside the plane, the engines roared and we rode down the airstrip until the plane lifted off into the sky over South Vietnam. I slid near one of the small windows to view the countryside. It was mostly dense green vegetation, flooded rice paddies and a dirt road now and then. I finally quit looking. I figured I would eventually see more of the countryside than I wanted to anyway. After a forty-five-minute flight we landed at Cu Chi, thirty miles northwest of Saigon. After another short bus ride I arrived at the 25th Division receiving area for another brief stay.

The base camp was like a small city where the Division headquarters, the 12th Evacuation Hospital (12th Evac) and many logistical and support units were located. The main roads were paved with asphalt and the rest were covered with gravel. Wood-framed buildings were scattered throughout the base camp. Cu Chi was built in a circle a couple of miles in diameter and was surrounded by sand bag bunkers built into a six-foot-high earthen berm called the perimeter. Army personnel manned the bunkers to keep the base camp secure. Outside the row of bunkers were coils of concertina wire. The concertina wire was similar to the miles of barbed wire used in Iowa to surround farm fields, except concertina wire has little razor-like blades with pointed tips woven into the wire. Those blades would snag on an intruder's clothing or cut someone trying to crawl through the wire.

The 25th Division Base Camp was named after the small town of Cu Chi, just outside the main gate. The area had once been a peanut plantation because the immediate area was well above the water table. That location had been selected for the base camp because the ground would hold the weight of planes, tanks and other heavy vehicles. Shortly after the base camp was built in 1966, Viet Cong (VC, meaning Vietnamese Communist) troops blew up an ammunition dump and then disappeared without a trace. The Army finally realized the base camp was sitting directly over a major tunnel complex built by the North Vietnamese Army (NVA) and VC. After months of effort, the tunnels were ultimately destroyed. However, the NVA and VC continued to use tunnels effectively all over South Vietnam to hide in and to store supplies and equipment. They would sleep and train in tunnels, and they had actually built underground hospitals.

After three days of orientation sessions that included explaining the rules of existence in Cu Chi and how the military operated in the area, I was taken by jeep to an infantry company as my permanent assignment. The jeep driver yelled at a man standing in front of the company headquarters, "Hey, Tom, I have some FNGs for you."

I looked at the two other men in the jeep and we shrugged our shoulders wondering, what are FNGs? I soon learned FNGs were "fucking new guys." The military had hundreds of acronyms, but I doubted that one was in any official manual. The three of us FNGs stepped off the jeep and walked over to the company headquarters to meet Specialist Fourth Class Tom Powers. He took our orders and checked us into the company. It was late afternoon. Tom said he would issue our weapons and gear and finalize processing us in the next day.

I settled into the little barracks across the street by claiming a bunk and throwing my duffel bag underneath it. There were about a dozen bunks in the barracks (or "hootch") used by men who were assigned to field duty, but were temporarily in Cu Chi. The men who were permanently assigned to our company in Cu Chi stayed in other buildings or hootches nearby. I had been assigned to Company A, 2nd Battalion, 14th Infantry Regiment, 25th Infantry Division. My final assignment would be to one of the three rifle platoons in Company A or Alpha Company as it was commonly called.

I had adjusted to the slowly deteriorating conditions since I arrived in Vietnam, but I knew there was much more in store for me when I went to the field. Most of the buildings in Cu Chi were simple wood frame buildings with corrugated metal roofs and large screen-covered openings on the sides to allow for ventilation. A four-foot-high wall of sand bags surrounded most of the buildings to protect anyone inside from shrapnel should an incoming mortar round land nearby. Unfortunately, if a round landed directly on a building, those inside were out of luck. One of the enemy's tactics was to fire mortar rounds into American military sites periodically in hopes of destroying property or wounding or killing GIs.

The latrines were similar to outhouses I had seen on farms in Iowa.

They were hot and smelly. There was also a small building with sinks and showers, with water provided from a large tank on the roof. The mess hall was a city block west of our hootch. At the end of the chow line I found two bowls containing malaria pills. One pill was to be taken daily, and the other pill was to be taken once a week to prevent our getting malaria from the mosquitoes.

That evening I found the first fringe benefit of being in Vietnam. Adjacent to our company area was a little club that opened at around 5:00 p.m. daily. It wasn't anything fancy, but they served cold beer for fifteen cents a can. I walked inside and met some of the other guys assigned to our company. Most of the men had served several months in the field and had been reassigned to the rear (meaning Cu Chi). Tom Powers was a big, husky guy who had been a machine gunner with the second platoon. He had recently been assigned to the rear and was in charge of the company's weapons. When replacement troops were assigned to platoons in the field they would often rotate the old timers (men who had been in the field the longest) back to the rear for the remaining months of their tour. A couple of other men were returning from a week of rest and relaxation (R&R) in Bangkok, Thailand.

I enjoyed making some new acquaintances that night. Regardless of who you were or where you were from, just being in Vietnam quickly made you one of the guys. The sad good-byes to my family and friends on the opposite side of the world were being replaced by the pleasure of meeting new friends in the relatively crude existence of Cu Chi. However, I also knew the peacefulness of that evening was only a brief pause on my way to facing the realities of the war.

During the next few days I attended more orientation and training sessions about serving in Vietnam and I checked in with the payroll office so I would get paid. We were also told it was the philosophy of the 25th Division to use firepower rather than manpower. That meant that, rather then engaging the enemy in a long firefight with rifles and machine guns and increasing the likelihood of serious American casualties, we would, when possible, withdraw from direct enemy contact and call in artillery or air support to knock out the enemy with the large artillery shells and bombs.

An instructor also explained an important American military philosophy regarding the grim reality of war. It was the tradition of the United States military to make every attempt to evacuate men who were wounded or killed in action from the immediate battleground. He solemnly said, "All of you will want to be evacuated if you are wounded or killed. You'll be expected to do the same for your buddies. Any questions?" There were none.

My indoctrination wasn't too demanding, leaving me time to check out Cu Chi. The PX, other little shops and a bank were in the center of the base camp. There was an NCO Club, Officer's Club, a chapel and two bathhouses where you could take a steam bath and get a massage. There were other little clubs scattered around like the one near our company area. Some clubs served mixed drinks for a quarter and others showed movies at night. There was also a Special Services Club with pool tables and games to play and books to read. There was even a swimming pool.

After I was issued my M-16 rifle I went to a rifle range to test-fire it and adjust the sights. I was also issued a helmet, a backpack, a pistol belt and web gear (shoulder harness), ammunition pouches, a gas mask, a canteen and everything else I would need, including a flak jacket, which was a thick, heavy vest to protect our chest, abdomen and back from shrapnel. I completed my final day of the orientation and training on August 3rd and was told I was ready for the "field," the countryside of South Vietnam. Tom Powers told me Alpha Company had run into an enemy bunker complex the previous day. One man in the first platoon had been killed and several men in the third platoon had been wounded during a firefight, and earlier, another man in the third platoon had been killed by a booby trap. I was being assigned to the third platoon, because they needed more men. I still had the khaki uniform I had worn to Fort Lewis and a few other items I knew I wouldn't need in the field. I put them in my duffel bag and left it with Tom Powers to lock up in a storage container.

After lunch the next day, a convoy of a jeep and two deuce-and-a-halfs loaded with supplies was assembled along the gravel road that led through the company area. I put on my helmet, grabbed my gear and my M-16 and climbed on the back of a deuce-and-a-half, ready for my trip to the field along with a couple of other men. There were no traditional front lines in South Vietnam like there had been in most previous wars. Our company operated out of smaller complexes called fire support bases and patrol bases and normally went out on patrols across the countryside during the day and set up remote ambushes at night.

We drove a mile and then reached the main gate of Base Camp Cu Chi. When we passed the guards at the gate the man who was manning the M-60 mounted on the deuce-and-a-half said, "You guys better lock and load."

The other men and I locked-in an ammunition magazine and loaded a round into the chamber of our rifles. We traveled through the village of Cu Chi and then turned west down an asphalt highway. It was Highway 1 that started in Saigon and led northwest to Tay Ninh near a mountain we could see in the distance called Nui Ba Den "Black Virgin" Mountain. Further west was Cambodia. There were lots of civilians riding along the highway on two- and three-wheeled motor scooters, and many kids and adults walking on the side of the road. They all moved aside as we roared past.

We drove a few miles west on Highway 1 and then turned northeast on a gravel road. We passed through the little village of Bau Dieu that consisted of primitive mud huts with tin or straw roofs. I saw no sign of modern civilization. I hadn't seen an automobile since we left Cu Chi. We drove less than a mile along the road and then stopped at a little compound occupied by a group of GIs. Tom Powers who was riding in the lead jeep, turned around and yelled, "Sergeant Hogue, this is where you get off." I had finally found my new home. I jumped down from the truck and waved to Tom as the convoy moved up the road.

On July 1, 1964, Army medical evacuation helicopter pilot Major James Kelly was killed in action in South Vietnam. Thereafter, his call sign, "Dustoff," became the nickname for medical evacuation helicopters.

Chapter 6

Meeting the Third Herd

I walked from the road onto a metal walkway that covered the muddy ground near the entrance to the compound and met a man who introduced himself as the platoon sergeant, Tom Brown. Staff Sergeant Brown was a fairly tall guy with sandy brown hair.

He reached out to shake my hand and said, "Hi, welcome to the third platoon. They call us the 'Third Herd.' "

I looked at the compound for a few seconds and then asked, "What's this?" I saw a group of four sandbag bunkers on the east side of the road surrounded by rice paddies on the remaining three sides.

"It's Venice East," Sergeant Brown replied. It was an outpost to guard the road at night to stop the enemy from setting land mines. Sergeant Brown said the road was used daily by military vehicles traveling to and from "Patton," our battalion fire support base (firebase). I could see the outline of bunkers that formed the perimeter of the firebase a half-mile to the northeast. He said we would be heading back there in several days after a few more men, like me, were assigned to replace some of the men they had lost two days earlier in the Ho Bo Woods.

I didn't understand exactly what was going on, but assumed I would soon learn. He led me through the entrance, a small doorway built into a ten-foot-high chain link fence that surrounded the compound. Sergeant Brown walked to one of the bunkers and said, "Hang on, you can meet our platoon leader." He leaned into the bunker entrance and said, "Hey, 3-6, want to meet a new NCO?"

Platoon leaders were nicknamed after their radio call sign. The call sign for the third platoon leader was "3-6." The second platoon leader was "2-6" and so on. "6" was the call sign for the Company Commander (CO) who was the next in the line of command above the platoon leaders. Our CO was a captain in charge of the four platoons in Alpha Company. The first, second and third platoons were rifle platoons armed with M-16 rifles, M-60 machine guns and M-79 grenade launchers. The mortar platoon provided support with 81MM mortars.

A few seconds later, a man my size and wearing glasses stepped from the bunker. He reached out to shake my hand and said, "Hi, I'm Steve Donaldson, platoon leader. Glad to have you with us."

Lieutenant Donaldson was a first lieutenant. As the platoon leader, he was in command of the platoon and delegated duties to the platoon sergeant and squad leaders, as he desired. If anything happened to him, the platoon sergeant would take command.

After talking with Lieutenant Donaldson for a few minutes, Sergeant Brown and I walked to a bunker facing the road that would be my new home. He then introduced me to more of the men. First I met Larry Jackson, the platoon's medic. "Doc" was a tall thin guy with a bushy mustache who had been in country for a few months. Men were sometimes assigned as medics if they refused to carry a weapon because of religious or personal beliefs. But Doc Jackson carried an M-16 along with the rest of us.

I was also introduced to Sergeant Jim Overbey. He was a slender guy from Kentucky with light brown hair. Jim was another shake'n bake who had arrived a week earlier. Sergeant Brown told me that Jim and I would be his squad leaders. I would have the first squad and Jim Overbey had the second squad.

I threw my gear inside the bunker and claimed a small area as my home territory where I would be sleeping on an air mattress that night. The bunkers were made of OD-green sand bags that had a plastic fiber material woven into the cloth to make them less susceptible to deterioration from constant exposure to the sun and rain in Vietnam. Large wood beams provided a framework and support for the bunkers. 4' x 8' sheets of perforated steel planking (PSP) supported the layers of sand bags and plastic sheeting that formed the top of each bunker. Bunkers provided protection from small arms (rifle and machine gun) fire and shrapnel from incoming rockets or mortar rounds. Whether or not a bunker could withstand a direct hit depended upon how well it was built and how many sand bags were used. I hoped never to find out for sure.

The name Venice East sounded like an exotic place, but it was actually another big step away from the modern world. The 100 foot square compound sat in the middle of an abandoned rice paddy and was surrounded on three sides by other rice paddies flooded with two feet of water. With all the water around us, I understood how the place had earned its name.

Four sand bag bunkers inside the compound were elevated on fifty-five gallon barrels filled with dirt. Walkways were built between the bunkers enabling us to move around inside without walking through the muddy water directly below. In the center of the compound was a fifteen-foot-high wooden tower. The tower housed radar equipment used at night to spot enemy movement in the area, and was also where we "pulled guard" at night. The chain link fence surrounding the compound would detonate an incoming B40 rocket (rocket-propelled grenade, RPG) the enemy fired from a rocket launcher. The RPG would detonate when it struck the fence rather than detonating when it hit a bunker or something inside.

Dave Hardy was one of the men in my squad who had been in country for a couple months. I spent a lot of time talking with him during my first few days in the field and asking questions about what I was supposed to be doing out there. Hardy was a slender twenty-year-old guy who was friendly and more than willing to answer my questions and share his experiences. I appreciated that. Although I had spent most of the past year in training to serve as an infantryman in Vietnam, I hadn't expected anything like Venice East.

Hardy told me about the company running into the enemy bunkers two days prior, on August 2nd. One man in the first platoon was killed by machine gun fire and nearly half the men in the third platoon received shrapnel wounds when the VC popped out of tunnels and began throwing hand grenades. Hardy then went on to tell me that they had lost George Conrad earlier that same day when a huge explosion literally tore his body into pieces. Dave said they had to pick up body parts and put them in a body bag. I could tell by the sad tone of his voice that it was difficult talking about losing a friend.

The company normally walked in two single columns when on patrols or Reconnaissance in Force (RIF), as the Army called them. They also would normally have one man walk roughly thirty meters to the side of each column for expanded vision over the countryside. That man was the "flank man" and it was called "walking flank." It was a dangerous place to be. Conrad was walking flank when a booby-trapped land mine killed him instantly.

Thousands of American artillery and mortar rounds were fired in

South Vietnam every day. However, a few of those rounds were "duds" and didn't explode when they landed. If the enemy found a dud round, they often made a booby trap by connecting a firing mechanism that was activated by stepping on it or tripping a wire attached to it which would detonate the round, often with deadly consequences. The NVA and VC used a variety of devices as booby traps, including land mines that contained enough explosives to destroy a vehicle, and "Bouncing Betty" mines. When triggered, the Bouncing Betty would pop out of the ground and detonate when it was two to four feet in the air.

The platoon sergeant, the medic and two radio/telephone operators (RTOs) were assigned directly under the platoon leader. Each RTO carried a PRC-25 two-way radio that was (naturally) OD green and had an antenna that extended several feet into the air. Chuck Gorman and Dennis Schultz were our RTOs who carried the twenty-five pound radios on their backs with a shoulder harness. We used a Phonetic Alphabet intended to ensure clear radio communication. Each letter of the alphabet was assigned a word. We would say Alpha for A, Bravo for B, and Charlie for C and so on. If an RTO wanted to radio that we saw VC he would say, "We saw some Victor Charlie."

The remaining men in the platoon were divided into two squads of seven to ten men each, depending upon the actual number of men in the platoon. Each squad had a two-man M-60 machine gun team consisting of a "gunner" who carried the weapon and 400 to 500 rounds of ammunition and the "assistant gunner" who also carried 500 rounds of M-60 ammunition in addition to his M-16 and ammunition magazines. The rest of us each carried a 100-round belt of M-60 ammunition that we could pass along to the team if needed. An M-60 machine gun could fire nearly 500 rounds a minute by connecting 100-round belts of ammunition together with the black clips attached to each shell casing. One man in each squad also carried an M-79 grenade launcher and the remaining men carried M-16 rifles. The two squads were pre-designated and normally had an NCO in charge for tactical maneuvers in combat situations or other duty that didn't require the entire platoon. The two squads normally rotated ambush duty assignments.

Each platoon was also assigned a Vietnamese soldier called a Chieu Hoi (which meant "open arms"). They were former VC or NVA soldiers who had either surrendered or were captured and then volunteered to support the South Vietnamese cause. Our Chieu Hoi was

named Hue and served as our scout. Although the idea of having a former enemy soldier working with us sounded crazy, the guys said Hue
had proven himself to be trustworthy. He carried an M-16 like the rest
of us. Hue's job was to help search for signs of the enemy during our
daily RIFs and help us communicate with Vietnamese people. Hue of
course spoke Vietnamese, and also spoke enough English to communicate with us.

Platoons were normally assigned to Venice East on a rotating basis
for a week at a time. The third platoon was there as a reprieve after the
firefight in the Ho Bo Woods. The platoon was slowly growing back
to a "normal" strength of twenty-five men. The atmosphere at Venice
East was pretty relaxed during the day. We didn't carry our weapons
and guys often "hung-out" along the road. But when darkness fell, we
got serious.

Our first task each evening was to arm thirty claymore mines
(claymores) which were placed around the perimeter. The blasting
caps were removed from the claymores every morning to prevent an
accidental detonation and were reinserted each night. Claymores were
rectangular antipersonnel mines an inch thick. There was a layer of
BBs in front of a layer of C-4 plastic explosive. The claymore was
detonated by a blasting cap that was connected to an electric wire leading to a detonator kept inside the bunkers. When you squeezed the
handle on the detonator it sent an electrical charge that fired the claymore. The claymores fired a huge shotgun-like blast of hundreds of
BBs in a convex pattern. We often connected two or three claymore in
a series, using blasting caps and detonation (det) cord. One detonator
could fire the connected claymores sending out a deadly wall of BBs.

After we closed the gate, we were barricaded inside the little compound for the night. We placed our ammunition and weapons in a con-
venient location in case we might need them during the night. Since
there were no lights, except for a few flashlights, the men started to
settle in when it got dark, while we set up guard duty assignments.

Two radar operators, not assigned to our platoon, rotated duty in
the tower at night to monitor the radar for enemy movement around
us. The rest of us rotated one-hour guard shifts along with one of the
radar operators. I didn't have guard duty during my first night at
Venice East. After dark I crawled inside my bunker and curled up
on an air mattress and covered myself with a poncho liner (a light

71

blanket with military camouflage design). It was a strange feeling lying inside a bunker with sand bag walls over a foot thick. Although I was in the middle of a war, that bunker gave me a feeling of security. I quickly fell asleep as the monsoon rain poured outside. That night passed without incident and we got up shortly after sunrise. Men began crawling out of their bunkers and taking a stretch while looking around at clear morning skies.

Lieutenant Donaldson stepped out from his bunker and said, "Sergeant Hogue, your squad has road detail today."

I replied, "OK," but I didn't know exactly what I was supposed to do. While I was putting on my gear I asked Dave Hardy, "What the hell are we supposed to do?"

He said it would be easy. We would follow two mine sweepers as they cleared the road and hope nothing happened. I thought, "I can handle that."

Two men carrying mine detectors led us in separate columns as we walked along the road. They slowly moved their mine detectors back and forth over the road to detect any metal objects. It took over half an hour to sweep the road from Venice East to the entrance of Firebase Patton. We then turned around and swept the road southwest through the village of Bau Dieu. The total distance was a mile and a half. When we neared Bau Dieu I noticed a little compound north of the village. I asked the guys what it was.

"It's an ARVN compound," someone replied. ARVN was the acronym for the Army of the Republic of South Vietnam. They were on our side. After we completed the sweep without detecting any land mines, we radioed the Alpha Company Command Post (CP) at Patton and told them the road was clear. The local civilians also waited until after we had cleared the road before they began their travels by walking or riding along on scooters or wooden carts pulled by cows or water buffalo. We walked back into Venice East and I took off my gear, wondering what was next. The rest of the platoon had disarmed the claymores and cleaned up the compound while we were gone.

A deuce-and-a-half arrived a short while later and dropped off a hot breakfast from the mess hall at Patton in several OD-green insulated food containers. A hot breakfast and dinner was normally delivered to Venice East every day.

We organized a chow line in a tent set up along side the road and loaded up on scrambled eggs and bacon on paper plates. They also delivered two cases of C-rations that we could rummage through if we got hungry during the day. Each case of C-rations contained a dozen smaller boxes that each contained a meal like potatoes and beef, spaghetti and meatballs, or scrambled eggs and ham. There was also canned fruit, peanut butter and jelly, crackers, and everyone's favorite treat, sponge cake. Additionally, there were little packs of coffee and hot chocolate mix, and most importantly, there were small P-38 can openers and packets of toilet paper in each case of C-rations.

After the road was cleared and the compound was cleaned up, we could relax for the rest of the day and do nearly whatever we chose. Men would catch up on letter writing, take a nap, play poker or hang out along the road and talk with kids and adults who were walking past or trying to sell them something. During my first full day there I joined a friendly quarter-limit poker game. But rather than using American money, we used Military Payment Currency (MPC). When we arrived in country we exchanged our money for MPC to control inflation and corruption in South Vietnam. The MPC was paper money that replaced both American coins and paper currency.

Vietnam was nearly 1,000 miles north of the equator. Summer was the rainy season, more commonly known as the monsoon season. The mornings were normally sunny and dry, but during the hot and humid afternoons, often within a matter of minutes, the skies would turn cloudy and it would begin to rain. We were fortunate at Venice East because we could seek shelter in the bunkers. The layers of plastic sheets on the top of the bunkers normally kept the rain from leaking inside. Because the monsoon season wouldn't end until October, we would have to put up with the rain and flooded countryside for a couple more months.

During my third day at Venice East they delivered what was called an S-P pack. The men acted like it was Christmas. The S-P packs that contained nearly everything we needed in the way of personal items and goodies were delivered weekly to each platoon. In addition to shaving cream and razors, toothpaste and soap, there were cartons of cigarettes, two packages of little Crooks cigars, candy bars and sta-tionery. Someone would control the dispensing of items to ensure everyone got his fair share from each pack. I didn't smoke cigarettes, but I did take a couple Crooks cigars and stashed them in a dry place to smoke later.

I soon learned there wasn't much I needed in the field that the Army didn't provide. Along with delivering hot meals and C-rations, they often delivered sodas. We could chip in and have beer delivered but the men stuck to an unwritten rule of generally not drinking in the field. It was more important to have a clear head out there and save the partying for when we were in the relative safety of Cu Chi.

My first few days at Venice East passed without any major incident. I spent a lot of time getting to know the men and learning as much as I could from the old timers who had been in the field several months. One of our RTOs, Chuck Gorman, was one of those "old timers" who had been with the Third Herd since that past May. He told me about a man in the first platoon who had been killed a couple months earlier when shrapnel struck and detonated a white phosphorous grenade he was carrying. The man was literally burned to death by the tremendous heat generated from the burning white phosphorous. None of us knew exactly what might happen next. But I knew one thing for sure, the relative peacefulness of Venice East wouldn't continue forever.

It was soon August 14th, my birthday. I had spent my last birthday in basic training, without any celebration. It appeared my twenty-third birthday would be just another day in South Vietnam. But, late that afternoon Sergeant Brown told me the CO wanted two men to pull guard at the ARVN compound that night.

I looked at him and said, "Oh Yeah, I suppose one of them will be me?"

Tom Brown smiled and put a hand on my shoulder, "Yep. Pick someone to go with you and grab your gear."

When I walked back to my bunker Dave Hardy asked, "What's up?"

I said, "Grab your gear, you're coming with me."

"What for?"

I smiled like Tom Brown had smiled at me and said, "We're spending the night at the ARVN compound."

"Oh, you're kidding, Sarge," Hardy said.

"I'm not kidding, grab your gear."

Hardy wasn't too happy I had picked him to join me, but he put on his gear without saying anything else. I guess that was why I liked him. He didn't complain like I knew some of the men might have. Neither of us knew exactly what we would be doing, and we definitely weren't too excited about only the two of us spending the night with the ARVNs. It sounded like a night of on-the-job-training for me.

We each took our M-16s, several hand grenades, a starlight scope and one of our radios to communicate with Venice East and our company command post at Firebase Patton. A short while later a deuce-and-a-half with a few men riding in the back stopped in front of the compound. Company Commander Captain William Branch was riding in the front and stepped out. Lieutenant Donaldson walked out to the road with Dave Hardy and me and introduced me to our CO.

Captain Branch said, "Sergeant, welcome to Alpha Company, I'm glad to have you with us," as we shook hands.

The CO explained to Lieutenant Donaldson and me that the ARVNs had observed enemy activity around the village the past night and the VC had fired some RPGs into their compound. The ARVNs asked to have GIs pull guard in their tower and call in mortar fire if needed. It sounded like they should be sending an entire platoon to provide reinforced support rather then sending two GIs. But I wasn't given the opportunity to recommend that option. After talking with Captain Branch for a couple more minutes he said, "Hop aboard." Hardy and I climbed in the back of the deuce-and-a-half for our short ride down the road.

With Venice East fading in the distance, I asked Hardy, "What the hell are they getting us into?"

"I don't know Sarge," was his reply as he shook his head.

A minute later we were at the ARVN compound north of the village of Bau Dieu. After Hardy and I jumped to the ground we walked with Captain Branch to the compound entrance and were met by two ARVN officers. The CO told the ARVNs that Hardy and I would spend the night at their compound.

Captain Branch pointed to a wooden tower in the center of the compound and told Hardy and me that was where we would pull guard for the night. He told us to call the CP for a radio check when we were settled in. The Alpha Company's Command Post at Patton was where Captain Branch and his staff were located.

Hardy asked the CO what call sign we should use.

Captain Branch said, "Just use Alpha Papa 3."

When squads or platoons set up an ambush at night, Alpha Papa was the phonetic radio term for Ambush Patrol. "3" was the designation for the third platoon. To keep it easy, Hardy and I were Alpha Papa 3 for the night.

Captain Branch said he would send a truck to pick us up in the morning. We waved to the guys in the back of the truck who were providing an escort guard as the driver turned it around and headed north towards Firebase Patton. Hardy and I walked through the main gate with the two ARVN officers.

Dave Hardy and I stopped when we reached the tower. The ARVNs kept walking on without saying a word. We never saw them the rest of the night. After Hardy and I climbed to the top of the tower we looked around and saw several wooden shacks and sand bag bunkers scattered around the compound. Coils of concertina wire were strung around the perimeter, and I saw one machine gun sitting on top of a bunker. There were also several women and children running around.

I looked at Hardy and asked, "What kind of an Army compound is this?

Hardy said, "The ARVNs are a pretty loose outfit."

"It looks like it," I said, "Now I see why they need us to fight their war."

The wooden tower was about fifteen feet high with a small platform at the top. There was just enough room for one of us to curl up and sleep on one side while the other man sat up and pulled guard. There was a two-foot wall of sand bags built around the edge of the tower floor, giving us some protection. But it looked like we were sitting ducks if enemy troops wanted to take a shot at us. B40 rockets had been fired into the compound the past night. Heaven help Hardy and me if a rocket hit the tower. Fortunately, there was a solid roof to protect us from the rain that would certainly fall during the night.

We did a radio check to establish communications with our command post. I also looked over the nearby countryside to identify the pre-established locations that had been coordinated with our mortar platoon. If I needed their support, I would first call in fire to one of those pre-established locations that I had marked on my map and adjust the fire from there.

There was also a little twist to the rules of engagement in the inhabited areas of South Vietnam. Those areas were considered "no-fire" zones during the day. That meant we weren't supposed to fire on anyone unless we were fired upon first. If we saw someone with a weapon or if it was otherwise obvious he or she was an enemy soldier, we could fire, but otherwise the civilians were generally free to move around in the no-fire zones without their lives being threatened by American fire.

The radar operators at Venice East frequently observed movement in and out of nearby villages at night. We had to assume they were the enemy. But because most of the Vietnamese people looked the same when we saw them during the day, we had no idea who were truly friendly civilians and who were VC who had hidden their weapons. However, at night the rules changed. Anyone moving outside the villages was considered the enemy and could be fired upon, with no questions asked.

It was five o'clock in the afternoon. There wasn't anything for us to do except wait a couple of hours until darkness. I sat in the tower looking over the compound and noticed a young woman walk to an open area near one of the little hootches. She pulled down her pants and squatted over a small hole in the ground.

I said, "Hey, Hardy," as I pointed to the woman, "don't they have outhouses?"

He said no, they just dig a hole in the ground. He told me if I listened closely when I walked by one of those holes I might hear the buzzing noise of maggots. The hole was in the open with no wall or anything to provide a little privacy. The people who walked near her paid no attention. After a few seconds the lady stood up, pulled up her pants and walked away.

I then thought of a way I might celebrate my birthday before dark. The kids in the compound had stopped by periodically and held their hands out hoping we would give them candy or something to cat. I had learned the kids and adults who had stopped by Venice East were always trying to sell us watches, jewelry, clothes and, yes, girls in exchange for money, cigarettes or even C-rations. Hardy and I had brought some C-rations with us, but neither of us was too hungry. I took two cans of C-rations and climbed down the tower hoping to make a deal with the kids.

I said, "Two beers," holding up two fingers.

I held out the C-rations indicating I would trade them for two beers. The kids understood and came running back a short while later with two cans of beer. I gave the kids the C-rations and climbed up the tower with the two beers.

After we opened our beers Hardy said, "Happy birthday, Sarge," as we tapped our cans together.

We laid back on the sand bag wall and talked while we drank a beer, and I quietly commemorated my twenty-third birthday in a way that I could never have imagined.

As darkness slowly arrived the ARVNs closed the main gate and activity along the road ceased. Many civilians traveled along the roads and across the countryside during the day, but they knew it wasn't safe to be outside their villages or hamlets scattered around the countryside at night.

It was finally completely dark, and I mean dark. There were no porch lights or streetlights in the nearby village of Bau Dieu; in fact, there was no electric power in any of the villages. I saw a few flickers of light from cooking fires or small lanterns, but for the most part, it was totally dark. It wasn't raining, but the clouds had moved in just before dark. There was no moon or starlight to help us see anything beyond the perimeter. There was a little movement inside the compound, but I could see a few ARVNs standing by their bunkers hopefully standing guard.

Hardy offered to take the first one-hour guard shift. I wrapped up in my poncho liner and settled in for an hour of sleep. We had rotated the one-hour guard duty in the tower at Venice East among all the men in the platoon. But this night, it would be one hour on and one hour off duty for the entire night for Hardy and me. So much for a good night's sleep.

I didn't sleep much during my first hour off guard. Eventually, Hardy shook me and said it was my turn for watch. As I sat up, Hardy said there was nothing happening. I moved next to the radio while Hardy curled up for his first hour of sleep. I turned on the starlight scope and scanned the countryside, but saw no movement. A starlight scope was a battery-powered night vision scope that magnified available starlight or moonlight enabling the operator to see in the darkness. It looked like a fat eighteen-inch-long telescope. Objects appeared as a slightly-fuzzy green image. The clouds obscured most of the moon and starlight, but I could still see the faint outlines of a few objects as I scanned the nearby countryside. I observed a few ARVNs moving inside the compound periodically, but for the most part, it was totally quiet while I sat in the tower with Hardy sleeping beside me. One of the company RTOs checked in with us every hour, on the hour, to make sure we were awake and OK.

He would say, "Alpha Papa 3, Alpha Papa 3, radio check."

We would simply acknowledge everything was fine by clicking the handset switch twice to avoid the noise of talking. Clicking the handset switch would "break squelch" and cause static that the RTO could hear. Maintaining silence wasn't so critical that night, but when on an ambush, being quiet was very important. I also had a watch with hands that glowed in the dark, so I didn't have to use my flashlight to see the time. Even if we had a flashlight, there were times when we didn't want to use it for fear of disclosing our position to the enemy. That night I didn't want to shine any light in the tower to give the enemy a target to shoot at.

As each hour passed with no activity I became a little more comfortable with our situation and was tired enough when I ended each guard shift that I quickly fell asleep. With everything being so quiet, it was sometimes a struggle to stay awake while staring into the darkness for an hour at a time. Around midnight, it started to rain. Although we threw our ponchos over us to keep most of the blowing rain off, it still quickly became a wet and miserable night in that little tower. As the morning light began to appear on the eastern horizon, it seemed we would survive our remote duty. The sun rose, bringing welcome daylight and a sense of semi-security as the countryside became visible, minimizing the likelihood of enemy activity. The enemy liked to use the cover of darkness when they attacked U.S. or ARVN compounds.

Hardy and I gathered our gear, climbed down the tower and stretched out the kinks after spending the night in that small confinement. The ARVNs opened the front gate and we walked to the road to wait for a ride back to Venice East. A short while later I noticed the mine sweeping team moving down the road toward us. Hardy and I decided we would walk back with them. I radioed the CP and told them not to send anyone to pick us up.

The following evening Bill Casey, a new guy from South Carolina, and one of the old timers, Zeke Weil, were the lucky ones selected to spend the night with the ARVNs. I was pulling guard in the tower at Venice East a few minutes after eleven o'clock that night when I heard explosions and small arms fire directly to our southwest. I couldn't see anything in the darkness, but assumed it was coming from the ARVN compound.

A minute later I heard Casey on the radio, saying, "This is Alpha Papa 3. We have incoming RPGs. We need a fire mission, over!"

The VC had fired RPGs into the ARVN compound again and Casey was calling for mortar support. Our mortar platoon fired several rounds east of the compound where the RPGs had been fired from while Casey and Weil and the ARVNs sprayed the surrounding countryside with M-16 fire. One of the RPGs wounded two ARVNs, but Casey and Weil survived unscathed.

The next morning we were told to pack up our gear and be ready to move back to Firebase Patton at ten o'clock. Two deuce-and-a-halfs brought another platoon to Venice East. While the new platoon moved in the Third Herd boarded the trucks and we were soon riding towards Patton.

➢ George D. Conrad, Jr. was from Plantation, FL. He arrived in Vietnam on June 17, 1969. He was killed in action on August 2, 1969 at the age of twenty-six.

➢ The man in the first platoon who was also killed on August 2, 1969 was twenty-year-old Venancio Vera. He had arrived in Vietnam on June 7, 1969.

The youngest American serviceman to die in Vietnam was PFC Dan Bullock. He altered his birth certificate to join the Marines. Dan Bullock was killed by enemy gunfire on June 7, 1969, at the age of fifteen.

Sergeant Richard Hogue in front of Venice East.
The elevated bunkers and guard tower are in the background.

Chapter 7

Welcome to the Woods

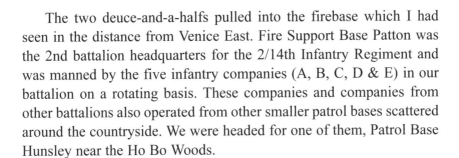

The two deuce-and-a-halfs pulled into the firebase which I had seen in the distance from Venice East. Fire Support Base Patton was the 2nd battalion headquarters for the 2/14th Infantry Regiment and was manned by the five infantry companies (A, B, C, D & E) in our battalion on a rotating basis. These companies and companies from other battalions also operated from other smaller patrol bases scattered around the countryside. We were headed for one of them, Patrol Base Hunsley near the Ho Bo Woods.

The firebase had been built in the early summer of 1969 as a state-of-the-art replacement for the original Firebase Patton located a quarter mile north, just outside the little village of Trung Lap that I could see in the distance. Lieutenant Donaldson told us to be on the landing zone (LZ) in thirty minutes. We were going to be picked up on the LZ on the east side of Patton and fly on Hueys to Patrol Base Hunsley to join the rest of our company. The Huey was a military utility helicopter designed to transport troops and supplies, and was also used to evacuate the wounded.

I took a few minutes to check out the firebase before we left. Patton's circular perimeter was about 250 meters in diameter, consisting of a continuous six-foot-high dirt berm with twenty-four large sand bag bunkers built into it forty meters apart. There was a gravel road circling the interior of the firebase just inside the row of bunkers, and a few other roadways leading into the center of the firebase.

There were 81MM and 4.2 inch mortar positions, and six 155MM artillery howitzers (called an artillery battery) spaced around the interior along with very large bunkers for the battalion headquarters staff and for company CP groups. There were also two ammunition dumps, a mess hall and a medical aid station. A large wood-framed tower rose about twenty-five feet in the air, where men kept watch over the surrounding countryside.

Three rows of coiled concertina wire attached to steel posts surrounded the entire firebase. There were two coils spread along the ground, one behind the other, with the third coil lying on top to make it difficult for someone to jump over the coils. They also had trip flares and claymore mines spaced around the entire perimeter. The trip flares were set into the ground with a stake or attached to a solid object. A small wire attached to a cotter pin was then stretched tight and attached to another object. If someone tripped the wire, it would pull the pin and release a spring-loaded cap, igniting the flare and lighting up the surrounding area.

The five companies in our battalion were normally rotated from Patton and other smaller patrol bases scattered around the countryside every couple of weeks. The living conditions and hazards of the duty varied among the various patrol bases. I guess the Army wanted to be fair and let everyone share in the good and bad experiences. After taking a few minutes to check out Patton, I walked outside the eastern perimeter to a flat grassy area used for the helicopter-landing zone. I was looking forward to my first chopper ride in Vietnam but wasn't too excited about what might be waiting for me at the end of the ride.

Most of the men were sitting on the ground or milling around smoking cigarettes and talking while they waited on the LZ that peaceful sunny morning. When we heard the sound of Hueys in the distance we lined up in groups on each side of the LZ so that we could quickly load from both sides of the chopper when it landed. Someone "popped" a smoke grenade that spewed colored smoke into the air to mark a landing spot for the lead chopper. When the choppers neared, one man in each group walked to the center of the landing zone and held his rifle horizontally over his head to mark the location for each chopper to land and pick up their men. The normal load for a Huey was six or seven men. Four choppers landed to carry twenty-one of us who were going out to Hunsley that day to join the rest of our company which had left earlier.

There were two pilots on each Huey and a door gunner on each side with an M-60. Four men sat on the canvas-covered bench seat that ran through the center of the chopper while the rest sat on the floor. The side doors were always kept open and sometimes were completely removed to enable men to make a quick entrance or exit. However, with the doors open you couldn't hear much over the sound of the swirling chopper blades.

After a fifteen-minute flight, the pilot began descending into the LZ outside Patrol Base Hunsley. I had become accustomed to the small villages and rice paddies and lots of civilians around Patton. But when I looked from the chopper I could see nothing but grass, trees, bushes and water. We continued our descent into the patrol base, which looked like a circle carved out in the middle of nowhere, south of the Ho Bo Woods. Normally two companies were assigned to defend it.

The Ho Bo Woods was a former French owned rubber plantation used by the NVA and VC as a base area. It was laced with tunnels and underground complexes and well concealed bunker complexes and fortified small base camps. The area consisted of sparse to dense woods with some open areas and abandoned rice paddies. It was basically a remote enemy controlled area with no civilians. The Army had been trying to chase the NVA/VC out of there for years and it was the scene of some of the bloodiest and deadliest firefights that had occurred around Cu Chi. Unfortunately, it had been pretty much a losing battle. On top of all that, the Ho Bo Woods was heavily infested with booby traps and land mines to discourage us from going out there.

After we landed outside the perimeter of Patrol Base Hunsley I walked toward the main gate thinking, "What the hell is this?" The patrol base was 100 meters in diameter with bunkers built into a three-foot-high berm surrounding the compound. I quickly found out why the berm was only three feet high. We were in the middle of "Charlie's" country and much more susceptible to enemy ground attacks. The 105MM artillery pieces at Hunsley could be lowered to fire at point-blank range over the berm to repel an enemy ground attack. Those howitzers could fire a beehive round containing 8,000 flechettes (a two-inch dart). At 150 yards the beehive round would kill anything in a path fifty yards wide. I hoped we wouldn't have to call on those beehive rounds to save our butts while I was there.

There was a wooden tower in the center of the patrol base and a few tents and other bunkers scattered around the interior. There were also circular mortar pits ten to twelve feet in diameter. A four-foot-high sand bag wall surrounded each pit to protect the men inside from incoming mortar-round explosions. Our mortar platoon set up one mortar tube in the middle of each pit.

The third platoon was assigned a group of bunkers along the

northeast perimeter. The bunkers were pretty small, making it a cozy fit. We left most of our gear outside to leave enough room inside the bunkers to sleep. Fortunately, we would only be out there a few days.

The mood of the men became more serious after our arrival at Hunsley. There was little laughter or horsing around like I had seen at Venice East. For the first time in Vietnam, although not scared, I definitely felt uncomfortable. Lieutenant Donaldson gathered the platoon to brief us on the plan for the night. Captain Branch had planned to send out two ambush patrols that night but the intelligence reports indicated there had been a recent buildup of NVA in the Ho Bo Woods. It was recommended we keep everyone inside the patrol base and be prepared for incoming mortar rounds and to defend against a possible ground attack.

My heart almost stopped when I heard the words "ground attack." "Take me back to peaceful Venice East," I thought to myself. Lieutenant Donaldson told us to double check our weapons and set up a guard rotation. It was starting to get dark. Several of us were outside a bunker organizing our gear while two men had started pulling guard duty. All of a sudden someone yelled from a nearby bunker, "INCOMING!" Almost immediately there was a loud BOOM! I saw the flash of a mortar round when it exploded by a nearby bunker as I instinctively turned and ran for our bunker entrance that was no more than four feet high and two feet wide. Amazingly, six of us made it through that small entrance in the matter of a few seconds without crunching each other.

More incoming mortar rounds continued to rain in on the patrol base while we huddled inside the bunker. Fortunately, someone must have heard the whistling sound of one of the first incoming rounds and had given everyone a little warning. One enemy tactic was to fire mortar rounds into a patrol base assuming we would all jump inside our bunkers, and then try to sneak through our perimeter and launch an attack before we could establish a defense. We waited inside the bunker while a series of fifteen to twenty incoming mortar rounds seemed to walk across the base. We needed to get outside to grab our weapons and stand guard along the berm, but we didn't want to get nailed by more incoming mortar rounds either.

While we were inside the bunker two men watched through the sight holes built into the front wall. If they spotted any movement near the perimeter they would detonate the claymores in front of our bunker. The incoming rounds stopped after a couple minutes.

I said, "Let's go, guys."

We quickly moved outside, slapped on our helmets and flak jackets, grabbed our weapons and ammunition and spread along the berm on each side of our bunker watching for any movement. Other men were popping out of their bunkers around us and setting up along the berm as our mortar platoon and the artillerymen were firing a barrage of outgoing rounds. Whenever we received incoming mortar fire our mortar and artillery crews would start firing outgoing rounds in all directions, even if that meant exposing themselves to the incoming rounds. If someone heard the pop of the enemy mortar being fired, they would get word to those crews to direct their fire in that direction. If it was unknown where the incoming rounds came from, outgoing rounds were fired all around the surrounding countryside.

As I looked toward the south side of the patrol base I heard someone yell for Doc Jackson. I told the men to stay along the berm while I went to see what happened. None of the men near our bunker had been hit but when I reached the south side of the patrol base along with Doc Jackson, we found a disaster. The mortar rounds had clobbered several men in the second platoon. Men were screaming in pain and yelling, "Doc! Help me!" The wounded men were scattered, lying or sitting on the ground.

Captain Branch walked up to me and told me to get some additional help for the wounded men. I ran back and told the men along the berm what had happened. I grabbed five men and told the rest to stay by the berm. The men with me quickly spread out among the wounded and helped the medics treat their wounds, ranging from minor shrapnel wounds to life-threatening injuries. It was agonizing to hear one man scream while I helped Doc Jackson put a large field dressing on his mangled shoulder. Two men had serious leg wounds but hopefully the doctors in Cu Chi could save their legs. Another man had received a blast of shrapnel in the stomach and was in terrible pain.

We soon loaded the most seriously wounded men onto litters that were stored at the patrol base and carried them toward the northern perimeter where the dustoffs would be landing to evacuate them. An RTO directed two choppers to the LZ that was marked with two strobe lights. When the dustoffs landed we quickly loaded the first group of wounded men aboard, took more litters from the choppers and returned for the rest of the injured men. A third dustoff soon arrived and flew the last of the eleven wounded men from the second platoon to the 12th Evac hospital in Cu Chi.

Those men were all alive when they left Hunsley, but several were in bad shape. The first few rounds had detonated near their bunkers on the south side of the patrol base and wounded the men before they could run for cover. Amazingly, one of the mortar rounds landed directly in front of the doorway to a bunker and wounded some of the men who were huddled inside.

We stood on 100% guard for an hour but everything remained quiet. When we went back to our normal one-hour guard rotation I quietly stood beside our bunker and thought how lucky the Third Herd had been that night. If we had been assigned to bunkers on the south side of the patrol base, we would have been the ones getting nailed. There was a higher power than all of us that determined our destiny that night.

I got up the next morning, put on my boots and walked outside my bunker to find a nice sunny day. Although we had air mattresses and hammocks to provide some comfort while we slept, it wasn't that comfortable night after night. My breakfast consisted of canned ham and eggs that I "doctored up" with some grape jelly to make them a little more palatable. I also learned that if we had time, we could burn a little piece of C-4 explosive to heat up a can of C-rations. I couldn't believe it until I saw someone do it one day. C-4 was a powerful white plastic explosive that looked like modeling clay that kids might play with. A blasting cap would be pushed into a stick of C-4 to detonate it. An exploding stick of C-4 would cause serious damage, but you could amazingly burn it without its exploding. It was probably expensive cooking fuel but, it was readily available and we used C-4 to heat C-rations whenever we could.

After my cold breakfast Lieutenant Donaldson briefed us NCOs regarding the day's RIF. We would be flown out to the eastern edge of the Ho Bo Woods and then walk back to Hunsley looking for any signs of enemy activity, and for the mortar tube that had fired the incoming rounds the past night. I lined out our route on my map and then went back to brief the rest of the men in my squad. Their first question was, "How many klicks is it?" A "klick" was 1,000 meters or .6 miles. The military referred to distances in meters rather than yards or miles. We would be covering twelve klicks (seven miles). There were several "ah-shits" and "damns" when the guys heard the news. I looked at my watch; it was 7:45 a.m. We had to be on the LZ in fifteen minutes.

Before I put on my gear I took off the OD-green boxer shorts I had been wearing under my fatigue pants and threw them into my backpack. GIs in the field in Vietnam had learned if they wore boxer shorts under their fatigue pants, they often developed chafing or a rash in their crotch from the moisture and from underwear rubbing while they walked. However, a simple solution was discovered: don't wear underwear. Sort of an "open air" approach. It worked for me.

I put on my web gear and pistol belt which were designed to carry other gear, like my canteen, a pouch for my compass, and a canvas ammunition pouch I used to carry my camera. I then threw on two bandoleers, each holding eight magazines of M-16 ammunition and a 100-round belt of M-60 ammunition. I also carried two smoke grenades and four hand grenades. The M-26 fragmentation grenade was oval-shaped with a flat bottom and it weighed 1.7 pounds. They also made what we called baseball grenades, but which were actually about the size of a tennis ball. Some men carried M-26s because they were more powerful while others liked the baseball grenades because they were lighter and could be thrown farther. I normally carried two of each type.

I put my map in the side leg pocket of my fatigue pants, slapped my helmet on my head and was ready for action. Well, almost. I had seen several guys sorting through a box of C-rations and taking a can or two with them. I walked to the box to see what was left. Ham and eggs? No way. Crackers? No, too dry. And then I found a can of fruit cocktail; perfect, I thought. I put the can in my pocket along with a plastic spoon. I carried a trusty little P-38 can opener and was set for lunch.

It would take two lifts (a lift was a group of four to six Hueys) to transport the company out and drop us off at a remote LZ in the boonies. The third platoon was on the first lift and we were soon aboard and flying high above the Ho Bo Woods.

We flew over the countryside for ten minutes to allow time for the artillery battery at Hunsley to "soften" the landing zone. Soften meant firing several artillery rounds near the LZ, hoping to scare off any

NVA or VC who might happen to be in the area. They would pepper two or three locations to confuse the enemy and not telegraph our actual landing site. When the artillery gunners had finished their job, they notified the pilots it was safe to drop us off.

The door gunner near me opened fire with his M-60 when we neared the LZ. It scared the hell out of me. What was he shooting at? It didn't appear we were taking enemy fire and I didn't see any movement on the ground. Chuck Gorman noticed the shocked look on my face and leaned over to me and said they were just spraying the area. It was no problem. I gave him an "OK" sign while the chopper continued to descend. The machine gun fire was another precautionary measure intended to make any enemy personnel in the area head for cover, letting us land in safety and allowing the choppers to get back in the air without being fired upon.

The LZ that morning was an open area covered with tall grass. I had been told that when we were dropped in a remote LZ that exposed the choppers to enemy fire, not to wait until the chopper was on the ground to hop off. Many pilots would hover a foot or two off the ground while men jumped off in the boonies, and then quickly lift off.

I was sitting on the floor next to the door and easily swung my legs outside the chopper and placed my feet on top of the round landing skid as we neared the ground. I was the first to jump. And boy, was I surprised. The grass was a lot taller than it appeared. When I jumped I thought we were only a couple feet off the ground, but we must have actually been four or five feet in the air. I wasn't ready for that kind of a fall, and I stumbled and fell when I hit the ground. I quickly picked up my helmet that had fallen off, stood up and moved away as the chopper roared off.

We spread out and established a defensive perimeter around the landing zone. Setting up a defensive perimeter usually meant placing men in a circle formation, facing outward to establish a secure area inside the circle. The choppers flew back to Hunsley to fly in the rest of the company.

A couple of the men who saw me jump from the chopper laughed after we settled in. One of them said, "Jumped a little early, didn't you, Sarge?"

I smiled and said. "Yeah, I think so." I shook my head in disbelief at what I had done. A combination of adrenalin from my first drop in a remote LZ and poor judgment about our distance from the ground made me look pretty silly.

Twenty minutes later the rest of the company arrived on a second lift of choppers, including Captain Branch who took charge of the RIF.

We lined up in two parallel columns twenty or twenty-five meters apart and started moving south along our designated route. First platoon led the RIF, followed by the CO and his CP group while the Third Herd brought up the rear. Each day the order of the platoons on the RIF changed. Obviously, leading the RIF was the most dangerous duty, especially for the first man in each column who was the "point" man. His job was called "walking point." He was not only the first to be exposed to enemy fire but was also the most likely to trip a booby trap should they be in our path. And they were.

We normally had the newest men rotate walking point until other men arrived to assume the duty. Walking point wasn't a friendly welcome to the field, but we had to establish a fair way to assign and rotate point duty. I didn't walk point because I was a sergeant. I normally was the third or fourth man in the column, near the middle of my squad, to take control if something happened. Lieutenant Donaldson and Sergeant Brown normally walked a little further back, enabling them to give directions to the entire platoon when necessary.

We tried to keep ourselves spaced ten meters apart as we walked along to avoid presenting a group target for the enemy and to minimize the extent of casualties from booby traps or hand grenades. The old saying "One grenade will get you all," suddenly made a lot of sense. One of my responsibilities while on a RIF was keeping an eye on the men to make sure they kept spread out and paid attention to what was going on around them. We kept our eyes moving all the time. We not only watched where we were stepping but also glanced out over the countryside for any movement or anything that looked suspicious. The NVA and VC were ingenious soldiers. They could conceal themselves in the vegetation, becoming virtually invisible until we were nearly upon them. They also could pop up from a tunnel, fire a few rounds at us and quickly drop out of sight before we could spot them to return fire.

I had a sling connected to my M-16. Being left handed I placed the sling over my left shoulder and rested my left hand on my rifle as we walked across the countryside. We didn't hold our rifles ready to fire unless we spotted something or expected to be walking up on enemy troops. We didn't talk too much during a RIF, and we often used hand signals to communicate. We tried to move across the countryside as quietly as sixty to seventy-five men could.

The first hour of the RIF was uneventful. I walked along not quite sure what to expect. We stopped for a break and sat down with the two columns of men facing outward watching out over the countryside. Anytime we were "outside the wire," (outside of a patrol base or firebase) we were always on the defensive, even when we took a break. I took my helmet off and took a drink of water and then poured a little water on the OD-green towel I carried around my neck and wiped the sweat from my face. Carrying a towel during a RIF to wipe off the sweat caused by the constant heat and humidity in Vietnam was one of the infantryman's "tricks of the trade" I quickly learned.

We had been resting for a few minutes when I heard the sound of gunfire coming from the front of our columns. I immediately grabbed my rifle and looked across the countryside around me. The gunfire continued but we weren't taking any incoming fire near me.

I then heard Lieutenant Donaldson yell, "Sergeant Hogue, take your gunner up front."

"What are we getting into?" I thought as I waved at my machine gun team, Bob Emery and Mike Stark, who were right behind me. We quickly moved to the front of our column where first platoon's machine gun teams were laying down fire along a hedgerow 100 meters to the northeast.

Captain Branch said, "Have your team spray those hedgerows. There's VC out there," as he pointed to the line of hedgerows in front of us.

Bob set his M-60 on a little mound, resting it on the two legs that folded down from the barrel. Mike quickly attached a belt of ammunition to the small string of ammunition Bob always kept loaded in the gun. Bob opened fire. Every fifth M-60 round was a tracer so the gunner could see where his rounds were going and could adjust his fire accordingly. I helped Mike lay out an additional belt of ammunition while the orange glowing tracers from the three machine guns filled the air as they raced into the hedgerow. Two men were firing M-79 grenades into the area. They exploded with a "ka-bam" when they landed.

Someone had spotted two VC moving into the hedgerow in front of us while we were taking a break. Anyone spotted in that remote area was considered to be the enemy. Our men had opened fire on them before they had a chance to do the same to us. Because we weren't taking any return fire, after spraying the area with M-60 rounds for a couple of minutes, the CO yelled, "Cease fire!

Captain Branch had called in a Cobra gunship to "pepper" the area before we moved through to search for the VC. Cobras were sleekly-designed, heavily armed helicopter gunships that could deliver awesome firepower. They were armed with grenade and rocket launchers and two six-barrel Miniguns that could fire up to 4,000 rounds a minute. The pilot sat in the front of the Cobra and the co-pilot, who was the gunner, sat directly behind him.

Many of the Cobras had huge teeth painted on the nose of the chopper resembling shark's teeth. I'm sure those Cobras scared the hell out of a lot of enemy troops when they looked up and saw a flying monster with shark's teeth coming at them and unleashing its weaponry. The Cobra arrived and fired several rockets and grenades into the hedgerow, sprayed the surrounding area with their Miniguns and then remained overhead on standby while we moved in.

We cautiously walked toward the hedgerow with every man holding his weapon ready to open fire at any movement. We spent nearly half an hour searching the area but didn't find any bodies, blood trails or signs of the enemy. Miraculously, VC hadn't been hit by our firepower. They were long gone. Captain Branch finally decided it was a bust, and we'd better start our trek back to Hunsley. We didn't get those two gooks that day, but I bet we scared the hell out of them.

We normally didn't walk too fast during a RIF. The point team moved cautiously while they watched for booby traps and signs of enemy activity. The point man had a compass and would be given a heading to follow or a target landmark to move toward while he watched for booby traps and land mines with each step he took. The second man in the column, called the "pace man," was responsible for looking over the terrain in front of him to observe for any movement. The pace man was also responsible for tracking the distance by counting his footsteps. When we were on company size RIFs, we normally walked in two columns; therefore, there were two point teams (point man and pace man) each tracking our direction and distance. With the point teams leading the way and several of us checking our topographical maps to monitor our travel, we could closely keep track of our location as we moved along the designated route.

We normally stopped only to check out anything that looked suspicious or unusual, or to take a short break. It was a hot and dry afternoon with no clouds in sight. I was getting beat. The lack of physical exercise during the past few weeks caught up with me. In one sense it was nice not to be drenched by a monsoon rain, but that afternoon, I would have actually enjoyed a shower from Mother Nature. Some of the other FNGs had tired looks on their faces while we made our way back toward Hunsley. After a couple more hours of uneventful walking through three-foot-tall grass, crossing a little stream and abandoned rice paddies, we finally pulled into Hunsley at just after four o'clock that afternoon.

Even happier than I to see Hunsley were Bob Emery and Mike Stark, my machine gun team. They were also on their first RIF and were both beat. Their only salvation was that they had fired a few hundred rounds of ammunition which lightened their load a little. I chugged most of my canteen of warm water when we got back to Hunsley. A shower would have felt great, but we didn't have much water to spare. I had to settle for pouring a little water over my head to wash off some of the sweat and dirt.

That evening we learned that all of the men in the second platoon who were wounded during our first night at Hunsley had survived. But most of them had serious injuries and would be flown back to "the world" to recover. When in Vietnam, we referred to the United States as "the world" because Vietnam was so strange and different from the world we had all previously known. It sometimes felt like we were on another planet.

We spent the next couple of days going on RIFs around Hunsley. We saw lots of enemy footprints indicating they were out there and found two supply caches containing food and ammunition, but we didn't see any enemy troops and didn't find any of the bunker complexes we knew were out there someplace. We were also fortunate and hadn't tripped any booby traps. The old timers said it was amazing we didn't run into something. But that was fine with me.

On our third day at Hunsley we returned from a short RIF just after noon. We were told to pack up our gear because we were being flown back to Firebase Patton. With sighs of relief, we packed up and walked to the LZ for the welcome flight back to Patton.

Patrol Base Hunsley was named after First Lieutenant Dennis Hunsley who served in the 25th Infantry Division and was killed in action on March 15, 1969. He had been awarded the Silver Star for gallantry two weeks before his death.

Patrol Base Hunsley was established to draw the VC out and provoke a ground assault. However, "Charlie" never took the bait for a ground assault at Hunsley while we were there. The VC had initiated ground assaults at other remote patrol bases previously and suffered heavy casualties from artillery fire and air strikes.

Back - Larry "Doc" Jackson and Bill Casey (sitting on a bunker)
Middle - Dennis Schultz and Staff Sergeant Tom Brown
In front - First Lieutenant Steve Donaldson

Chapter 8

Glad to Be a Ground-Pounder

I sat on the floor of the Huey and relaxed as it lifted off while I enjoyed the changing scenery flying southwest toward Patton. The area around Hunsley was high ground covered with thick vegetation which wasn't flooded like much of the rest of the countryside during the monsoon season. When we neared Firebase Patton I saw more and more water and flooded rice paddies and streams filled to their banks. From the air, groups of rice paddies looked like a large lake divided into little squares by the man-made earthen dikes.

I also vividly noticed the scars on the landscape left by years of fighting. The ground was dotted with large and small craters from exploding artillery shells and bombs. Clusters of ten or twenty craters could be seen where a firefight had occurred and where artillery shells or an air strike had bombarded the area. Those craters, filled with water from the monsoon rains, created a pretty scene from the air; however, there was probably a tragic story associated with many of those clusters of craters.

After we landed on the east side of Patton we walked through the perimeter and settled into a group of bunkers along the west side. The large bunkers at Patton provided a reasonably comfortable place to sleep and store our personal items. Captain Branch and his staff settled into their Command Post, a group of bunkers near the interior of the firebase. His staff (CP Group) included a medic, a demolitions expert, a forward observer to call in mortars, artillery or air strikes, three RTOs and First Sergeant William Seavey, who tried to keep us in line.

Most first sergeants were nicknamed "Top." Top had served as a Marine in World War II and served in the Army during Korea and Vietnam. Like many first sergeants he sometimes got carried away with enforcing some of the military rules. Top tried to make sure we shaved every few days and that we kept the areas around our bunkers clean. Yes, even in the middle of South Vietnam, we had to keep things clean. But it wasn't just because of Top. There were lots of rats, mice, snakes and flies that were attracted to trash, especially any food left around. It was important to keep our so-called living quarters clean to keep the critters away. The flies were around during the day; the mosquitoes came out at night, and the rats and mice were around all the time.

Mail was delivered that afternoon along with other supplies. Like in the movies, someone would take the stack of mail for our platoon and call out the name written on a letter or a package. The men who received a letter would find a quiet spot and spend a few minutes reading about what was happening back in the world. I received a letter from Mom, dated August 17, 1969. She started the letter by saying that Steven Crumb had been killed in Vietnam on August 13th. I stopped reading. Steven had grown up on a farm south of Schaller and graduated from high school one year behind me. The realities of the war in Vietnam had finally hit Schaller, Iowa by taking the life of one its own. Steven and I weren't close friends, but I had known him most of my life. It was a shock knowing he had been killed. The letter went on to say President Nixon had briefly stopped sending troops to Vietnam the day Dean Christiansen was to leave. Dean had been reassigned to Fort Ord, California, a lucky break for him.

After mail call, most of us cleaned our weapons. We normally cleaned our rifles every couple of days whether we used them or not, because our lives depended upon them. The M-16 was a great rifle but had the reputation of jamming if not kept clean. The two machine gun teams worked together to clean their guns, which was more effort than cleaning an M-16.

Our machine gunners had the most physically demanding job in the platoon, which meant that the burly guys often became our machine gunners. Bob Emery was an eighteen-year-old, husky, blond-headed guy from Michigan who had been assigned to the third platoon a few days after I arrived. He had been sent to Germany since he was only seventeen at the time, but he had volunteered for Vietnam soon after he turned eighteen. Bob came to me on his first day with the platoon and volunteered to be my machine gunner when he learned that I needed a permanent gunner in the first squad. After taking one look at Bob I said, "The job is yours." Another blond-headed guy, Michael Stark from Wisconsin had arrived with Bob. I assigned Mike as Bob's assistant gunner.

The M-79 grenade launchers looked like a fat sawed-off shotgun.

It could fire buckshot-like pellets at short-range targets and fired a golf-ball-size grenade over 300 meters. It was nice to have a weapon that could fire an explosive round, but the M-79 grenades didn't have nearly the destructive force of a hand grenade. We probably scared the enemy more often than we injured them. Each platoon also carried several Light Anti-Tank Weapons (LAWs). The NVA and VC didn't have armored tanks but the LAWs could destroy bunkers or other solid targets.

The routine at Patton was much more relaxed than at Patrol Base Hunsley. I didn't notice anyone peeking over the berm to see what was happening outside. Historically, there had been no enemy assaults at Patton but there had been several mortar attacks. We didn't carry our rifles with us when we were inside the firebase and didn't pull guard at our bunkers during the day. Men rotated lookout from the tower at the center of the firebase during daylight hours.

The afternoons were always hot, unless it was raining, so most of us would take off our fatigue shirts and just wear trousers when we were inside a firebase or patrol base. Some of us would run around in our OD-green boxer shorts, or other shorts and take off our jungle boots and wear thongs or sandals. Late during my first afternoon at Patton I saw three of the guys grab their towels and begin walking toward the center of the firebase.

One of them said, "Hey, Sarge, want a shower?"

"Shower?" I said, "where?" I hadn't heard anything about showers at Patton. I grabbed my towel as they waved for me to follow them. I hadn't had a real shower since I took a quick shower in the little makeshift shower at Venice East. That shower was nothing more than a small barrel of water elevated on wooden framework with a showerhead attached at the bottom. I quickly found my towel and caught up with the guys. I looked in amazement when I saw several showerheads spraying water on men who were lathering up to clean off the dirt and grime. I stripped off my pants and joined the others under the showers. The water was cool but on that hot afternoon it felt great as I washed several days of dirt and grime off my body.

There were no walls around the showers and we could be seen by anyone in the general area (not that we cared). I chuckled to myself while I looked around at a dozen men taking a shower under blue skies. We looked like a little nudist colony. A well had been drilled at

Patton shortly after the firebase was built. At four o'clock every after-noon a pump was turned on that fed the showers for an hour or so. Even a cold shower was a luxury in the field.

The mess hall at Patton was another luxury. The cooks served a hot breakfast every morning, and dinner starting around five o'clock each afternoon. After my shower, I joined the chow line that formed at one end of the mess hall. In a few minutes I walked out of the mess hall with a plate of food that looked a lot better than the C-rations I had been living on the past few days. We normally walked back to our bunkers to eat because the mess hall didn't have tables and chairs inside. The meals were served on paper plates and we used plastic utensils. We threw everything in the trash when we were through.

The schedule for the daily assignments (normally a RIF) was usu-ally determined by the battalion headquarters staff, based upon obser-vations by U.S. troops in the field, aerial sightings or intelligence reports about enemy activity. However, sometimes they sent us into an area simply because no RIFs had been conducted there recently. The orders would be passed down to our CO who would then brief the pla-toon leaders early each evening for our mission the following day. If the area to be patrolled was a long distance from the firebase or patrol base, we would be flown out on choppers early in the morning to search the designated area and normally would be flown back that afternoon. If the RIF covered a local area we would walk out and back.

I had a topographical map covered in plastic to keep it dry. When I was briefed about our daily mission I would map out our route on the plastic cover with a grease pencil. It was important to know where we were at all times in case we needed to call in mortar or artillery fire, or an air strike, or if we had casualties and needed to call in a dustoff. The maps were lined with numbered horizontal and vertical grid lines that formed thousand-meter squares. If we needed support we could identify our location by referring to the numbered grid lines.

After Lieutenant Donaldson was briefed regarding a RIF he briefed us NCOs, who in turn, briefed the remaining members of the platoon. We thought we would be working out of Firebase Patton for a while, but Lieutenant Donaldson informed us that evening that plans had changed. We were going to be operating with a mechanized unit for a few days. Mechanized units were infantry companies who used armored personnel carriers (APCs) and armored tanks to travel across the countryside. Alpha Company was a traditional infantry company. We were nicknamed "ground-pounders," meaning we walked most of the time. But riding rather than walking sounded OK to me.

We settled in for our one-night's stay at Patton and set up a guard schedule. We kept two men on guard at each bunker from dusk to dawn, pulling one-hour shifts. When we established a rotation for guard duty early each evening, everyone knew who followed who and knew where his relief man was sleeping. The rule was, you made sure your relief man was on guard before you went back to sleep. We had air mattresses to sleep on inside the dirt or wooden-floored bunkers, and most of us had a hammock we could tie to the huge wooden rafters that supported each bunker. I preferred to sleep in a hammock if I had a choice. My towel served as my pillow and I covered myself with a poncho liner. I soon learned to sleep like a baby, rocking in my hammock.

I took first watch on guard that night wearing my helmet and flak jacket. Although our flak jackets offered good protection, we sometimes didn't wear them on guard because they were heavy, uncomfortable and made you hot. If Top caught us on guard without a flak jacket he would yell and cuss until we put one on. I also had my rifle and a couple hand grenades by my side. We often set an M-60 on the top of the bunker with a few hundred rounds of ammunition ready, just in case someone tried to surprise us. There were little walkways on each side of the bunkers to provide access through the berm to the front of each bunker. One man would normally stand in each walkway while on guard.

I pulled my first hour of guard without incident and woke up the next man, who got up and took my place beside the bunker. I then took off my boots, rolled into my hammock and fell asleep. The night passed without incident. At nine o'clock the following morning we boarded a convoy of deuce-and-a-halfs, traveling several miles west on Highway 1 and then turning north where we met up with the mechanized unit along a dirt road.

I stepped down from the truck and walked toward a group of APCs when I heard someone yell, "Hey, Hogue, what the hell are you doing out here?"

I looked around and saw a man jump off an APC, waving at me. It was John Jarvis. We had gone through NCO School and OJT together. We smiled when we met and shook hands, each glad to see a familiar face. He was in charge of one of the APCs. We talked for a few minutes about our brief time in Vietnam and then had to mount up on the APCs to move out.

The APCs were square track-driven vehicles made of thick metal. They were smaller than a tank and didn't have an artillery gun. They normally had a .50-caliber and M-60 machine gun mounted on top. APCs were as their name implied, armored personnel carriers designed to carry personnel in the battlefield. There was a large open space inside where personnel could ride, with a large rear door that lowered to the ground to enter and exit. There were also two round hatches on top you could crawl through to enter or exit. However, the APCs had weaknesses. Although the sides were made of heavy aluminum metal, an enemy anti-tank round could penetrate the side and detonate inside the APC. That meant almost certain death to those riding inside. Additionally, the bottom of the APC wasn't thick enough to withstand most land mine explosions. Therefore, we rode on the flat top of the APC. Although that exposed us to enemy fire, it was considered safer than riding inside.

It was a wild ride atop those APCs. We held on for dear life while the driver maneuvered through rice paddies and across terrain covered with bumps and holes. We would travel on the APCs for a while and then hop off to search certain areas on foot while the mechanized units stood by. After hours of riding and then walking, and then riding and walking again, the process didn't make much sense to me. Although we obviously had a lot of personnel and firepower, unless we ran into a large number of well-fortified enemy personnel, I assumed they would hide or run away unnoticed when they heard us coming. I doubted a small number of NVA or VC would take us on.

We had traveled on high ground during most of the morning, making it easy for the vehicles to keep moving. But after noon we ran into mushy terrain that was flooded from the monsoon rains. The APCs and tanks struggled to move through the mud and muck. Late that afternoon one of the APCs became stuck in an abandoned rice paddy. The driver of another APC attached a cable and tried to pull it out and almost buried his vehicle. After spending most of an hour trying to get the APC unstuck, the two drivers gave up. A large towing vehicle would have to be driven out the next morning to pull it out.

Since it was getting late, we established a perimeter around the stuck APC in a "night laager" position. Establishing a laager position meant setting up a defensive position in the boonies with no bunkers or other pre-established defenses. We tried to dig small foxholes and build dirt mounds for cover, but that was a hopeless cause. The holes quickly filled with water. We rearranged ourselves to use rice paddy dikes for cover. After working with the mechanized units only one day it became evident it wasn't as much fun as I had imagined.

Our night laager looked like a wagon train from the 1800's circled for the night. Only we had a lot more firepower than the cowboys had against the Indians. I ate part of a can of cold potatoes and beef for dinner that evening and threw the rest away. It tasted lousy, although I did luck out and find some sponge cake.

When darkness fell we settled into rotating guard duty and tried to sleep when we weren't on guard, in the rain that continued for several hours. The night passed without any action but I woke up cold and wet. Most of us moved on that morning while two APCs and fifteen men stayed behind until help arrived to free the stuck APC. I thought mechanized unit commanders would have learned long ago it was a waste of time trying to move tanks and APCs through the soggy countryside and let us ground-pounders search those areas on foot. But I guess not.

We eventually moved to higher ground and away from any inhabited areas and were out in the boonies by afternoon. The mechanized guys said they had been in that area and lost several men during a firefight with the VC a couple weeks earlier. We stopped several times and found trails that had recently been used, but we didn't have any enemy contact.

We finally stopped in an area called a "hard spot" to rendezvous with another mechanized company for the night. American units had previously used that remote location to establish a defensive perimeter. The vegetation surrounding the hard spot had been cleared away to give us good visibility and there were foxholes already dug around the perimeter. We interspersed groups of men in the foxholes between the APCs and tanks.

Late that afternoon we received word the mechanized company that was to join us had been ambushed four klicks southwest of our location. They had sustained heavy casualties and needed help. Three APCs, one tank and their men were ordered to move out to help them make their way back to our position. The APCs and the tank headed out while the rest of us went on guard. It was believed an enemy unit was moving through the area and possibly headed our way. With all of the noise we had made, our presence was certainly known if they were out there.

It had been dark for an hour when the mechanized units pulled into the hard spot. Several of us were standing a short distance from one APC when they dropped the rear door. We were all speechless when we saw the bodies of twelve men lying inside, stacked one on top of another. It was a gruesome sight. Lieutenant Donaldson asked me for three men to help unload the bodies from the APC. I hated to ask anyone to perform that task, but it had to be done.

When some men in the first platoon were told to help move the bodies, I heard one of them say, "I'm not going to touch those bodies."

His platoon sergeant grabbed his arm and said, "If that was your dead ass in there we'd carry you out. Now get over there and do your job!" The man walked toward the APC without saying another word.

Medical evacuation helicopters (medevacs) were on the way to evacuate several wounded men first and then the twelve bodies. One by one the bodies were carried from the APC and laid on the ground nearby. Several of us found ponchos to cover them. The men who had survived the ambush were in shock, some of them crying and consoling each other.

John Jarvis, my friend from NCO school, quietly walked up to me. Neither of us had known any of those men but seeing twelve fellow Americans lying dead on the ground was a shock for both of us. I couldn't imagine what it would be like losing twelve men in the Third Herd in one day. Later that evening we learned the mechanized unit had been ambushed while traveling through an area a short distance west of where we had earlier traveled. About a dozen NVA troops had abruptly popped up from holes in the ground covered with brush and vegetation (spider holes) and weren't seen until it was too late. All of the NVA were eventually killed, sacrificing their own lives knowing they would take some of us with them.

One of the men who survived described the action by saying "Those men dropped off the APCs like dead flies." He then looked at me and said, "War is hell, but actual combat is a mother-fucker," and turned and walked away. I hadn't heard that crude description of combat before, but

I couldn't disagree with it either. It was hard to believe that only a handful of NVA had inflicted so many casualties while facing the awesome firepower of the mechanized company.

During the rest of the night we periodically sprayed the surrounding countryside with machine gun and rifle fire to deter an enemy attack. We had obviously made our presence known and took a "better safe than sorry" approach by blasting the countryside. After a long night the sun rose to reveal over 150 men, a dozen APCs and four armored tanks.

We spent the third day working our way back toward Firebase Patton and, fortunately, had no enemy contact. We drove through the little village of Trung Lap north of Patton and then headed southwest on the road leading to Patton. The APCs and tanks stopped at the front gate of Patton to let us off. I quickly found my shake'n bake buddy, John Jarvis and shared a good-bye.

I walked through the main gate of Firebase Patton thinking about what had happened the past three days. I decided if I had to be in the infantry I was actually glad to be a ground-pounder. After watching the APCs struggle through the mud, and then seeing the bodies of twelve men who had been picked off from the top of their APC, I was ready to take my chances humping through the boonies on foot. My job wasn't the safest job in the Army, but I wasn't ready to trade my old buddy John Jarvis for his job.

Although over 58,000 Americans were killed in Vietnam, an estimated 924,000 NVA and Viet Cong troops were killed during the war. An estimated 415,000 Vietnamese civilians were killed and 935,000 were wounded during the Vietnam War.

Some Vietnam veterans believe the APC wasn't intended to be used the way it was in Vietnam. They were designed to accompany tanks and protect troops after they dismounted and maneuvered. The APCs were often used like Cavalry units and ridden into battle in Vietnam. Unfortunately, mechanized units often suffered higher casualty rates than ground units in Vietnam.

Chapter 9

Fire Support Base Patton

We were all glad to be back at Patton and happy to be surrounded with a six-foot berm again and have a bunker to sleep in. Most of us soon headed for the showers and then enjoyed our first hot meal in three days. That evening the second squad, led by Jim Overbey, gathered their gear and left to pull an ambush. One squad from our company would normally set up an ambush every night at a pre-established site within 1,000 meters of the firebase or patrol base we were assigned to. The ambush team would rotate guard duty throughout the night, and if any enemy troops passed close by, they would ambush them by opening fire. We called it "popping" the ambush.

The night passed without incident except for more monsoon rains. The men from second squad returned from their uneventful ambush. The ambush team normally got the day off following their ambush to catch up on sleep, since the men spent much of the previous night on guard duty. I headed for the mess hall for a warm breakfast to start my day before we headed out for another RIF.

Our RIF took us west of Firebase Patton. We left through the main gate a little after eight o'clock, first heading through some rice paddies and open fields. Because the rice paddies were still filled with a foot or two of water, we normally walked on the grassy earthen dikes that surrounded each paddy. I had been told during NCO School we shouldn't walk on the dikes because the enemy planted booby traps on them. Lieutenant Donaldson told me they rarely booby-trapped the dikes in inhabited areas because the local civilians working in or around the rice paddies walked along the dikes daily. Booby traps would wound or kill more civilians than GIs. He warned me if we were operating in uninhabited areas we had to be much more careful about walking on the dikes.

Rice paddies were built in squares or rectangles 100 to 125 feet square. The earthen dikes were two or three feet high and normally less than two feet wide at the top. During the springtime the civilians

107

planted little rice plants in the paddies. The monsoon rains then flooded each paddy during the summer. The rice grew in the water until the monsoons ended each fall. The paddies then dried up and the rice was harvested.

As we continued on our RIF we passed through hamlets with four to six hootches clustered together. We searched a few hootches to let the local civilians know we were keeping an eye on them. The VC and VC sympathizers were out there, even if we didn't recognize them, working the local civilians to support their cause. The VC often used cruel and life threatening tactics to recruit civilian support. For many civilians it was either support the VC or be killed.

The local adults normally kept their distance while looking at us as we passed by, but the kids often came up begging for food or candy. One youngster, about ten-years old, came up to us on wooden crutches. His left leg had been amputated just below his knee. He may have tripped a booby trap and became one of the innocent civilian casualties of the war.

When we moved through one hamlet, a Vietnamese woman came running toward us carrying a young girl. Someone yelled, "Watch that woman!" She could have been on a suicide mission and toss a hand grenade or have a concealed pistol. Several of us pointed our rifles at her, waiting to see what she might do. Someone yelled, "dung lau!" (Dung lau is Vietnamese for "stop.")

Lieutenant Donaldson yelled, "Easy on the trigger, guys!"

The woman ignored our rifles and commands to stop, and continued moving toward us, frantically talking in Vietnamese and pointing with one hand to the little girl she was carrying. The little girl was crying and we soon saw the child was bleeding. The woman finally stopped when she was a few feet away from our column and then laid the little girl on the ground. Doc Jackson, and company medic Sidney Morrison walked up to the little girl, who was crying in pain, to check her out. Two men also quickly searched the woman. She had nothing concealed under her clothing. The woman pointed to the ground and then swung her arms outward, we thought, trying to indicate something had exploded.

Doc Morrison told the CO that the girl had serious shrapnel wounds and needed hospital care. Captain Branch radioed for a chopper. Our Chieu Hoi, Hue, talked with the woman and confirmed she was the girl's mother. After a short while, a chopper landed and the girl and her mother were placed aboard along with one of Captain Branch's staff to escort them to Cu Chi. The mother would be interrogated further to determine what actually happened.

Later that day Steve Robinson yelled, "Fire in the hole!" as we were walking along. He pulled the pin from a hand grenade and dropped it down a well. The grenade exploded three or four seconds later sending a gush of water eight feet in the air. The enemy sometimes used the water wells scattered throughout the countryside to hide supplies or ammunition. They would seal items in plastic to keep them dry and drop them in a well. The package would sink to the bottom and enemy troops would come by later and fish it out. An exploding grenade wouldn't destroy the well, but it would dislodge anything lying on the bottom and send debris floating to the top. We didn't often find anything in the wells, but the men enjoyed dropping in a hand grenade and watching the plume of water soar into the air.

We worked our way back to Patton that afternoon without finding any signs of enemy activity, but the pouring monsoon rain soaked us. I put on dry fatigues after the rain stopped an hour later. Along with the mail and other supplies arriving on the supply convoy from Cu Chi that day, there were sodas and blocks of ice. I took a can and laid it on its side on a block of ice. I rolled the can with my hands while the turning can wore an indentation into the ice. After rolling the can for two or three minutes the soda was ice cold, "Rolling a soda," another trick of the trade in Vietnam.

Another special treat for all of us was receiving "care packages" from home. Almost every day one of the guys would receive a package containing homemade goodies. We often gathered around the man while he opened his package, hoping he would share the goodies inside. My mom sent many care packages of homemade chocolate chip cookies that were normally devoured in a few minutes by the Third Herd.

My squad had ambush duty that night, and after some late afternoon chow it was time to get them ready. Lieutenant Donaldson gave me our ambush location and I marked it on my map. A dozen men including my machine gun team, an RTO and Doc Jackson would walk 700 meters east of Patton to set up an ambush. We would each take all the gear we normally carried, plus our poncho liner and a claymore mine. It was still daylight when we walked along the path through the concertina wire on the northeast side of Patton. I gave a compass heading to our point man Carlton Quick that would lead us to our destination. Quick led the single column toward our ambush site while Ed Leberski walked second and counted paces.

When we neared the site I motioned to Quick to lead us into a group of trees a short distance to the south, which would conceal us until it started to get dark. We didn't want to set up the ambush with too much daylight because that increased the risk of being spotted by the enemy. Just before darkness fell, I walked directly behind Quick and guided everyone into the ambush site. We set up near a little path that ran past a group of rice paddies. We would set up behind a rice paddy dike ten meters south of the path, to give us concealment.

We set up the ambush with three groups of four men spaced a short distance apart, like the three points of a triangle. Two positions faced the path and the third position faced the rear to protect our backside. I designated "fields of fire" for each position, by identifying a target to their left and right as their primary responsibility to fire upon, enabling us to protect ourselves in all directions. While we settled in, one or two men at a time placed his claymore mine in front of each position. The electrical wire attached to the blasting cap inside each claymore was then strung along the ground, back to the detonator we kept near each position. When finished, a dozen claymores surrounded our ambush site. If enemy personnel passed by we would first fire the claymores without revealing our exact position. We would then throw hand grenades, and, lastly, open fire with our rifles and machine gun. At least that was how it was supposed to happen.

It was dark by the time we were completely settled in. I was in one of the positions facing the trail to call the shots if something happened. We assigned guard duty, with one man staying up at each of the three positions while the rest of us found a spot to sleep. Over a foot of water in the rice paddy made it impossible to sleep. The men not on guard spaced themselves along the top of the dikes surrounding the rice paddy, hoping to catch a little sleep.

I didn't have my first guard shift for a couple of hours, but it was going to be tricky trying to sleep on a two-foot-wide dike. Before I lay down I rubbed mosquito repellant on my hands, neck and face. I had learned during my first night in the boonies, you needed to put mosquito repellant on any exposed skin or the mosquitoes would eat you alive. I added one more defense against the mosquitoes. I took my mosquito net and pulled it over my head to cover my entire face.

With repellant on my skin and my mosquito net in place, I curled up in my poncho liner with my towel under my head and fell asleep to the hum of mosquitoes flying around my head. I was awakened about an hour later by the pitter-patter of rain on my poncho liner. Within minutes it began pouring. I was soon completely soaked. We had been issued waterproof ponchos but we didn't carry them on ambushes because the rustle of the heavy plastic made too much noise. The rules while on an ambush were "no lights" and "minimal noise."

The foot of water in the rice paddy soon no longer mattered. There was nothing I could do except wrap up in my soggy poncho liner and try to stay halfway warm. I didn't fall asleep again before it was my turn for guard duty. I sat there on guard with water dripping off my helmet, staring out into the darkness. When we pulled guard on an ambush, we kept our M-16 by our side. We also kept the claymore detonators handy and had several hand grenades lying nearby. Pulling guard seemed like a hopeless cause that night. The clouds obscured any light from the moon or stars and the rain made it impossible to see more than a few feet in any direction. Someone could have walked along the trail and I might not have seen them. I looked around with the starlight scope but it was useless. I hoped "Charlie" was as miserable as we were and was holed up somewhere rather than roaming the countryside. After what seemed like an endless night, the sky brightened as the sun began to rise. When daylight arrived we gathered our claymores, loaded up our gear and headed back to Patton to dry out and relax during our day off.

On the morning of August 24th, a lift of Hueys picked us up from the LZ at Patton. I enjoyed the chopper ride, but they dropped us in the middle of a swamp east of the always-dangerous Ho Bo Woods. Lieutenant Donaldson was the first to jump out the door of the chopper I was riding on, and landed in water almost up to his armpits. The rest of us had no choice but to join him with a "splash." We would have been in trouble if the VC had wanted to hit us as we slowly sloshed through waist-deep water for almost 100 meters, until we reached shallow water and finally worked our way onto dry ground.

Fortunately, it was a warm, clear morning and we would soon dry out. We organized ourselves with the first platoon leading the RIF, followed by Captain Branch and his CP group, the third platoon behind them and the second platoon bringing up the rear. Everyone was pretty serious. The stories about working in or near the Ho Bo Woods were very disheartening. Several companies, including Alpha Company, had taken heavy casualties when they ran into heavily fortified NVA bunker complexes out there. Our job was to try to find one of those complexes.

We had been walking north from our LZ for an hour through mostly flat terrain with scattered trees and hedgerows. Suddenly, a signal came from the front of the columns for everyone to get down. I passed the signal on back and kneeled to the ground holding my rifle in my hands. It was quiet and we didn't see any movement nearby. A couple minutes later Lieutenant Donaldson waved for us NCOs to come over to him. He told us there was a bunker complex directly in front of us, and we were moving up on the right flank.

The third platoon slowly maneuvered forward to the right of the bunkers. Second platoon was doing the same on the left side while the first platoon and the CP group moved forward in the center. I expected all hell to break loose at any moment as we moved closer and closer to the bunkers. Amazingly, we didn't encounter any enemy fire. A Chieu Hoi from the first platoon boldly walked up to one of the bunkers. It was empty, but "Charlie" had been there. There was a pot on a small cooking fire that was still hot. Where were they?

Men carefully checked two other bunkers which were also unoccupied. The men in the first platoon found a tunnel containing supplies and small tools and then the CO was told a booby-trapped hand grenade was spotted just inside a second tunnel entrance. Captain Branch knew the NVA often planted several booby traps around their bunker complexes. Because we had found one device, he wanted to pull back before someone accidentally tripped one. Just as the CO gave the word to start moving back, BOOM! The Chieu Hoi from the first platoon tripped a booby-trapped grenade near a bunker where several men were standing.

The explosion threw a cloud of dirt and debris in the air and sent everyone to the ground.

Someone immediately yelled, "We need medics up here!" No one in the third platoon had been close by. We were all OK. Lieutenant Donaldson motioned for us to stay in place while he walked over to see what had happened. I soon heard over the radio that eight men had been wounded, including Captain Branch, who had a shrapnel wound in his arm. Lieutenant Donaldson was taking charge of the company. Two Chieu Hois, Lieutenant Cannava (our Artillery Forward Observer), an RTO from the first platoon and three other men were down. Lieutenant Donaldson told Sergeant Brown to take charge of the third platoon.

We had been lucky that only one booby trap had been triggered, with so many men stomping around while we searched the area. The wounded men were soon moved away from the bunkers and the entire company pulled back and set up a perimeter around an LZ for the dustoffs. One medevac soon landed and evacuated the most seriously wounded men. Several of us loaded the other injured men onto two more medevacs that arrived a few minutes later. We then organized ourselves and continued moving south away from the bunkers. A few minutes later, artillery was called in to destroy those bunkers.

As the 155MM artillery shells bombard the bunkers, we learned one of our sister companies, Delta Company, had also found a bunker complex several klicks to the northwest; however, it sounded like they found the NVA at home. Delta Company had suffered two KIAs and had nearly a dozen others wounded during a two-hour firefight with the NVA. We hurried back south until we found a clearing to use as an LZ. A lift of Hueys arrived a short while later to shuttle us over to help Delta Company. We were told to expect a "hot" LZ, which meant to expect enemy fire. The door gunners sprayed the nearby countryside while we descended into another small clearing. As the choppers flew off, we heard rifle fire just to our east.

After our entire company arrived we moved out and found Delta Company. They had run into a bunker complex fully occupied by the NVA. Delta had finally withdrawn and called in artillery and an air strike to demolish the area.

We joined Delta Company to sweep through the demolished area in two columns, with us on the left and Delta on the right. As we began to move forward, an NVA soldier surprisingly appeared from the middle of the rubble and began walking toward us with his hands in the air to surrender.

The men from Delta Company began yelling, "Shoot him! Shoot the bastard!"

Most everyone was pointing his rifle at the NVA soldier. I was surprised someone didn't shoot him.

Lieutenant Donaldson quickly walked forward yelling, "Hold your fire! Hold your fire!" The NVA soldier stopped near the center of the clearing.

Quickly, two men from Delta Company ran toward him. When the two GIs reached the NVA soldier one of them pointed his M-16 and appeared ready to shoot him. Lieutenant Donaldson yelled at the GI, "Don't even think about pulling the trigger."

The GI kept his rifle pointed at the NVA's head for a few seconds longer and then lowered his weapon. I thought it was over. But then, the same GI took the butt of his M-16 and smacked the NVA as hard as he could on the side of his head and yelled, "You fucking gook bastard!"

The NVA soldier slumped to the ground while other men restrained the angry GI and pulled him away. I thought the NVA was dead. Obviously the man from Delta Company was distraught after losing his friends and was in no mood to accept a peaceful surrender. Amazingly, the NVA soldier survived the blow to his head and was flown to Cu Chi for interrogation.

As we cautiously moved through the area I saw for the first time the awesome destructive force of artillery shells, bombs and napalm. I hadn't seen the area previously but there wasn't much left. The smell of thousands of pounds of explosives filled the air while smoke and steam rose from bomb craters twenty feet wide and six to eight feet deep. Hedgerows and trees had been blown into splinters. We found the remains of what had been three log bunkers. The enemy would cover the log framework of their bunkers with branches and dirt and after a while grass and vegetation would grow over them, making them look like part of the natural landscape. From a distance, what might look like a natural mound or small hill was really a well-concealed bunker.

We saw a few bodies, or parts of bodies, along with several weapons that had been nearly destroyed by the air strike. The men in Delta Company estimated there were forty NVA engaged in the firefight that day. The actual number of NVA killed couldn't be determined, but the Delta Company CO reported a body count of fifty. However, the enemy body count was meaningless for most of us, because two Americans had made the ultimate sacrifice that day.

It was almost six o'clock when we landed back at Firebase Patton that evening. Everyone was tired and hungry after humping through the Ho Bo Woods for nearly ten hours. All I had eaten during the day was my trusty can of fruit cocktail while we waited to be flown over to help Delta Company. I headed for the mess hall and enjoyed a warm meal along with a quart of chocolate milk served in wax-coated paper containers. The only problem with the milk over there was that we had to get used to the preservative they put in it. But funny tasting milk was better than no milk at all.

While we settled back in at Patton, we learned Captain Branch had received a minor shrapnel wound in his right arm and would rejoin us in a week or two. Lieutenant Cannava had been hit in the hand, but he would fully recover. The first platoon's RTO lost a testicle and the two Chieu Hoi and three other wounded GIs also had serious injuries. They wouldn't be returning to the field.

The 155MM howitzers at Patton fired periodically day or night after they received a fire mission from the field. They also fired harassment and interdiction (H & I) fire at night. They would fire rounds periodically at select targets where friendly troops weren't located in the hopes of hitting enemy personnel who might happen to be in the area. The howitzers were mounted on self-propelled tank chassis, and we often heard the engines fire up to move the gun mount before they fired a round. Additionally, the artillerymen normally yelled, "Fire in the hole," before they fired so that men close by could cover their ears and prepare for the tremendously loud "BOOM" that accompanied each round.

One evening I was standing guard by our bunker on the north side of Patton. There was a 155MM artillery piece sixty meters behind our bunker. Without warning, they fired a round directly over our bunker with the loudest BOOM I had ever heard. I ducked and felt my heart pounding. I was OK, but that shot scared the literal hell out of every man who was standing guard along the northern perimeter.

Several new men had joined the Third Herd since I arrived in early August, and some of the old-timers gladly packed up their gear when they received an assignment in the relative safety of the rear. Staff Sergeant Tom Brown moved on, and Sergeant Rick Shields, who had recovered from being shot in his leg in July, returned to take over as platoon sergeant. Rick was a dark-haired, friendly twenty year-old from Los Angeles. He had been drafted and was a shake'n bake like me, with no plans for making the Army his career.

Most of the FNGs were Privates First Class (PFCs) directly out of AIT. Bill Casey, the easygoing guy with a southern drawl from South Carolina became one of our RTOs, replacing Chuck Gorman who moved on to the CP group. David DiBasio was a carefree Italian from Boston and was quickly nicknamed "Wop." Carlton Quick, from Griffin, GA was a soft-spoken little guy with a southern accent. Bob Ryken was a lighthearted guy from California who brought his guitar to play in his spare time, and Ed Leberski was a tall and slender guy from Pennsylvania. Danial Heiderich was a good old boy from Oklahoma and was nicknamed "Whitey" because he had light blond hair, while red-haired James Mincey, from South Carolina was naturally nicknamed "Red." A fellow Iowan, Mike Myers, from Marshalltown was nicknamed "Babysan" (Vietnamese slang for "baby") because he didn't look old enough to be in the Army. Glennon (Glenn) Haywood, Terry Thornton, Vic Ortega, Robert Draughn and Junior Houchens had also joined the third platoon since I arrived.

There were also a few men who had been in the third platoon for a while longer than I. Doc Jackson, Hal Harris, Steve Robinson, Dennis Schultz, David Hardy and Randal Johnson had each been in the field for a few months, along with Vern Reden, an Indian from South Dakota who was nicknamed (what else?) "Chief."

We often called each other by our last name or nickname. I had earned the nickname of "Hound Dog." While many of the men had little or no body hair, I had lots of hair on my chest and back. Wop thought I was as hairy as a "hound dog" and gave me the nickname.

The latest new arrival was Ron Peterson, who appeared more apprehensive than normal about being in the field. The first morning after Ron arrived I told him to be on the LZ and ready to fly out at eight o'clock. He never showed up and we left without him. When we returned that afternoon I found Peterson sitting by his bunker. He said he had gone to the latrine that morning and missed the choppers. I accepted his explanation, considering it was his first morning in the field. But, the next day the same thing happened. Peterson didn't show up on the LZ and we left without him. I again found him by his bunker when we returned. Peterson's explanation that day was that he lost track of time and missed the choppers, again. I didn't believe him.

I took him aside and I said, "Peterson, what the hell's going on?" He reluctantly admitted he was afraid to fly on a chopper. I told Peterson that flying on a chopper should be one of the slightest of his worries. If something was going to happen to him, it would probably occur on the ground, not in a chopper.

I said, "I'll make sure you are on the LZ tomorrow!"

The following morning several of us kept an eye on Peterson, and I personally escorted him to the landing zone. When the choppers landed, two men each grabbed an arm and ushered him aboard. We sat him in the center of the canvas seat, away from the doors. Peterson tightly held the bottom rail of the seat while we lifted off. I looked at him and gave him a thumbs-up as we flew along, but he just looked straight ahead, holding onto the seat.

I was normally one of the last men to board a chopper after I made sure everyone else was aboard. I usually sat on the floor and sometimes dangled my legs out the door and let them swing in the breeze while we flew high above the countryside. I couldn't imagine someone being afraid to fly in a chopper, because I loved it. After a couple days of dragging Peterson onto a chopper, he overcame his fear and showed up with the rest of us on the LZ whenever we flew out on an air assault mission.

During the first week of September, Lieutenant Donaldson was reassigned to our battalion headquarters. He had been a good platoon leader and I appreciated the great advice he had given me along the way. We all wished him well in his new assignment. Twenty-year-old Second Lieutenant Craig Fielding, was assigned as our new platoon leader. He was from Salt Lake City and practiced the Mormon faith. Lieutenant Fielding told us he didn't drink and didn't cuss, much. We soon noticed he was gung ho, the John Wayne type. Every day was like a new adventure for him. He volunteered to go on ambushes with us at night, which the other platoon leaders rarely did. We all liked Lieutenant Fielding but couldn't understand how he could be so enthusiastic about serving in Vietnam.

One morning we were leading a RIF when we came across a grove of trees that looked like it had been occupied recently. The grass was trampled, and we found an abandoned cooking fire. We set up a defensive perimeter and searched the area that was on high ground. Captain Branch, who had just returned to the company, suspected there might be tunnels or underground storage caches there.

Someone soon found a tunnel and yelled, "Fire in the hole!" They dropped a hand grenade down the tunnel and it detonated, sending dirt flying up from the entrance. We normally dropped a grenade down any tunnel we found before we did anything else, intending to kill or injure anyone inside or to detonate a booby trap the enemy might have planted near the entrance. We also dropped a smoke grenade into the tunnel and then covered the entrance, hoping the smoke would come up elsewhere to reveal other entrances. We didn't see any other smoke. It must have been a small single-entrance tunnel.

Lieutenant Fielding was chomping at the bit to crawl inside to check it out. When Captain Branch saw him kneeling by the entrance he yelled, "Hey, Fielding, you're not going inside there." He didn't want his new platoon leader crawling in a tunnel. Lieutenant Fielding's job was to command his platoon, not be a "tunnel rat." Bob Ryken was small enough to squeeze through the tiny entrance and volunteered to crawl inside with a .45 automatic pistol and flashlight. Bob popped up after a couple of minutes with a brown cloth bag filled with clothes.

We confiscated clothing, rice and weapons from two other tunnels but didn't find any NVA or VC. After we searched the tunnels, we blew them up with bangalore torpedoes. We often carried a few bangalore torpedoes, five-foot-long metal tubes, filled with C-4. They could be connected together if needed to blow away hedgerows or destroy whatever else we chose to. We pushed one bangalore torpedo into each tunnel and detonated them.

After destroying the tunnels we moved on without any enemy contact. The NVA, and more so the VC, normally moved around the countryside in small groups of six or less. If they saw up to one hundred GIs coming their way, they often found a hiding spot unless we happened to see them first. Although I wasn't looking for a firefight I also knew that unless we could inflict enemy casualties, they would be back another day trying to inflict casualties upon us. It was like a game of hide-and-seek except we weren't playing a game. We were facing deadly consequences in Vietnam.

The U.S. military dropped six million tons of bombs and fired over fifteen million tons of artillery shells during the Vietnam War.

Sergeant Rick Shields (standing) and Carlton Quick cleaning
weapons at Fire Support Base Patton.

Chapter 10

In the Boonies

During the second week of September, we packed up and moved several miles northeast of Patton to a small company-size patrol base, simply named Delta. I stored most of my personal items and gear I wouldn't need during our daily RIFs in a gray metal ammunition box that was about eighteen inches square. The lid had a waterproof seal to keep the contents dry. That morning I strapped the ammunition box to my backpack, threw the backpack over my shoulder, grabbed my rifle and ammunition and walked to the landing zone outside the perimeter wire at Patton, ready to move on.

A large Chinook helicopter would fly each platoon to Patrol Base Delta. Chinooks were huge and looked like a big OD-green colored banana, with windows on the side. The twin rotor blades stirred up twice as much dirt and debris as a Huey, forcing us to keep our distance until the Chinook landed. We then quickly walked up the ramp that dropped down from the rear of the chopper. Most of us found a seat on the long canvas-covered benches inside while others just sat on the floor. The pilot revved the engine and we slowly lifted off toward our new home. It was a fairly short but bumpy flight. The ride on a Huey was normally pretty smooth once we were in the air, but the huge, rotating twin blades on the Chinook shook and vibrated the huge chopper the entire trip.

We landed outside the northern perimeter of Patrol Base Delta. Delta was less than 100 meters in diameter with bunkers built into a three-foot-high berm. The interior was similar to Patrol Base Hunsley with a few tents and scattered bunkers, mortar pits and three 105MM artillery pieces. When I looked beyond the perimeter I could see fairly open countryside with no villages or hootches. It looked like we were in the boonies. We soon settled into another group of small bunkers and made ourselves at home.

Captain Branch wanted each platoon to go out for a couple hours that afternoon to make a sweep of the surrounding area to see what we might find and to help many of us newer guys learn the area. Each platoon saddled up and took off in a different direction. During our route that took us southeast of the patrol base, I had my first close look at the effects of Agent Orange. Agent Orange was a chemical defoliant sprayed from specially equipped helicopters or C-123 transport planes that killed most every bit of vegetation it touched. Engineers often came through after spraying an area and bulldozed most of what was left, leaving almost nothing for the enemy to use as a hiding place. That was fine for us, but it was an eerie feeling to walk through areas where there had previously been lush green trees and undergrowth. There was nothing left but dead vegetation lying in small clumps or flat on the ground, sometimes for hundreds of meters in any direction. We didn't find any signs of enemy activity during our sweep and walked back into Delta by four o'clock.

The first platoon went out on an ambush the first night at Delta. Early that evening we checked the claymores and trip flares in front of our bunkers to make sure they were operational. We set up a schedule for guard duty and prepared for another night in Vietnam. A few hours later I was standing guard by my bunker along with a new man, John Potts, who had arrived a few days earlier. There was nothing but silence and darkness outside the patrol base.

Unexpectedly, I heard a faint "pop" sound in the distance directly in front of me. My eyes opened wide as I turned and shouted "INCOMING! INCOMING!" while I hurried for our bunker. When I reached the bunker entrance I looked for Potts. He was frozen in place beside our bunker. I stepped back and peered out over the perimeter for an instant thinking he had spotted something. I didn't see anything. I yelled, "Potts, get your ass in here!"

Potts jumped as though he had been in a trance and then turned and quickly followed me into the bunker just as a mortar round exploded near the perimeter in front of our bunker. Several more rounds quickly followed. The men inside the bunker woke up when I ran inside and they sat up when they heard the sound of the exploding mortar rounds. There was a brief silence, and then our mortar platoon and the 105MM battery began firing outgoing rounds.

I told the men to get out on guard while I ran over to our mortar pits. I wanted to tell our mortar platoon the direction I thought the incoming rounds had come from. Wearing my helmet and flack jacket

I ran over to the mortar pits and pointed northeast, the direction I believed the mortar rounds had come from. They directed several rounds in that direction for a few minutes and then stopped firing. There was silence again.

When we checked around the patrol base it appeared only a couple of rounds had landed inside the perimeter and fortunately had caused no injuries or damage. The entire company stayed on full guard for a while but all remained quiet. We finally went back to our normal guard rotation for the rest of the night. The next morning Captain Branch had us up early to grab some chow in preparation for an early start in the hopes of finding that enemy mortar tube or any trace of the VC or NVA who had fired the mortars at us.

There wasn't a mess hall at Delta, but there was a mess tent where the cook prepared some hot food or served the food delivered each day in insulated containers for the morning and evening meal. The food out there was better than surviving on C-rations, but I soon learned the scrambled eggs prepared out there were horrible. They were made from powdered eggs and actually had a slight greenish tint. They didn't taste like eggs; in fact, they didn't have much taste at all. Even ketchup didn't help. Most of the guys would take a few bites and throw the rest away. Even a stray dog that hung around the patrol base wouldn't eat those scrambled eggs.

The entire company headed northeast on a RIF before eight o'clock that morning. We soon ran into heavy vegetation with tall grass, trees and hedgerows. They hadn't sprayed Agent Orange out there and everything was growing wild, fed by the monsoon rains. We knew there had been enemy troops out there, and we took our time hoping to avoid walking into an ambush or tripping any booby traps they might have left behind. By mid-day, we hadn't found any signs of enemy activity. Captain Branch called for a Huey gunship to scout the area around us, two klicks north of the patrol base.

The third platoon led the way as we started moving west in two columns. Our point men, Robert Draughn and Carlton Quick, were both having trouble finding a clear route, and we slowly wove through and around hedgerows, bushes and trees. We all stayed closer to each other than normal to keep in sight of each other. Two long bursts of gunfire suddenly erupted from a cluster of trees less than fifty meters in front of us. Everyone immediately hit the ground. The vegetation was so thick I couldn't see more than a few feet in any direction when I crouched to the ground.

I yelled, "Is anybody hit?"

"No," was the reply as guys cautiously looked around for any movement, ready to duck if enemy fire erupted again. There was no more gunfire coming from the trees, but Captain Branch was on the radio telling the gunship overhead to check out the trees directly west of us. The pilot immediately flew in that direction and one of the door gunners began firing his M-60 machine gun as the chopper circled the trees. We stepped up the pace as we closed in on the trees without receiving any more enemy fire. The chopper pilot radioed they had seen two enemy personnel in the trees and had opened fire on them. They hadn't seen any other enemy troops in the area but we knew they could have quickly taken cover and might still be nearby.

The third platoon spread out when we reached the trees and maneuvered forward on line as we led a sweep through the area with the gunship circling overhead. A door gunner dropped a smoke grenade near the trees where the enemy troops had been seen. We cautiously walked toward the purple smoke and came upon two VC lying on the ground, both dead. Their bodies were covered with blood and riddled with bullet holes.

The CO had the first and second platoon establish a defensive perimeter around the trees while the third platoon continued to search the area. We hoped to find their mortar tube or mortar rounds, but we found nothing except two AK-47 Russian-made rifles, some ammunition and a small bag of rice. However, the grass in the area had been trampled indicating other troops had been there. We believed the two VC had spotted us while serving as "lookouts." They had remained behind to provide cover while the others sneaked away. Unfortunately for them, they were sitting ducks when spotted by the gunship.

I picked up the AK-47 lying by one of the bodies. I had seen AK-47s during training, but wanted to hold one the enemy had actually used. I pulled out my camera and asked someone to take my picture holding the weapon. Some of the other guys quickly did the same to have a memento of the little bounty we had captured. Although we hadn't found the mortar tube, the gunship eliminated two VC and stopped any plans they had for us. We took their weapons and supplies with us and left the bodies lying where they had fallen from the trees.

We continued on by circling south back to Patrol Base Delta without spotting any other enemy movement.

Although we normally out-manned and out-gunned the enemy, they operated effectively in small groups that were much more mobile than we were. They could fire mortar rounds at us during the night or open fire on us like the two VC did that day, and then they were gone. For all we knew, the enemy troops who had fired the mortar rounds toward Delta the past night were miles away ready to use the mortar tube elsewhere, or they could have crawled into a tunnel for the day, ready to pop out after dark and drop more rounds on Delta.

When we got back to the patrol base later that afternoon, I took off my gear to relax for awhile before our scheduled ambush. To our surprise, a group of ARVNs had been assigned to Delta to work with us. Although the United States military was leading the battle against the VC and NVA, the ARVNs were also fighting them. Part of our job was to work with the ARVNs in hopes they someday would assume a greater fighting role, thereby enabling the United States to reduce its involvement and eventually pull out of South Vietnam. The process was called "Vietnamization." It was a good idea, but from what I had seen of the ARVNs they had a long way to go before they would be a formidable fighting force. Supposedly, President Nixon was trying to initiate peace talks with the North Vietnamese and withdraw American troops from South Vietnam. But until the fighting actually stopped and we were safely back in the world, those peace talks weren't helping any of us GIs who were serving in Vietnam.

We were told some of the ARVNs would be going with us to set up the ambush that night. Rick Shields, Jim Overbey and I were taking nine other GIs and six ARVNs on the ambush. After a quick dinner, Lieutenant Fielding gave us our ambush assignment. We would head south of the patrol base, walk through a group of hootches and then establish an ambush 100 meters beyond.

Rick, Jim and I wanted to have an experienced point man lead the ARVNs and us that evening. We asked Hal Harris who had walked point after he joined the platoon that past summer. He agreed to lead the ambush patrol.

We GIs were ready to leave on schedule, but we had to wait for the ARVNs. We were slipping behind schedule as Rick waved at the six ARVNs to hurry up and join us. The sun was getting low in the western horizon when Harris finally led us through the perimeter wire followed by Carlton Quick and then John Potts.

Rick walked near the front of our single column to help guide Harris while us GIs followed and the ARVNs brought up the rear. It was almost dark when we neared the group of hootches 600 meters south of the patrol base. I was about to walk through a hedgerow when I heard two loud explosions in front of me and I hit the ground.

Bursts of rifle fire immediately followed and knocked some branches off the hedgerow directly over me. The rest of the men had disappeared. I saw the hedgerow directly in front of me and nothing but darkness behind me. My heart pounded as I held my rifle with the safety turned to automatic while I tried to figure out what was happening and where the rest of the men were. Rifle fire and what sounded like hand grenade explosions continued in front of me.

I yelled, "Where are you guys?" I couldn't hear anything over the noise of the gunfire and explosions. Intermittent rifle fire continued while I crawled through the hedgerow hoping to find one of the guys. When I reached the far side of the hedgerow I came face-to-face with a Vietnamese soldier. I froze! I could see that he wasn't wearing a helmet. I didn't know if it was an ARVN or VC. The VC normally didn't wear helmets, but many of the ARVNs also didn't wear helmets. I thought about shooting him for an instant, but since he hadn't already tried to kill me, he had to be one of the ARVNs. I tried to talk to him but he didn't understand a word I was saying. He just looked at me. I crawled to my right and finally saw Dennis Shultz and Mike Myers kneeling near one of the hootches. It suddenly became strangely quiet.

Dennis Shultz our RTO was talking with the command post at Delta. I heard him say, "We have a KIA."

I couldn't believe what I heard. I asked Schultz where Rick was. He pointed in front of the nearby hootch. I told Schultz and Myers to follow me while I led them forward. I soon found Rick with the rest of our men.

Rick said, "We were ambushed," and then hesitated a few seconds, "Harris is dead. Quick and Potts are wounded!"

A Huey gunship had been called in and soon began circling overhead to give us cover and dropping flares to light up the area so that we could organize the men and account for everyone. A rocket-propelled grenade had killed Hal Harris instantly. His body had been carried back and laid on a poncho liner beside a nearby hootch. Quick and Potts could both walk, but they needed further medical attention. The rest of us were uninjured.

Rick, Jim Overbey and I briefly huddled and agreed we should get out of there and get the wounded men back to Delta. We weren't going to surprise anyone with an ambush. Unfortunately, we had been the ones surprised by an ambush. Rick radioed Captain Branch and told him what happened. The CO agreed we should return to the patrol base.

I quickly told the men what we were doing. They knew it would be dangerous to walk back to Delta in the darkness, but they also wanted to get the hell out of there before something else happened. We somehow organized the ARVNs and got the message across that we were moving back to Delta.

After every man was accounted for, Rick Shields and Dave Hardy led us north in a single column. I joined Doc Jackson, Jim Overbey and Mike Myers to carry Harris' body back to Delta. I hadn't looked closely at his body and was shocked when I reached down to grab a corner of the poncho liner. Hal's body had literally been torn into pieces. His right leg had been completely blown off and was lying grotesquely on the poncho liner. His lower right arm had also been nearly severed and there was a golf-ball-sized hole on the right side of his head. I didn't say a word. I took a deep breath and lifted my corner of the poncho liner as the four of us moved out.

No one knew for sure how many enemy troops we had run into or if any of them had been killed or wounded during the brief firefight. I hoped and prayed they weren't waiting for us somewhere in the darkness on our way back. It was slow going as we cautiously walked through the dark. The four of us carrying Harris had to stop periodically to take a short break and to switch arms. Harris was a pretty good-sized guy; after a while, it felt like the arm I was using to carry him would fall off.

After what seemed like forever, we neared Patrol Base Delta. We stopped while Schultz radioed the command post to alert the men on guard around the perimeter that we were coming in so that they wouldn't fire on us thinking we were the enemy. It wasn't an exceptionally warm night, but sweat was running down the faces of the four of us who had been carrying Harris' body as we waited outside the perimeter trying to catch our breath. When we knew it was safe, we moved toward the perimeter and walked through an opening in the concertina wire. The four of us carried Harris' body into the mess tent and laid him inside. Someone found a poncho to cover him. I walked away in almost disbelief about what had happened.

We checked to make sure the rest of the men were OK and provided a report to Lieutenant Fielding and Captain Branch.

Rick simply said, "We were ambushed."

Rick said that Hal Harris was walking point when he was killed as we passed through some hootches. The VC threw hand grenades and fired their AK-47s. Rick explained that our men had returned fire and thrown several grenades, but it was too dark to see anything out there. Captain Branch asked about the rest of the men. I told him that Carlton Quick and John Potts had minor wounds but everyone else was OK.

After talking with Lieutenant Fielding and Captain Branch for a few minutes, Rick and I went back to see how the rest of the men were doing. Doc Jackson was checking Quick's wounds again. He had a shrapnel wound in his left shoulder and needed to be medevaced to the 12th Evac in Cu Chi. I then found John Potts. He hadn't actually been wounded, but he was in total emotional shock. He had been behind Harris and Quick and was right in the middle of the action. I tried to talk with Potts but he jabbered incoherently, walking around staring off in the distance. He wouldn't make eye contact with anyone and didn't seem to comprehend what anyone said to him. I don't think he even knew where he was.

Doc Jackson tried to talk with Potts but had no better luck than the rest of us. Doc and I agreed Potts should be flown out with Quick on the dustoff that was on its way. Potts had been with us for less than a week. That night's action was the first he had seen. All of us were in varying degrees of shock, but the rest of the men appeared to be in control of themselves. For many of us in the third platoon, Hal Harris was the first man we had seen killed in action. It was difficult to comprehend that he was dead.

A medevac landed outside the main gate a short while later. Quick was able to walk on his own but two of us guided Potts to the chopper. The swirling chopper blades scared the hell out of him. We had to force Potts on board. If we had let go of him I believe he might have taken off running into the darkness, not realizing what he was doing. Doc Jackson told the medic on the chopper what was going on with

Potts so he would keep a close eye on him. A litter carrying Harris' body was then loaded on board. We backed away when the medevac lifted off and quietly stood there for a moment to pay our respects and say good-bye to our friend and comrade Hal Harris as the chopper disappeared into the darkness. I assumed Quick would return to the platoon after he recovered from his wound. But I didn't know if we would ever see Potts again. One week in the field may have destroyed him emotionally for life.

Hal Harris knew walking point would be dangerous, but he willingly assumed the risk to help the rest of the platoon. Rick Shields, Jim Overbey and I felt terrible that we had asked Harris to walk point. It was a decision that cost him his life. Several of us lingered around our bunker for a while talking about the ambush.

I overheard Jim tell someone he had shot two of them.

I asked, "Jim, you shot two gooks?"

"No," he said, "I shot two water buffalo!"

Jim had been in front of me when we neared the hootches. When he crawled forward he saw something moving to his left and he opened fire with his M-16. He didn't realize until later it had been two water buffalo tied up near one of the hootches.

What many of us thought would be another routine ambush patrol turned out to be a first-hand taste of combat. That night truly brought the realities of war directly before my eyes. Hal had eaten chow with several of us earlier that evening. He put on his gear along with the rest of us and led us on the ambush without reservation. Thirty minutes later, he was dead. That night I learned to no longer take anything for granted. We had walked through many similar groups of hootches that I had considered to be safe. After that night I knew no place was truly safe over there.

It was almost midnight when I walked back to my bunker and crawled inside hoping to get a little sleep. I lay down on my air mattress and pulled my poncho liner over me. I tossed and turned, trying to get the thoughts of the past few hours out of my mind. Before I eventually fell asleep I remembered I had written a quick letter to my folks that afternoon after we returned from the RIF. I dated it September 14, 1969. That night was exactly one month after my 23rd birthday and a night I will never forget.

Early the following morning, the cook yelled for help after he walked into the mess tent. Several of us ran over and saw the shocked look on his face as he pointed inside. The cook said, "What the hell is that? Get it out of here!"

When Hal Harris' body was carried from the mess tent to the medevac, his severed leg had somehow been left behind. Finding Harris' leg was a gruesome way for the cook, and the rest of us, to start the day. A couple men took Hal's leg and buried it outside the perimeter.

After breakfast the third platoon led the rest of the company back to the site where we had been ambushed. The two water buffalo Jim Overbey had shot were lying dead on the ground east of the first hootch. Although it was obvious people had been living in those hootches, no one was around. Food, utensils, personal items and clothing were inside the hootches, and there was a huge pile of rice stored by one of the hootches. Either the VC forced the civilians out or the occupants were VC sympathizers who may have helped with the ambush.

We didn't find any enemy bodies or weapons, but there were dozens of empty AK-47 shell casings in the area. Knowing the VC were in the area, we burned the food and clothing we had found. Captain Branch also called for explosive charges to be flown out. After they arrived, we helped our demolitions man set a charge inside each hootch and then pulled back a safe distance. The huge charges exploded, sending a cloud of smoke, dirt and debris in the air, and left nothing but flattened hootches in piles of burning rubble. It may have been cruel to destroy those primitive homes, but we frankly didn't give a damn. Hal Harris died in the middle of those hootches. We returned to Patrol Base Delta that afternoon with smoke rising to the sky behind us.

After we returned to Delta we learned one of our sister companies, Charlie Company, whom we had replaced at Delta, had sent ambush patrols through those same hootches their last two nights at Delta. That meant the third platoon had unknowingly become sitting ducks, with the VC waiting for us when we again walked through the same group of hootches. An apparent lack of communication between Charlie Company and Alpha Company had cost Hal Harris his life.

We didn't have much time to dwell on Harris' death. The next morning Alpha Company and the ARVNs were told to pack our gear. We were moving to a patrol base with the strange name of Dong Tien, southeast of the Ho Bo Woods. There was a lot of bitching and moaning when the men got the word to pack up again and meet on the LZ north of Delta. Around mid-morning a lift of Hueys flew us toward the Ho Bo Woods. The countryside near Dong Tien was covered with thick vegetation, giving the enemy plenty of concealment. It would be hard to spot anyone out there even from the air.

When I walked in from the LZ at Dong Tien I found another small patrol base with the traditional circle of bunkers built into a small berm and surrounded by rows of concertina wire. The first 150 meters surrounding the patrol base had been sprayed with Agent Orange and were partially cleared to give us visibility, but beyond that there was nothing but thick green vegetation. When we returned after a short RIF with the ARVNs late that afternoon, some of the men in the company were missing a radio or camera they had left behind. We normally left our personal gear in or around our bunkers when we went out on a RIF and rarely had a problem with anything missing.

Since most of the GIs had been on the RIF except our mortar platoon, we guessed some ARVNs had taken the missing items. The ARVNs were assigned bunkers along the opposite perimeter but the mortar guys said they noticed two of them wandering around our bunkers that afternoon and had told the ARVNs to move away. Some of our guys wanted to go search ARVN's bunkers for the missing items, but Captain Branch didn't want to cause an uproar. He told the ARVN commander to keep his men on their side of the patrol base from then on. After that day, we left one man behind to protect our possessions whenever ARVNs were in a patrol base with us. What a sad state of affairs. The ARVNs were stealing from us while we were risking our lives in their war.

The following morning, September 16th, we were organizing ourselves outside of the patrol base before a RIF. The ARVNs didn't intermingle with us often, but one of them came up that morning and asked to bum a cigarette from one of the guys. That man was a friendly little guy who tried to talk using the little English he knew. He wore sandals while all of us GIs and most of the ARVNs wore jungle boots, and he carried an M-16 but no ammunition other than the one magazine in his rifle. I looked around and noticed most of the ARVNs were carrying extra ammunition magazines but none of them carried as much gear and ammunition as we did. They weren't prepared for any long battles.

The ARVNs led the RIF while we followed in two columns behind them. We had been walking most of the morning when the columns stopped. The word quickly came back that the ARVNs had spotted an enemy bunker complex. The company cautiously moved foreword and set up a perimeter along rice paddy dikes in front of the bunkers. Amazingly we received no enemy fire as we closed in.

Captain Branch laid out his plan. He had called for some forty-pound explosive charges to be flown out. If we didn't run into any enemy troops, we would place the charges in the bunkers to destroy them. Everyone held their places for nearly twenty minutes watching over the nearby countryside, but we didn't see any movement.

After the charges were unloaded from a Huey, our company demolitions man moved forward while several men carried the charges to the front of our perimeter. Jim Overbey, Mike Myers and RTO Dennis Schultz were with the point group for the third platoon, and moved toward the bunkers with the demolitions man and some of the ARVNs who were to stand guard and help place the charges. The men began to set the charges when BOOM! BOOM! Enemy RPGs exploded around them and enemy rifle fire came from NVA troops who had been concealed in another bunker complex, behind a hedgerow north of the original bunkers we had spotted.

We couldn't see the NVA because of the thick vegetation but the smoke and flashes from their weapons revealed their location. Several of us took cover as green tracer rounds from an enemy machine gun flew over our heads. The ARVNs and our point group dove for cover and returned fire while the rest of the company sprayed the surrounding area with rifle and machine gun fire and fired M-79 grenades, directing as much firepower as we could toward the NVA. The deafening noise from the rifles and machine guns continued as I emptied several magazines of ammunition into the nearby hedgerow.

After the first rockets were fired, the ARVNs who were with our point group and demolitions man returned fire, but then quickly began pulling back. I looked forward and saw the little ARVN guy, whom I had seen with only one magazine of ammunition, stand up and fire his M-16 into the bushes in front of him until his magazine was empty. He then ran back sat down behind us. I thought, "You son-of-a-bitch! You fire one magazine of ammunition and then run behind us and hide while we fight the rest of the battle."

Unfortunately, the ARVNs had left six of our men all alone by the original bunker complex taking enemy rifle and rocket fire. Dennis Schultz radioed Lieutenant Fielding saying they needed more covering fire so they could get out of there. Lieutenant Fielding told Schultz to have the men crawl straight back toward the rest of us while we concentrated our fire to the north.

Lieutenant Fielding spread the word to direct all of our fire on the northern hedgerow where the initial enemy fire had come from. Additional men joined us along our northern perimeter, and we all bombarded that hedgerow with fire from our M-16s, three M-60s and four M-79 grenade launchers. After a couple of very long minutes, Jim Overbey and the rest of the men with him crawled away from the bunkers and rejoined the rest of us who were spread out behind the rice paddy dikes. Miraculously, we hadn't sustained a single casualty.

But the battle wasn't over yet. Just when we thought we had nailed all of the NVA or they had made a run for it, a group of over a dozen NVA was spotted moving behind another hedgerow and someone yelled, "There's more gooks on the right!"

Ed Leberski dropped one man with his M-16 and Wop hit two more with his M-60. Rick Shields also dropped another NVA with his rifle while the rest of us began firing where several of the NVA had hit the ground. Most of us couldn't tell if we were hitting any enemy troops while we sprayed the area where they had last been seen, but we were making it nearly impossible for them to survive or escape. The barrel of Wop's machine gun was smoking hot after firing hundreds of rounds during that firefight. And it smoked even more when he stopped firing for a minute and poured silicone lubricant on it to keep it cool so it wouldn't warp.

Captain Branch then called for a cease-fire and ordered us to slowly pull back about 100 meters. His Forward Observer was calling in artillery to be followed by gun ships and then an air strike. We didn't know for sure what we had run into, but the CO wasn't taking any more chances in fighting it out until he called in the heavy stuff. To sweep through the area and encounter further firefights would most certainly result in American casualties. Pulling back and letting the big boys "sock-it-to'em" sounded like a damn good idea to the rest of us.

A couple of minutes after we had pulled back, the first 155MM artillery round from Fire Support Base Patton landed near the bunkers with a crackling explosion. Over a dozen more rounds followed and landed across the area in front of us while we ducked for cover each time we heard the whistle of an incoming round. We got peppered with debris after each round exploded. 155MM artillery rounds looked like huge two-foot-long bullets and made a thunderous explosion when they detonated.

When the artillery stopped, two Cobra gunships fired dozens of grenades and rockets and sprayed the area with thousands of rounds from their Miniguns. The bunkers and area surrounding them were slowly being demolished. I could smell the explosives and smoldering debris in the smoke-filled air. The Cobras continued their mission for ten minutes while we scoured the countryside for movement and watched the awesome air show.

Someone then yelled, "The air strikes are on the way."

I looked over my shoulder and saw an F-105 Thunderchief swoop toward us and then release a huge bomb while directly overhead. The bomb sailed through the air, heading toward its target in front of us. I ducked as the first bomb exploded and shook the ground beneath me. A rain of dirt clods and debris began falling all around us. Several more jets followed, dropping 500-and 1,000-pound bombs that literally leveled the countryside to our west and north while continuing to pelt us with debris with each exploding bomb.

Some of the chunks of dirt and debris might have caused serious injuries if they had landed directly on someone, but we all escaped with only close calls. It was one hell of a show of firepower and a demonstration of the 25th Division's philosophy of using "firepower rather than manpower." I liked it.

When the air strikes ended there was silence. I looked toward the west and saw smoke and dust streaming from the ground in front of us. But there was one final weapon to employ. Flame baths of napalm in 55-gallon drums were dropped from helicopters. We could feel the heat from the huge balls of orange flame while huge plumes of black smoke rose into the air. Napalm was a flammable substance used in flamethrowers and aerial bombs. When the napalm ignited, it spewed a flaming jelled liquid that stuck to whatever or whoever was nearby. I couldn't imagine any NVA troops surviving the barrage of artillery rounds, rockets, bombs and then napalm.

Lieutenant Fielding told us we were moving out to sweep through the bombed out area. We organized ourselves in two columns and cautiously walked forward and weaved around huge bomb craters as we moved through the area that was completely decimated. The hedgerows and trees were flattened and laid scorched by the napalm. We found a few body parts in the remains of the bunkers, along with pieces of destroyed rocket launchers and one NVA flag. Although we believed there had been over thirty NVA in the two groups that had put up a fight with us, most of their remains were either destroyed or buried under the dirt and debris. Captain Branch reported a body count of 36 later that day.

It felt strange when I walked through that ruined area. Where there had been two enemy bunker complexes filled with who knows how many NVA, nothing but wasteland remained. We walked on for another klick or two with no further enemy contact. The best news of that day was that amazingly we made it through with no friendly (American or ARVN) casualties. The NVA, with the protection and concealment of their bunkers, could have inflicted heavy casualties upon us. We had been fortunate.

When I took off my gear after we returned to the patrol base I finally felt like we had accomplished something for a change. It was a combination of good military tactics and the good Lord watching over us that helped us all survive that day. Although we had kicked the NVA's butt, the big picture still didn't make a lot of sense to me. We fought what was termed "guerrilla" warfare in Vietnam. Rather than having established battle lines, with the opposing forces mounting huge arsenals of weapons and men to conduct major battles for control of an area, in South Vietnam the NVA, and more so the VC, roamed the countryside in small groups engaging in smaller encounters with the American and ARVN forces.

Although there had been some major battles involving hundreds of enemy forces in areas closer to the Demilitarized Zone (DMZ), across much of South Vietnam the NVA operated from isolated strongholds like the Ho Bo Woods. They deployed small groups to set booby traps and land mines, to build punji pits with sharp bamboo stakes, and to fire sporadic mortar rounds into patrol bases. They used their mobility to avoid or elude American forces and would use their vast network of tunnels to avoid detection.

The NVA and VC had us fighting their kind of war because they knew they would soon lose to our awesome firepower if they engaged in conventional warfare. Although the NVA and VC had suffered significantly more casualties than the Americans since the beginning of our involvement in Vietnam, we hadn't gained any significant advantage. If both sides continued to contribute personnel and equiupment, that kind of war could go on forever. I had been going out on RIFs nearly every day for two months and we hadn't accomplished anything except getting some of our guys killed and wounded.

We then got some good news. Stand down!

➤ Private First Class Hal Harris was from Detroit, MI. Hal arrived in Vietnam on May 28, 1969. He was killed when the third platoon was ambushed on September 14, 1969. Hal was twenty-two years old and would have celebrated his 23rd birthday on September 18th. He was married with one child.

"Hal was a good man. When Hal was walking point in July 1969, he spotted a booby trap and prevented casualties that might have occurred had someone tripped it. He was wounded on August 2nd and I recommended him for a Bronze Star (for valor) for his actions that day." (Steve Donaldson, Hal Harris' former platoon leader)

An estimated nineteen million gallons of Agent Orange chemical defoliant were sprayed on an estimated five million acres in South Vietnam between 1962 and 1971. In more recent years, considerable debate has arisen regarding the exposure to Agent Orange causing certain serious illnesses among Vietnam veterans.

Bomb craters filled with water during the monsoon season.

Chapter 11

Stand Down

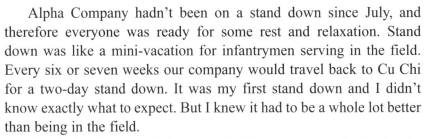

Alpha Company hadn't been on a stand down since July, and therefore everyone was ready for some rest and relaxation. Stand down was like a mini-vacation for infantrymen serving in the field. Every six or seven weeks our company would travel back to Cu Chi for a two-day stand down. It was my first stand down and I didn't know exactly what to expect. But I knew it had to be a whole lot better than being in the field.

The timing for a stand down couldn't have been any better for the Third Herd. We needed a couple of days to refresh our minds and put the night of September 14th behind us. After one more night pulling guard at Dong Tien we were up early and packed our gear for a chopper ride to Cu Chi. Chinooks shuttled in a new company to take over the patrol base. After a Chinook landed to drop off a platoon of new men, one of our platoons loaded on board and relaxed during the bumpy ride to Cu Chi.

After arriving at our company area, we cleaned our weapons and took care of any problems we might have been having with them. We then checked in our weapons with Tom Powers who kept them locked inside the company headquarters building. Most of the men shaved and took a long shower because we hadn't taken one since we had left Patton the previous week. We then put on brand new fatigues that made us all look like FNGs. It felt great to be clean and have fresh fatigues, but more so, it was a relief to be in the peaceful environment of Cu Chi and not have to worry about the hazards of combat. I had the rest of that day and the next to do pretty much whatever I wanted.

There was an area in Cu Chi reserved for companies on stand down called the Cu Chi Hilton. It wasn't exactly like a Hilton Hotel, but there were clean wooden barracks, showers and a mess hall. It was where I would call home for two days. After lunch I walked to the PX with several other men. The PX was like a department store. They had clothing, personal hygiene items, small appliances, cameras and film, radios and a host of other things GIs might need for their day-to-day living. We could also order stereo equipment, china, cameras and other items from a catalog, to be delivered to Cu Chi or sent home. All I needed was a few rolls of film for my camera.

I had a Kodak Instamatic camera that I kept wrapped in plastic and carried in a canvas ammunition pouch clipped to my pistol belt when I was in the field. Almost all the guys had a camera and took lots of pictures. I left two rolls of film for developing. I was anxious to see the picture of me holding one of the AK-47s we captured from the two VC soldiers who had been shot out of the trees.

I left the PX and joined several guys at the Special Services Club. There were pool tables, ping-pong tables and other games, as well as a small library inside. We also talked with two American Red Cross girls who worked there. I had seen lots of Vietnamese women in the villages around Firebase Patton, and there were also a lot of Vietnamese women working inside the base camp, but it was nice to see "round-eyed" (American) women again. I played a couple games of pool with the guys and then moved on to our stand down area. There would be a trailer full of cold beer arriving later that afternoon, and then at seven o'clock a band would entertain us for an hour or so. I lay down in a bunk in our barracks to take a nap, something I hadn't had much opportunity to do in the field. I woke up an hour later and heard someone say that the beer was on the way.

"All right!" I thought. I hadn't had a beer since the one I drank with Dave Hardy on my 22nd birthday. I walked out to the open space near the barracks, which was a grassy area with a few trees that made a peaceful spot to relax and enjoy ourselves. Most of the men in Alpha Company were mingling around and talking while they patiently waited for the beer to arrive.

A few minutes after five o'clock, Tom Powers drove into the stand down area with a jeep pulling a trailer full of iced-down beer to the cheers of Alpha Company. We mobbed the trailer in a semi-orderly fashion until everyone who wanted one had a cold beer in his hand. We smiled and toasted each other with our beers and talked, while not wandering too far from the trailer. It was great to enjoy a brief reprieve from the war that continued in the countryside surrounding Cu Chi. For the first time in over six weeks I could totally relax for awhile and forget about fighting the war.

Captain Branch mingled with us while he enjoyed a cold beer. He had served a previous tour of duty in Vietnam as an ARVN advisor. He had begun his second tour that past June and became the Alpha Company CO shortly thereafter. Captain Branch was a friendly guy and laughed and joked along with the rest of us that afternoon. For the first time in my brief Army career, his rank didn't matter. I wouldn't have felt comfortable back in the world drinking beer with a captain. But that afternoon, Captain Branch was just one of the guys.

I then talked with our Battalion Chaplain. I had met Chaplain Wideman a few weeks earlier when he visited Patrol Base Delta. Several of us gathered around a 105MM artillery position where he conducted a brief chapel service. At the conclusion of the service, he gave each of us a silver cross on a chain. I had also removed an M-16 round from its brass casing and heated it with C-4 to melt the lead enough to stick the ends of a small loop of wire into the backside of the round. I slipped the chain through the wire loop and wore the M-16 round along with the silver cross around my neck. Rick Shields had done the same thing with the AK-47 round they removed from his leg in July. Most of the men wore some type of necklace or bracelet to establish their own unique identity. Some of them were as simple as a braided bootlace.

I then ran into Chief near the trailer. We smiled at each other as we reached in and pulled a cold beer from the ice. Lieutenant Fielding then walked up and said, "Hi, guys, where's the soda?"

"Soda?" I said, "Have a beer."

"Oh no, I don't drink beer, just soda." Fortunately there were a few sodas in the trailer for the non-beer drinkers.

I later found Carlton Quick standing with some of the guys. I hadn't seen him since he had gotten on the chopper the night of September 14th. I walked up and put my arm round Quick's good shoulder and asked how he was doing. Quick replied, "I'm fine, Sarge," as he smiled and raised the beer in his right hand. His left shoulder was bandaged and his left arm was in a sling. Quick said they had pulled two pieces of shrapnel out of his shoulder in the hospital. He was still a little sore but would be ready to rejoin us in a couple weeks. Quick was happy to see his buddies in the Third Herd, and it was great to see him, especially since he seemed to be doing fine both physically and emotionally. Quick said he didn't see anything before he was wounded by shrapnel from an enemy grenade.

I asked Quick if he knew anything about John Potts. He said Potts was still in the psych ward as far as he knew. He had walked over to visit Potts one day but they wouldn't let him in. Most of us doubted we would ever see Potts again. And we didn't. John Potts never returned to the third platoon.

Our party in the middle of the Cu Chi Hilton continued with most of the guys drinking beer until it was all gone. But that was probably for the best. Many of the men were feeling pretty good by then. If there had been more beer some of them would have been falling-down drunk before long. Most of the men were only nineteen or twenty years old and probably drank more beer that night than they had ever drunk before. Having recently turned twenty-three, I was the oldest man in the Third Herd.

After the beer was gone, most of us walked toward the grandstand where the band was preparing to entertain us. There was a covered stage for the band, with wooden benches in front for us to sit and enjoy the show. A short while later four young Korean girls walked out on stage to a huge reception of cheers and whistles from the rowdy group of Alpha Company GIs. We had seen many Vietnamese women in the field when we were operating around Firebase Patton but nothing like the girls in the band. Seeing those young ladies in short dresses revealing their curvy figures was an enjoyable treat on our first night of stand down.

The girls played songs like "Tie a Yellow Ribbon Round the Old Oak Tree," "The Green Green Grass of Home" and "I Left my Heart in San Francisco" that reminded us of the world we left behind. Those songs could have easily made us sad and homesick, but for an hour or so we all forgot about being half way around the world and the hazards we faced every day. We enjoyed the music while we sang along and cheered the girls throughout the entire show. It was great.

After the show everyone scattered. Some of the men headed to a club, others were going to play poker, while some of the guys were drunk and needed to find their way back to the barracks. Dave Hardy and a couple of other guys and I decided to walk back to the barracks to see what was happening. As we neared our barracks, Chief came staggering out. After the beer ran out, he and a couple of other men had started on a fifth of whiskey. Chief saw us and waved a .45 automatic pistol in the air.

Bang! Chief fired a round into the air. I yelled at Chief to put the gun down, but he ignored me, of course. He started walking away and fired another round into the air. We had to get the gun away from him before he shot himself or someone else. Hardy wrapped his arms around Chief, while I carefully reached for the pistol and pulled it from Chief's hand without too much resistance.

We helped Chief back inside the barracks and put him in a bunk. I told him we would give him the pistol in the morning. I don't remember what happened to that pistol but I know we never gave it back to Chief. Someone said he had taken the pistol from a dead NVA soldier in July. After our little battle with Chief I decided it was too late to get involved in a poker game. I took off my boots and crawled into a bunk to enjoy a comfortable night's sleep.

I slept in for much of the next morning. The only thing I had to do the second day of stand down was attend an awards ceremony that afternoon. When I finally got up and walked outside I ran into Rick Shields and a couple of the old timers from the Third Herd who had been assigned to the rear. They were headed to the steam bathhouse. Rick said, "Come on with us, Hound Dog."

They had also invited Lieutenant Fielding along as a friendly gesture towards our new platoon leader. As we walked toward the steam bathhouse, the men who had been there before told me what to expect. It cost a few bucks to get in, of course. You could sit in a sauna or a steam machine and then get a massage from one of the young ladies working there. The military maintained control over the steam bathhouses and there weren't supposed to be any sexual favors available. But the guys said to ask for whatever you wanted when you were getting a massage and see what happens.

We paid a girl on our way in and were given a white towel. We walked to a changing room, took off our fatigues and boots and put them in a little basket that we checked in with another girl. We each wrapped a towel around us and moved into the bathhouse. Going to a steam bathhouse was a totally new experience, thanks to good old Uncle Sam. I first sat down inside a sauna with a couple of the guys to check it out. Naturally, it was hot, but it soon became way too hot for me. I said, "I'm out of here, guys."

Outside the sauna was a row of one-man steam machines. The

front of each machine opened to get in and out. I thought I might as well try one. There were Vietnamese girls in the room who spoke English and helped with whatever we needed. When I walked toward one of the steam machines one of the girls walked over and opened the door. I stepped in and she held her hand out and said, "Towel?"

A GI in a machine down the line chuckled and said, "Just give her the towel."

I said, "Oh, yeah," and removed the towel from around my waist and handed it to her. When I sat down inside, she closed the door and placed the towel around my neck. There I was sitting with my head sticking out the top, just like I had seen in the movies. Now that felt good. It was warm but not too hot. The steam generated inside the machine rose around my neck while I relaxed and checked out the three Vietnamese girls as they helped other men in and out of the steam machines. After relaxing for a while in the steam machine I decided to move on to see what else they had to offer. I asked one of the girls to open the door. She pulled the towel from around my neck and opened the door. I took a couple steps outside the machine and smiled when I took the towel from the young lady and wrapped it around my waist.

One of the girls told me to walk down a hallway to my right if I wanted a massage. I walked along the hallway and was greeted by another young Vietnamese girl. She led me into a small private room, with a table in the middle covered with a foam mattress and a sheet. She patted her hand on the sheet and said, "Lie down."

I lay down on my stomach. Without saying another word she began to massage my body using some type of oil or lotion. I just relaxed while she massaged my shoulders, arms and back and then worked on my legs. She chuckled when I turned my head and smiled when she began giving me a quick little massage on my butt through the towel that was still covering me. It felt great. "What a way to go," I thought. She then told me to roll onto my back, and began massaging my chest and arms and again worked her way down to my legs. I didn't say much while she was massaging me. I simply relaxed and enjoyed her gentle touch.

After she had massaged most of my body she stopped and appeared to be finished. Being a first-timer in the bathhouse, I didn't know what would happen next. The girl placed her hand on the towel

144

that covered me, indicating there was one more place she could massage and said, "Five dollar."

I had learned when dealing with the civilians most everything was negotiable, so I automatically said, "three dollars."

She came back saying, "four dollar."

I said, "OK." I wasn't exactly dealing with high finances. I gave her four dollars. The young girl slowly reached under my towel and gently began a very "personal" conclusion to my massage. After receiving the first massage of my life, I got up and picked up my wallet and began walking out of the room. I looked back at the young girl, smiling, and said, "Thank you." She gave me a little smile and waved as I walked on to get my clothes.

When the rest of the men from the Third Herd began straggling in after their massage, we began exchanging experiences with our masseuse. A couple of the men got a massage, and that was it. And then there was Lieutenant Fielding.

Someone asked, "Hey 3-6, how was your massage?"

He smiled and said, "Oh, it was great," and paused for a second and then added, "My masseuse offered me sex. But I said no."

"What?" was the reply from a couple of the guys.

Lieutenant Fielding said he just couldn't do it. It wasn't right. The rest of us looked at each other and shook our heads when we heard his tale. The one girl who was willing to have sex ended up with Lieutenant Fielding, who turned her down. Although most GIs would have had sex with those girls, we respected Lieutenant Fielding's beliefs. Asking those girls for sexual favors may not have been the right thing for any of us to do, but there were a lot of things that weren't right in Vietnam. It wasn't right for Hal Harris to have died a few days earlier, and it wasn't right that men were probably dying somewhere in Vietnam while we enjoyed ourselves in that steam bathhouse. We all knew that any day could easily be our last. Consequently most GIs took the opportunity to enjoy themselves when they could. After our trip through the steam bathhouse, we ate lunch in the mess hall and enjoyed rehashing our morning of rest and relaxation.

I took an hour after lunch to get a quick letter off to my folks and to Jan Griffin. I tried to write a letter to them every few days. I also wrote letters to other family and friends whenever I had time. In my letters to my folks I only gave them general details about what I was doing. I told them we went out on patrols every day and stayed at a firebase at night. I definitely didn't tell them that we had lost Hal Harris that past week. They would have been worried sick if I had told them what actually happened in the field. I was a little more open in my letters to Jan, but asked her not to share any details if she happened to talk with my folks. I did mention that I had enjoyed my first steam bath, but didn't share the details about my first massage with either my folks or Jan.

It was almost two o'clock when I finished writing the letters and dropped them in a nearby mailbox. One fringe benefit of serving in Vietnam was that we didn't have to pay postage on our letters. What a deal, risk your life for your country and they give you free postage.

I found most of the company gathered with their platoons for the awards ceremony. The military's way of recognizing special or heroic achievements was to award medals based upon the nature of the achievement. Most of us weren't in Vietnam to become heroes or to see how many medals we could earn, but most men accepted their recognition with pride and proudly wore their medal(s) while they had their picture taken.

First Sergeant Seavey called the company to attention and then turned the ceremony over to Captain Branch. The CO asked for a moment of silence and then Chaplain Wideman said a prayer for Venancio Vera (first Platoon), George Conrad and Hal Harris (third platoon), who were the last three men in Alpha Company to be killed in action. Captain Branch expressed his personal sadness concerning those men but reminded us all it could have been worse considering what we had encountered the past couple of months.

The men receiving medals stood in a separate line to accept their due recognition. Captain Branch stood in front of each man while the citation for his medal was read. The CO pinned the medal on the man's fatigue shirt, said a few personal words and exchanged salutes. Several men received a Bronze Star for heroic action, a few men received Purple Hearts for being wounded in action and others received Air Medals awarded for completing twenty-five air combat missions (flying out in choppers).

After all of the medals were awarded, we were dismissed. We congratulated the men who had received medals and I took pictures of Doc Jackson, Rick Shields, Dennis Schultz and a few other guys in the third platoon wearing their medals. There were no medals for those of us who had recently arrived in country, except for Carlton Quick who received a Purple Heart for being wounded the night we were ambushed.

The one award most infantrymen earned was the Combat Infantryman Badge (CIB). The CIB was a rectangular metal badge with a silver muzzle-loader rifle centered on a light blue background and a silver wreath surrounding the rifle. The CIB was awarded to Army infantrymen who served in combat. You had to serve at least thirty days in the field as an infantryman, or have faced enemy action, to earn the badge. Most of us in the third platoon who had been in the field the past month had earned our CIB and proudly wore the cloth replica insignia on our fatigues.

After the awards ceremony, many of the men who had received medals wanted to celebrate, not so much because they received medals, but because they were alive to receive them. Many men never lived to see the medals they earned in combat. I joined a group of men at the club near our company area that had opened early because we were on stand down. A bond of comradeship had quickly developed between most of the men in the company because we risked our lives every day performing the most dangerous duty in the world. Once a man showed he was willing to carry his own weight and fight along-side his comrades, he was welcomed into the family of fellow infantrymen. I was no longer an FNG and wasn't called a "shake'n bake" except in a joking manner.

It was great spending time with several newfound friends while we relaxed, sharing a few cold beers together. We laughed while we picked on each other about things we had done, like my jumping out of a chopper for the first time, or simply joked about where we were from. Rick Shields and Bob Ryken were from California. We accused them of being gay. Guys from the South were all hillbillies, and men from Montana or Wyoming were jokingly accused of having more sex with sheep than women. Mike Meyers and I were simply dirt-busting Iowa farmers. It was amazing how we got along and had fun as though we had known each other for years.

We enjoyed ourselves for a couple of hours and then went back to the stand down area to take advantage of another trailer load of free beer. Why pay fifteen cents a beer when you could drink it for free?

The second night of stand down progressed much like the first.

147

Most of the men pounded down free beers, and after the beer was gone, we again cheered and sang along while another all-girl band played songs that reminded us of our world so far away. A bottle of whiskey was passed around during the concert, and I took a couple swigs during the hour or so the girls were singing. By the end of the show I was feeling no pain. The beers I had drunk that afternoon and the sips of whiskey during the concert had done me in. For once I made a smart move and headed for my bunk to crash for the night.

Morning arrived way too soon. We had to literally pull some of the men out of their bunks to get them moving to make it to the convoy taking us back to the field at 10:30 that morning. We returned to our company area, got our rifles and gear, and reluctantly climbed aboard what we called the "Cu Chi Express," a convoy of deuce-and-a-halfs. While we rode toward the main gate of Cu Chi, men exchanged stories of what they had done for the past two days and laughed about the good time they had. Some of the men had smoked pot, others had found hookers, and a couple of men bragged about how much money they won playing poker. But when we passed through the main gate and entered the countryside, we again "locked and loaded" our weapons and left the good times behind.

Stand Down

First Sergeant William Seavey was one of the few men awarded the Combat Infantryman Badge for service in World War II, Korea and Vietnam.

The Congressional Medal of Honor, the nation's highest military decoration, was awarded to 241 men for their actions in Vietnam. 64% of those awards were made posthumously. Staff Sergeant Hammett Bowen was serving with Charlie Company (one of our sister companies) on June 27, 1969 when his platoon came under enemy fire. After returning fire, Sergeant Bowen ordered his men to fall back. As they moved back, an enemy grenade was thrown amid Sergeant Bowen and his men. Sergeant Bowen shouted a warning and hurled himself on the grenade, saving the lives of his fellow soldiers. Sergeant Bowen's extraordinary courage and concern for his men cost him his life. Staff Sergeant Bowen was posthumously awarded the Congressional Medal of Honor.

Left to right - Junior Houchens, Dave Holt, Bill Tally,
Sergeant Jim Overbey and Mike Myers.

Chapter 12

Back in the Field

Going back to the field was a big letdown after two days of fun and relaxation in Cu Chi. But we were happy to learn we would be working out of Firebase Patton for awhile. When we turned off of Highway 1 and headed toward Firebase Patton, we passed through the little village of Bau Dieu and the ARVN compound where I had spent my birthday. We then passed Venice East and waved at the men manning the little guard post and enjoying their relatively easy duty.

While I was settling into my bunker at Patton I saw Steve Robinson, one of the men in my squad, carrying a little gray monkey that he had bought in Cu Chi. Steve handed the monkey to me. He tugged at my fatigue shirt with his little hands and then crawled up on my shoulder and began playing with the hair on my head. The monkey soon became our mascot. We left him inside the firebase when we left each day, and he would be anxiously waiting for Steve and the rest of us when we returned. Many of us enjoyed the simple entertainment of playing with the monkey and letting him climb all over us from time to time.

Fortunately, we didn't go out on a RIF that afternoon, giving us some time to rest up from our two-day stand down. While I pulled guard by our bunker during our first night back in the field, I thought about my nearly two months in the field and how my personal outlook had changed. I had learned that on any given day I could be seriously wounded or killed without warning. I had also seen the peace and quiet of a day or night instantly change into terror most people could never imagine. Unfortunately, there wasn't much I could do to change my situation. I could only pray for the best.

After an uneventful night at Patton we were up early the next morning preparing for a flight near the Saigon River. One of the first things I did that morning was to take a long drink of cool water from my canteen. The water they supplied us was loaded with chlorine and tasted like water from a swimming pool. The water in my canteen would heat up during the day, and although it would quench my thirst, drinking warm water wasn't very enjoyable. Shortly after I arrived in the field, I started most days with the simple pleasure of a drink of cool water from my canteen.

Shortly after eight o'clock we lifted off for an early morning aerial tour of the Vietnamese countryside. I noticed a lot of water below while we descended into our landing zone fifteen minutes later. Although it was nearing the end of the monsoon season there were still frequent rain showers. The rice paddies were still full of water and most of the low-lying areas of the countryside remained flooded.

The landing zone was on high and dry ground, but that didn't last long. As we moved north along our designated route, we soon began walking through a grassy swamp one klick west of the Saigon River. At times, the ground seemed to bounce when we walked, like walking on a trampoline. I would take one step in ankle-deep water; the next step, the water would be knee deep. We had been flown out there to look for enemy troops that supposedly had been spotted.

Before long, the entire company of over eighty men were all soaked. We had crossed a waist deep channel of water and then moved north where we came to a stream fifty meters wide. Our designated route took us across the stream and continued north where we would rendezvous with choppers at a landing zone over four klicks away. Whoever had planned the RIF didn't know how much water was out there, or (more likely) he knew about all of the water, but didn't give a damn because he wouldn't be coming out with us. Regardless, we were nearly surrounded by water.

Captain Branch wanted to try crossing the stream. The point team from the first platoon slowly led a single column of men into the water. Suddenly, the point man, who was in chest deep water, slipped and went under. His helmet fell off and floated away in the current, upside-down. The man behind him quickly went to his rescue. They both struggled to keep their heads above water while other men moved toward them to help.

As the men struggled to regain their footing one of them yelled, "The current's too fast, we can't stand up!" The point man wasn't even halfway across the stream. With all the gear, ammunition and weapons each man carried, it appeared impossible to cross the stream safely. Captain Branch waved for the men to come back. The men helped each other struggle back from the swiftly moving water, finally making it safely back to the edge of the stream, but they were soaked to their heads. The CO altered our course to head west parallel to the stream, through more knee-and waist-deep water. If enemy troops had come through there, they probably thought what most of us were thinking: Let's get the hell out of here and find some dry land. After another hour of sloshing through more swampland, we finally found high ground and made our way to a newly established LZ. The day had proved to be nothing but a waste of time for the company.

After we reached the landing zone, we established a perimeter to wait for the choppers that were scheduled to arrive in twenty minutes. We took that time to check for leeches. Although we wore elastic bands around the bottom of our pant legs to hold them tight, leeches still found a way to get inside and latch onto our skin. You normally couldn't feel a leech, so we always checked ourselves after we had walked through water that was more than ankle deep.

When I pulled up my right pant leg, there was an ugly leech. It was small, the size of the tip of my little finger. Those leeches were brownish-gray in color and slimy, like worms. They got bigger as they hung on to you and sucked your blood into their bodies. Some men had found leeches the size of their thumb in the past. If we touched the leech with the tip of a lit cigarette or put a drop or two of insect repellant on one, it would normally release its bite and fall off. We didn't want to just pull them off because their fangs might stick in our leg and cause an infection. Almost all of the guys found one or two leeches on them before the choppers arrived.

As we heard the distant sound of the choppers, we gathered our gear and organized to get aboard. The wind blowing through the chopper during the ride back to Patton began drying out our soaked fatigues and gear. When we arrived at our bunkers inside Patton, I immediately took off my boots and soggy socks and wet fatigues and put on dry clothes.

After dinner we organized guard duty and settled in for another night in Vietnam. After I finished my first guard shift at ten o'clock and had rolled into my hammock inside our bunker, I heard a loud BOOM! outside. The men who had been on guard came running inside saying we had incoming. I scrambled to get my boots on while two men peered through the viewing holes in front of our bunker.

There were several more explosions from incoming rounds, and then there was silence. After a minute of silence we hurried outside, put on our flak jackets, grabbed our weapons and spread out along the berm near our bunker like we always did when we received incoming rounds. Someone then ran over and told me two of our men had been wounded. I ran to the bunker west of ours and found Doc Jackson and another man tending to one of the injured men lying on the ground.

I leaned over Doc's shoulder and saw it was Chief. "Damn," I thought. He was due for reassignment to the rear soon. It looked like he was going to the rear the hard way. Doc looked at me and said Chief would be OK.

I then heard Ron Peterson yelling nearby. I rushed over and I saw he had taken a blast of shrapnel in his right thigh. Two men were trying to stop the blood gushing from the wound, as Peterson yelled in panic for them to get away. He didn't want anyone other than Doc Jackson to treat him. I told Peterson to calm down; I would get Doc. I rushed back and told Doc Jackson that Peterson wasn't letting the other guys treat him. I stayed with Chief while Doc ran off to treat Peterson.

We were all trained in basic first aid and prepared to help anyone who was wounded, but in his shock of being seriously wounded, Peterson didn't want the rest of us to touch him. A medic from another platoon soon arrived to help Doc Jackson bandage Peterson's leg and help calm him down. Peterson had been in country less than two months, but it looked like the war was already over for him. Chief was doing fine. He had been peppered with shrapnel on his face, arms and legs, but his wounds didn't look too serious. I tightened the bandages Doc had put on. Although he was in pain, Chief lay there not saying much. I told him it looked like he would be OK and that a medevac was on the way.

It sounded like a loud Fourth of July as outgoing mortar and artillery rounds were fired over our heads. It would have been pure luck if they actually hit the culprits who had fired the mortars at us. But I knew one thing, with the number of rounds they were firing, they had to be scaring the hell out of whoever was out there.

After the outgoing firing stopped a few minutes later, I noticed a commotion a short distance away toward the center of the firebase. We soon learned our Battalion Sergeant Major had been seriously wounded. He was taking a leisurely shower in a shower stall outside his bunker when one round landed next to it. We put Chief and Peterson on litters and carried them to the nearby medical aid station. In a short while a medevac was on the landing pad in front of the aid station. We quickly loaded the Sergeant Major and our two wounded buddies, and they were on their way to the 12th Evac in Cu Chi. So much for a quiet night at Patton.

We often went several days, or sometimes a week or two, without anything serious happening. During those times, some of the men started thinking that combat duty might not be quite so hazardous after all. But then BAM – something like that night's incoming mortar fire brought us back to reality. One moment there was peace and quiet, and the next, men were lying on the ground fighting to stay alive.

The following morning Alpha Company went out on a RIF near the firebase. Before we left, we heard that surgeons in Cu Chi were forced to amputate the Sergeant Major's leg. Ron Peterson's leg was a mess but they were able to save it. Chief was listed in fair condition with multiple shrapnel wounds. They would all be flown back to the world in a couple of days for further medical care.

Alpha Company headed north along the road toward the village of Trung Lap less than half a mile away. As we neared the village, we were greeted by a group of kids with their hands out, hoping for anything we might give them. If we had candy, we would throw it in the air and watch the kids scramble for it. Although our primary task was to search for any signs of the enemy, we also performed some public relations work in addition to giving the kids candy and C-rations in an effort to keep the civilians on our side. While we searched their hootches, the medics took time to check a child when a mother carried them up and tried to explain what was wrong. Our medics treated the kids for cuts and bruises and minor ailments, but couldn't treat anything too serious. The U.S. military periodically sent medical teams into the villages to provide additional medical care for the civilians. They didn't want any serious disease to get out of control and spread to the GIs.

Our Chieu Hoi, Hue, was very helpful in communicating with the civilians. Most of us GIs knew a few words in Vietnamese but not enough to carry on a conversation. Hue was also helpful while we searched the village looking for anything unusual. He knew what to look for better than most of us GIs.

As we slowly worked our way through Trung Lap, I received further exposure to rural Vietnamese civilian life. There were a few little shops that sold food, clothing or personal and household items. Most of the hootches had clay walls four to six inches thick and four to five feet high, with an open space between the top of the walls and the roof, which was made of corrugated metal or straw. There were usually no doors, just an open entrance, and the interior was sometimes divided into two or three smaller rooms. The floors were dirt, sometimes covered with a bamboo mat, and there was normally a belowground storage area built into the floor making a cool place to store some of their food. Although their homes were primitive, they protected the people from the hot sun and monsoon rains.

There was no electricity, no running water or indoor plumbing and no other modern conveniences. Some of the civilians had bicycles or motor scooters, but most people just walked everywhere they went. They often used a cow or water buffalo to pull a two-wheeled cart to transport items too large or too heavy to carry themselves. I saw no cars or trucks, nor did I see any horses. I thought horses would have made great transportation for them, but they were probably too expensive to buy and to feed.

Although those people lived the most primitive existence I had ever personally seen, they survived in relatively good health. They appeared to have enough food to eat that was mainly rice, and vegetables they grew in the many gardens we saw. The adults wore loose fitting shirts and slacks or shorts; some wore sandals while others were barefooted. Some of the babies and young children ran around naked but most of the kids wore shorts and were barefooted. After we entered the village and while we searched the hootches, I noticed peculiar odors. Some of the smells were from small cooking fires, but there were also other strange odors inside the hootches. Some of the guys swore they could smell a Vietnamese person because they had a different body odor than we GIs. Maybe that's what I smelled.

We spent over an hour searching through Trung Lap which was no more than 500 meters long. After not finding any weapons or other signs of enemy presence, Captain Branch directed us on to our next checkpoint; a hamlet two klicks east of Trung Lap. When we arrived we immediately began searching the four hootches as five or six civilians stood around watching us. Finally, Bingo!

We found medical supplies, syringes, medicine and bandages and a cache of AK-47 ammunition. There was also a stash of clothing that appeared to be more than just extra clothing for the inhabitants. We immediately gathered the civilians together and held them under guard. They were no longer considered innocent civilians. Hue and the Chieu Hois from the first and second platoons helped Captain Branch interrogate the civilians. They basically pleaded innocent to everything we had found. Captain Branch radioed the Battalion CO to report what we had found. The Battalion CO wanted the civilians taken to Cu Chi for interrogation and the hootches destroyed.

A short while later, a chopper delivered four large demolition charges. An intelligence officer who arrived on the chopper immediately tied the hands of the civilians. Once they were placed aboard the waiting Huey, they were on their way to Cu Chi. We helped our demolitions man set a charge inside each hootch and then pulled back. We watched as a huge explosion leveled each hootch to the ground, spewing a giant cloud of dust and debris into the air. That little hamlet was literally wiped off the map.

It was difficult to imagine what life was like for the Vietnamese civilians who were surrounded by war. It appeared the majority of them were supportive of our being there; however, there were obviously others who sided with the North. Although we had destroyed four hootches and confiscated medical supplies and ammunition, we didn't know whether the inhabitants were VC sympathizers who willingly hid the supplies, or if the VC had forced them to cooperate under the threat of death. Many Vietnamese civilians innocently lost their homes and their lives while they struggled to exist in the middle of that lousy war.

It was mid-afternoon when we began our trip back to Patton with the third platoon in the lead. Captain Branch stopped us after we had moved about one klick south and walked to the front of the columns. We were supposed to continue south and then circle northwest towards Patton. But the CO told us he wanted to head straight west towards Patton as he pointed to the guard tower in the distance. He hoped to get back by four o'clock to enjoy the country music that was played on the Armed Forces Radio Network between four and five o'clock each afternoon.

We headed through mostly open countryside and rice paddies and walked through the southeast path in the concertina wire at Patton a few minutes after four o'clock that afternoon. The CO was happy. As I took off my gear by our bunker, someone turned on a radio and several of us stomped our feet and clapped our hands to the beat of country music. Although I knew Captain Branch took his role as our CO seriously, it was nice to have a leader who gave us a little slack now and then. I headed for the showers.

A couple of nights later I took my squad out on an ambush. We had no difficulty in setting up the ambush and had an excellent site behind a little rise to view a trail that crossed the countryside. I took first watch that night, quietly sitting on the ground looking into the darkness for any movement. Midway through my first hour on guard I heard the sound of the "155s" firing from Patton. A couple seconds later I heard the whistle of the huge round soaring over our heads, and then, a few seconds later, a distant boom as the round detonated on impact far to the east. I had grown accustomed to artillery and mortar rounds whistling overhead while we were on an ambush. I could only hope each round kept sailing on to its intended target.

We quietly rotated guard during the night and I wrapped in my poncho liner while I slept. It was quiet, but for some reason I abruptly woke. I looked at the man who was supposed to be on guard at my position. He was slumped over, asleep. He jumped when I nudged him. I whispered, "Wake up!" I then moved to the other forward position and found the man who should have been on guard also asleep. I couldn't believe it. I shook him and said, "Stay awake." When I moved to the rear position I found one of the guys awake and on guard.

I sat there for a minute thinking about the scary situation I had found. Two of the three men who were supposed to be on guard had fallen asleep. How many times had it happened before? Pulling guard on ambush and looking into the darkness for an hour at a time was a boring job. But you were expected to do whatever it took to stay awake. Enemy troops could have walked up on us and we all could have been history. I was pissed at that moment. How could they fall asleep knowing everyone's life was on the line? I thought I knew why. Fortunately we made it through the remainder of the night without incident and without anyone else falling asleep on guard.

I didn't say anything to the men the next morning. I wanted to talk with Rick Shields and Jim Overbey concerning what happened rather than just yell at the two men who had fallen asleep. During the past few weeks several of us had noticed some men having trouble staying awake while on guard at our bunkers. We also noticed a couple of men dozing off while we took breaks during RIFs. The word was a few men in the Third Herd were smoking pot and taking speed. They would find a little hideout somewhere inside the firebase or patrol base and have a little party rather than getting some much needed sleep at night. The combination of drugs and lack of sleep was taking its toll on those guys. Even if they stayed awake while on guard, they weren't as alert as they should be. We believed there were only three or four guys who were putting everyone else at risk.

Rick, Jim and I proposed some new rules to Lieutenant Fielding. He agreed without question. We gathered the entire platoon later that afternoon and laid down the new rules. The first rule wasn't new, but needed to be reemphasized. No drugs in the field. Although the military didn't condone drug use, it was difficult to stop. Drugs were cheap and readily available most anywhere in Vietnam. Hopefully by bringing the drug issue out in the open, the rest of the platoon would put enough pressure on those few men to make them stay straight in the field.

The second new rule was there would be two men on guard at each ambush position. We had been keeping only one man on guard at each position enabling us all to get a little more sleep. But after the past night, we decided it was better to lose a little sleep than never to wake up again. The two men on guard at each position could keep each other awake. Everyone agreed with the new procedure, or at least no one verbally disagreed.

Rick and I had a private conversation with the two men who had fallen asleep on the ambush and with the other guys who we believed had been doing drugs. We simply told them to knock off the dope or we would go to the CO if the problem continued. They also knew the rest of the platoon wasn't happy with them. The drug problem in the third platoon ended.

A couple of days later we pulled an all night mission. During the afternoon a truck convoy took us to a location 20 miles southwest of Patton. We would work with another company to surround a small village with suspected VC living there. Sometime after midnight we would begin walking three klicks southeast from a patrol base and surround the village before daylight. At dawn, the other company would sweep through the village. Alpha Company would be waiting outside to stop any VC who tried to escape. It seemed like a good plan, but I wasn't looking forward to walking across the countryside at night.

I ate some dinner and then caught some sleep. Shortly before 2:00 a.m. we packed up and were on our way. We started walking through rice paddies because it was too dark to walk along the narrow dikes. The water in the rice paddies around Patton had been slowly receding, but we must have been in a low-lying area because the water in the paddies was still nearly knee deep. We moved through rice paddy after rice paddy, through some hedgerows, and then through more rice paddies. The area was way off the map I had. I hoped someone knew where we were.

After walking for over an hour, we slowed down when we came upon a three-foot-high dirt berm. Dave Hardy was directly in front of me and just dropped out of sight. He had slipped into a small bomb crater that couldn't be seen because of the water. He soon popped up out of the water and Carlton Quick and I grabbed him and pulled him out. He was OK, but we were all a mess. Hardy was completely soaked and covered with mud and Quick and I were also a muddy mess. It quickly became another long, miserable night. We were all tired, wet and muddy as we neared the village two hours later. We stopped in a group of rice paddies and spread along the dikes. We couldn't see it in the dark, but apparently the village was out there somewhere.

When daylight arrived the other company entered the village from the west. We had the other three sides surrounded, with the third platoon spread behind a dike seventy-five meters east of the village. We would have to keep our fire low if any enemy personnel were spotted to avoid exposing the GIs inside the village to "friendly fire" (fire from American troops). A few minutes later, we heard gunfire coming from inside the village. We heard over the radio that two VC had been killed and several more surrendered without putting up a fight. However, three were making a run to the east. When we spotted the three VC running toward us, we opened up with M-16 and M-60 fire, dropping them in a muddy rice paddy. Anyone trying to escape had little chance of survival with eighty GIs unknowingly waiting for them.

After half an hour without any more action, we headed south to check out other hamlets nearby. The bullet-riddled bodies of the three VC were left where they had fallen in the rice paddy.

When we took a break on some dry ground later that morning, most of us found a leech or two sucking on our legs. What a way to start the day. We spent the rest of the morning checking several hootches in two hamlets. We found no more signs of the enemy. After what happened earlier, any other VC were either well hidden or were long gone. We arrived back at the remote patrol base shortly after noon and then rode on a convoy of deuce-and-a-halfs back to Patton.

We spent the next hour cleaning our weapons and gear and then hit the showers to wash away the mud and gunk left by our past night's escapade. While we were taking showers, someone noticed two Red Cross girls standing on a large communications bunker less than 100 meters away. The Red Cross girls visited Patton periodically to talk with the men and try to boost our morale. We waved at the girls and motioned for them to join us for a shower. That would certainly have boosted our morale. The girls appeared to ignore us, but then one of them waved at us before she stepped down from the top of the bunker.

That night I was standing guard near our bunker, watching out over the perimeter and chatting with Vic Ortega who was standing guard on the other side of the bunker. I heard footsteps behind me and turned to see First Sergeant "Top" Seavey walking in the darkness toward me. Top started yelling and cussing at us for not wearing our flak jackets. I said, "Sorry, Top, I forgot," while Vic scrambled to find his flak jacket.

Top said, "Oh bull shit, Hogue!"

"All right, Top," I said, "I'll put it on." Top moved on, ready to check on the guys at the next bunker. But he was right. I hadn't forgotten about wearing my flak jacket. I had been lax, preferring to be comfortable and thinking nothing would happen. I knew better.

Top was normally a pretty decent guy and often joked around with us during the day. But Top liked to prowl around the perimeter bunkers at night and raise hell with us when he saw something he didn't like. We normally just took it in stride. After nearly thirty years in the Army, it was just Top's way of doing his job.

For the next week we had fairly easy duty. After areas of the countryside had been sprayed with Agent Orange, the engineers used bulldozers to plow down the dead vegetation. Our job for a few days was simply to pull guard for the bulldozer operators. We would establish a perimeter around the area to be destroyed, and when the engineers finished, we would move on to the next area and establish a new perimeter. It wasn't exciting duty; in fact, it became boring. We didn't encounter any enemy action and the days got real long and hot.

The Third Herd's next assignment was to provide guard for another group of engineers for a couple days and nights while they built a temporary bridge in a swampy area west of the Saigon River. Again, we set up a perimeter around the engineers during the day while they built the bridge. Before dark, we pulled back onto high and fairly dry ground to dig in for the night. We set out claymore mines around us and pulled guard all night. Other than walking through swampland and getting wet every day, our time guarding the engineers was uneventful.

It was during those relatively peaceful days that I had time get to know some of the men better. I could talk and shoot the bull with the men while we were sitting in a daytime perimeter.

Terry Thornton was from Oklahoma. He was married and had a young daughter. Terry was genuinely concerned about his welfare in the field and leaving his wife and daughter without a husband and father. He was seriously considering reenlisting to get out of the infantry. He had arrived in country a couple days after I did and had seen what could happen. I told Terry that if he wanted to play it safe, I would send him back to Cu Chi to talk with the enlistment folks. Terry said he would think about it and let me know.

I also talked with James "Red" Mincey one day. Red told me his older brother had been in the Marines and died of malaria in Vietnam in 1968. Red had talked with his CO during AIT regarding his brother, but they sent him to Vietnam anyway. Red said he was willing to stick it out in the field with the rest us, but I told Red I would talk with Captain Branch about getting him transferred to the rear. His family had sacrificed enough.

And then there was Bob Emery, the eighteen-year-old who had been sent to Germany but volunteered for Vietnam. One day I asked Bob why. Bob said if he was going to be in the Army he wanted to be in a real war, not playing war games. Besides, he hated it in Germany because the brass (senior officers) were a pain in the ass. Regardless of how Bob got to Vietnam, I was glad to have him.

162

I noticed after I arrived in the field that none of us had been issued bayonets. The M-16 rifles were designed for a bayonet to fit over the end of the barrel to use in hand-to-hand combat. None of us wanted to experience hand-to-hand combat, but we all had received hours of bayonet training during basic and AIT. I never did get an answer about why we weren't issued bayonets.

Most of the men carried a hunting-type knife with a 4" to 6" blade as an alternative. We didn't carry a knife so much to use as a weapon, but rather as a handy tool. I had asked my parents to send me a small hunting knife shortly after I arrived in the field. I carried my knife in a sheath attached to a loop on my fatigue pants with a metal snap ring called a "carabiner." Carabiners were used to loop the rope through when rappelling and often used to attach cargo straps to choppers.

One of the challenges for many of us was sharpening our knives. Daniel "Whitey" Hiederich was a country boy from Oklahoma who knew how to sharpen knives, and he became the expert Third Herd knife sharpener. Whitey had shown me how to rub the blade against a sharpening stone just right to get it razor sharp. After awhile I was able to sharpen my knife just like Whitey had shown me. But some of the guys gave up trying to sharpen their own knives and would just ask Whitey to do it.

After pulling guard for the engineers, we returned to the routine of daily RIFs with the rest of the company. Late one morning the third platoon was leading a recognizance in force southwest of the Ho Bo Woods. The area was covered with tall grass, scattered bushes and hedgerows. It had been a calm morning when I heard someone near the front of our column yelling for help. I knew it wasn't a booby trap because I hadn't heard an explosion. I walked through a small hedgerow and saw two men gathered around Junior "Houch" Houchens who was sitting on the ground. I walked closer to see that Houch had stepped into a two-foot-deep punji pit with his left leg. Houch looked up at me and said, "I think I'm OK." I turned to call for Doc Jackson, but he was already walking forward. When Lieutenant Fielding walked up, I told him what had happened and then helped to set up a perimeter while Doc checked Houch's injuries.

The NVA and VC built punji pits that were simply a hole dug into the ground with pointed bamboo stakes pushed into the pit with the points up. They often dipped the stakes in human waste hoping to cause infections. The pit would be concealed with branches and vege-tation. If a man stepped on the cover it would give way and he would plunge into the pit and be spiked with the pointed stakes, often caus-ing serious injury. Houch had fallen into a pit in which some of the stakes had fallen over, creating a clear spot that Houch happened to hit. He only had a few scrapes on his left leg. If his foot had gone a few inches in any direction we would have been calling in a dustoff for him.

Doc treated Houch's scrapes and said he would be OK. He could get checked out further at the aid station back at Patton. We cleared away from the punji pit and let Houch throw a hand grenade into it to destroy the stakes and blow away the cover to reveal it to any other friendly troops who might pass through the area another day. We con-tinued moving on through the area which was mostly tall grass and scattered bushes.

Less than an hour later I heard someone else yelling, "Ouch! Damn it! Ouch!" I looked forward and saw Ed Leberski standing near a bush, jumping around in circles and slapping himself all over. I guessed he had run into a nest of fire ants, reddish-brown ants that lived in large nests. We were in an area that was dry and prime land for fire ants. Ed had either stepped on a nest or they had been on a bush he brushed against.

Ed threw his helmet on the ground, dropped his M-16 and began taking off his gear. The ants had gotten under his fatigues and were bit-ing him all over. Ed continued to yell and cuss while he frantically pulled off his gear. There wasn't anything the rest of us could do except watch. The red ants would continue to bite until they were knocked off his body. Some of us couldn't help but chuckle as we watched Ed quickly pull his shirt off and drop his fatigue pants down to his ankles. It was like a striptease in the middle of the boonies. We then helped Ed slap the ants off, using our towels until we believed we had gotten all of them.

Ed was nearly out of breath after his encounter with the red ants. He stood there for a moment and then slowly pulled up his pants, look-ing for more ants that might still be there. We helped Ed shake his shirt and his gear to knock off any fire ants that might be clinging on, wait-ing to attack again. Ed finally smiled when we told him how funny he looked jumping around and ripping off his gear and fatigues out there.

He said, "They hurt like hell," and he pointed to the little red marks the fire ants had left with each bite.

The rest of us took another route to avoid the nest of fire ants Ed unfortunately had found. Besides enemy troops and booby traps, we faced a variety of obstacles in the field. Punji pits, fire ants…and snakes. There were several varieties of snakes including boa constrictors, pythons, and deadly cobras. Cobras would try to bite anyone who walked upon them, and they could actually spit blinding venom up to six feet away. A cobra's bite was usually fatal.

We saw snakes everywhere, and we normally dealt with them with a burst of M-16 fire. We didn't take any chances and didn't take the time to determine whether it might have been a harmless snake or a king cobra. Most of the men believed, "The only good snake is a dead snake." A cobra had been killed inside Patrol Base Delta early one evening while we shared the patrol base with the ARVNs. The ARVNs took the snake and cooked it for dinner.

I hadn't heard much from my buddy Allen Schwab from Schaller since I arrived in Vietnam, but I did get one letter from him after I had been in the field a couple of months. He was with the Americal Infantry Division which operated in the northern part of South Vietnam generally referred to as the "highlands." A natural hazard they encountered up there was tigers. He mentioned in his letter that a tiger had attacked and killed a man in his company while the man sat on guard one night. I hadn't seen a tiger and hadn't even worried about tigers until I read Allen's letter. I wrote Allen back and told him thanks for telling me about the tiger. Now I had something else to worry about.

And so it was. Each day in Vietnam I learned something new. When I arrived in country I thought my only enemies were the NVA and VC. But I soon learned there were also many natural enemies. Even the malaria carried by an innocent-looking mosquito could kill you.

Near the end of October we went back to Cu Chi for a stand down. My second stand down was much like the first. I got new boots and a clean uniform, drank free beer and cheered the all-girl band that entertained us each evening. I also saw my old NCO School buddy John Jarvis. He had landed a job maintaining the area where the bands played and arranging for them to play each evening. John had survived his time in the field without a scratch. It was great to see him again. The two days on stand down flew by while I enjoyed a relaxing time with my friends in the Third Herd and Alpha Company.

The monthly base pay for a Sergeant E-5 was $265. Military personnel serving in Vietnam also received $85 per month combat/hazardous duty pay.

Left to right - Bob Emery, Sergeant Richard Hogue and David "Wop" DiBasio at Fire Support Base Patton with M-60 machine guns.

Chapter 13

Dry Weather and Danger

While we were on stand down, Carl Seals, a little guy with reddish-brown hair, joined the third platoon along with Chuck Merritt, another fellow Iowan. Two new NCOs, Sergeants Mike Daniels and John Matson, also joined us and were assigned as team leaders in charge of four or five men within each squad. Our platoon sergeant, Rick Shields, had arrived in country early that past summer and would soon be due for a job in the rear. We actually had more NCOs than we needed, but it would work out when Rick was reassigned.

Rick, Jim Overbey and I each spent time with the two new shake'n bakes, explaining what we expected of them and how we operated in the field. Sergeant Matson began to assume his responsibilities, but Daniels didn't seem to give a damn about what we had to say. During the next few days several men complained to me about Sergeant Daniels, who was assigned to my squad. The guys said he was basically one of the laziest men they had ever seen. When we were out on RIFs, Daniels just walked along and didn't take any initiative to keep an eye on his team. He was one of those men who could easily get someone else killed. I had a private talk with Daniels and told him he needed to shape up if he expected to survive in the field. But I saw little change in his behavior.

We were working out of Patrol Base Delta when another group of ARVNs joined us one evening to go out on an ambush just after the first of November. I vividly remembered what happened the last time we went on an ambush with the ARVNs. We lost Hal Harris. I was in charge of twelve GIs, and one of the ARVNs who spoke some English, identified himself as the leader of a dozen ARVNS. We GIs led the way and walked quietly toward the ambush site while keeping a watchful eye over the countryside. But the ARVNs leisurely moved along, not seeming to be concerned about much of anything. They talked and laughed like they were headed for a picnic. I told their leader to keep his men quiet and they finally quieted down.

It was nearly dark when we reached the ambush site along a dirt road. I told the ARVNs to set up on the south side of the road behind a hedgerow that provided concealment. I set up our position to their left where the road curved north. As we normally did, we set up two four-man positions along the trail to observe in both directions and placed one position to our rear. We set out claymores in front of our positions, and within a few minutes we quietly settled in for the night.

The ARVNs took forever to settle in. They mingled around alongside the road for several minutes and finally organized themselves behind the hedgerow. We began pulling guard with two men awake at each of our positions, but the ARVNs took a totally different approach. All but one of them lay down and went to sleep. That single ARVN stayed on guard while the rest of them slept, and, I guess, hoped he would stay awake. I didn't notice how often they rotated guard duty, but it certainly was one hell of a risky approach to pulling guard on an ambush.

I was in the right forward position along the trail with Sergeant Daniels and two other men. I had learned from one of the guys in our CP group that Daniels had been assigned to us because he was kicked out of another company for being a loafer. We had someone else's dead wood and I wanted to keep an eye on him. Later that evening, Daniels and I were pulling guard. It was quiet, and we hadn't observed any enemy activity. Halfway through our shift I looked over and saw Daniels' head hanging down. He had fallen asleep. I nudged him so hard he nearly fell over. I whispered, "Wake up!" I could have slugged him.

Daniels said, "I wasn't asleep."

"Bull shit," I whispered, " you were sleeping!"

That was it. I wasn't going to let Daniels mess up the Third Herd. He was worthless. When we returned to the patrol base the next morning I told Rick Shields and Lieutenant Fielding I wanted that son-of-a-bitch Daniels out of the platoon. I said, "He's going to get someone killed out there."

Rick looked at me with a surprised expression; he hadn't seen me so angry before. Rick and Lieutenant Fielding both agreed with me. The three of us went to see Captain Branch. I explained to the CO what Daniels had been doing, or rather not doing since he arrived, and I repeated my story about his falling asleep on guard during our ambush the past night. I asked the CO to have Daniels reassigned.

168

Captain Branch said he understood and would take care of it.

I smiled and said, "Thank you, sir, I owe you one."

"Don't worry about it, Hound Dog. I don't want his kind in Alpha Company." Captain Branch gave me a friendly pat on my shoulder as we left his bunker.

Two days later there was good news and bad news. The good news was Sergeant Daniels was told to pack his gear. He was being reassigned, again. I'm sure he knew why, but he didn't say a word to me or anyone else before he left. The bad news was Captain Branch was being reassigned to our battalion headquarters to gather intelligence information about NVA and VC activity. Captain Branch had been a terrific CO. He cared for the welfare of every man in the company. We all hated to see him go, but for his sake, his new duty would be safer than walking through the boonies every day with us.

Captain Larry Dalton was assigned as our new company commander. No one knew too much about him except that he was gung ho. Maybe he and Lieutenant Fielding would hit it off.

On November 6, 1969, Alpha Company was assigned to Patrol Base Hunsley. The last time we were there the second platoon lost eleven men the first night. A lot of the men grumbled about going back to Hunsley, but I knew complaining wouldn't change anything. After serving as an infantryman in Vietnam for three months, I knew the living conditions were always lousy, and we could encounter danger nearly everywhere. My biggest challenge was to stay alive for nine more months regardless of where I was assigned.

Our platoon had ambush duty the first night after we arrived at Hunsley. Lieutenant Fielding planned to take the entire platoon because of the increased probability of encountering larger numbers of enemy troops roaming near the Ho Bo Woods. Rick Shields, Jim Overbey and I double-checked the men while we prepared for the ambush to make sure their weapons were clean and that they had all their gear and plenty of ammunition.

Lieutenant Fielding appeared excited about being near the Ho Bo Woods. We had a lot of brave and dependable men in the Third Herd, but most of us didn't welcome enemy action. In fact, most of us were happy to see day after day pass without any action because that meant we had one less day to survive before we could go home.

We left before five o'clock that afternoon and headed north toward a trail almost two klicks away that was supposedly heavily used by the NVA and VC. We moved cautiously through the heavy vegetation, continually looking around for movement and hoping to avoid walking into an enemy ambush.

We arrived safely near the ambush site well before dark and settled into a concealed area. Shortly before dark, we moved toward the trail to set up the ambush. We split into two groups with Lieutenant Fielding and Jim Overbey in charge of fifteen men who set up along the well-defined trail and Rick Shields and I in charge of seven men to cover the back side of the ambush site. We quietly settled into two half-circle positions to form a perimeter. Several men stayed on guard while we took off our gear and set out claymores. We placed one machine gun team at each end of the forward position enabling them to lay down fire in either direction along the trail, and we designated fields of fire for groups of men to cover the entire area around us.

While we settled into our positions and arranged our gear for the night, unbeknownst to anyone, Lieutenant Fielding had slipped away and boldly walked a short distance down the trail to the west to set up a trip flare. If someone came along the trail they would trip the wire and ignite the bright flare to expose themselves. It wasn't something we routinely did on ambushes.

Rick Shields made a final check along our position and then walked toward the trail to make a final observation before dark. Rick noticed Lieutenant Fielding kneeling beside the trail and then saw him get up and turn toward the forward position. Rick also noticed he wasn't carrying his rifle. At the same instant, Rick heard noises coming from down the trail behind Lieutenant Fielding. Three VC were approaching with a dozen or more following behind. The VC hadn't seen Rick but they had spotted Lieutenant Fielding and raised their weapons toward him. Lieutenant Fielding wasn't aware of the VC. He was defenseless and in a real predicament.

Without hesitation, Rick opened fire with his M-16 on automatic, spraying rounds and hitting three of the VC. He turned and yelled, "Blow some claymores! There's gooks down the trail!" as he started running back toward our ambush site.

When Rick opened fire, Lieutenant Fielding turned and saw the VC and immediately plunged for cover in the tall grass beside the trail. However, most of the men in the forward position hadn't seen

Lieutenant Fielding and didn't know he was near the trail in front of them.

The sound of loud BOOMs filled the air as several men detonated their claymores, spraying a hail of BBs toward the trail and stirring up a huge cloud of smoke and dust with each explosion. Rick was knocked to the ground by the back blast from one of the claymores. One of the men helped him up and pulled him inside our perimeter. Rick was dazed but otherwise was uninjured.

I jumped when I heard Rick firing. I immediately grabbed my M-16 and surveyed the backside of our site looking for any signs of trouble. I didn't see any movement, but after I heard Rick yell, I told the men near me to throw some hand grenades. I yelled at Red, who was beside me, "Detonate some claymores!"

I ducked as two claymores blasted in front of us and then I rose to my knees to throw a hand grenade as near darkness surrounded us. The men facing the trail were firing their M-16s and throwing hand grenades at the enemy troops who were probably struggling to find cover as our machine gun teams filled the air with orange tracers. We all scrambled for cover from a small amount of enemy rifle fire while we unleashed everything we had, hoping to kill or force back the VC. I could barely hear myself as I yelled to the men near me to continue spraying the area with M-16 fire and to throw more hand grenades.

When I saw Rick in the middle of our site, I quickly crawled over and we huddled for a few seconds as the gunfire continued. He yelled, "3-6 is out near the trail!"

"What the hell was he doing out there?" I yelled back.

Rick took a few seconds to catch his breath and then yelled, "I don't know, but we have to find him." Rick and I moved to the forward position and asked the men if they had seen Lieutenant Fielding. No one had. We quickly told Jim Overbey and the rest of the men that Lieutenant Fielding was somewhere in front of them and to be careful with their fire as the firefight continued with a thunderous noise. After a few minutes we ceased firing and held our breaths, waiting to see what might happen. There was silence. Then someone heard moaning in the tall grass beside the trail. We hoped it was Lieutenant Fielding. Rick looked at me and said he would go find him.

"All right," I said, "We'll give you some cover."

Rick slowly crawled through the tall grass while the rest of us stood watch, our hearts pounding, and holding our weapons ready to fire. After a couple of very intense minutes, Rick found Lieutenant Fielding and pulled him back inside our ambush site with the aid of two other men. Lieutenant Fielding had been hit with BBs from our claymores and continued to moan in pain. Doc Jackson immediately checked the extent of his injuries. The front of his fatigue shirt was soaked with blood from serious chest and abdominal wounds. Doc said if 3-6 was going to survive, we had to get him out of there soon. Bill Casey, one of our RTOs, had spoken on the radio with Captain Dalton at Hunsley advising him of our situation. Casey told Doc Jackson a dustoff was on the way.

While most of the men watched for movement around us, Rick, Jim Overbey and I talked and agreed that as soon as Lieutenant Fielding was evacuated we needed to get out of there ourselves. Trying to make a sweep along the trail would be too risky. Although we believed we had inflicted heavy casualties on the VC, more of them could be hiding in the darkness planning their next move. We didn't want to stay any longer than we had to. We quickly spread the word for the men to start packing up to move out after we evacuated 3-6.

Doc continued to do all he could for Lieutenant Fielding, who was semi-conscious and having trouble breathing. Doc was anxious to get him on a dustoff. The rest of us began gathering up our gear while glancing beyond our perimeter. Amazingly, no one else had been hit. We had been lucky.

A Cobra gunship that the CO had called in began circling overhead. We identified the center of our site with a strobe light placed inside an upside-down helmet. Putting the strobe light in a helmet made it visible from the air, but minimized the light directly around us to limit exposing ourselves to the enemy. After the pilot acknowledged our position, we took cover while the gunship fired several rockets around our position and circled again to unleash a barrage of Minigun fire before the dustoff dropped in to pick up Lieutenant Fielding. With the Cobra circling overhead we expanded our perimeter and the Huey landed on the back side of our ambush site. We quickly placed Lieutenant Fielding on a litter and loaded him aboard.

While the chopper flew off toward Cu Chi, we worked in groups to retrieve the claymores that hadn't been fired. Men followed the wire from each detonator to find the claymores, while others stood guard.

We didn't want to leave any claymores out there to fall into enemy hands. The combination of the darkness and heavy vegetation made it impossible to see more than a few feet, and also made it scary as hell. Rick had been in touch with the CO at Patrol Base Hunsley. Captain Dalton wanted us to work our way back if we could. It would be another dangerous trip, but we had to move. The enemy knew where we were; the longer we stayed the more danger we could be in.

Rick asked our Chieu Hoi, Hue, to help lead us back to Hunsley. Hue was more familiar with the area than the rest of us and was the best man to take the lead. After a few minutes everyone was ready. Hue, with Rick Shields right behind, led the column through the rear of the ambush site. We simply played the odds by moving away from where we knew the enemy had been and hoped any remaining VC hadn't circled around to our rear to wait for us.

Rick wanted me to stay at the rear of the column to keep the guys moving and be sure we didn't lose anyone. He kept RTO Dennis Schultz with him and I had Bill Casey with me to maintain communications. The Cobra gunship continued to circle overhead. We considered trying to keep him with us as we traveled back to the patrol base but thought that would only telegraph our movement to the enemy. Schultz radioed the pilot and said we would move on without him.

We walked slowly as we moved through heavy vegetation in strange territory. We stayed close together to maintain contact with each other, or someone could easily be lost, especially those of us at the tail end of the column. I glanced to my rear occasionally but couldn't see anything. It would be my luck; some VC would surprise us and start picking us off from the rear.

Rick stopped the column periodically to give us a short breather. Rick and I kept in touch by radio to make sure everyone was still together. He also had to work with Hue to determine where we were and adjust our course to keep us moving toward the patrol base. We were all hot, sweaty and dead tired but willingly kept moving for nearly two hours until we finally reached Patrol Base Hunsley. We had taken a fairly direct route going out in the daylight, but I'm sure we weaved back and forth many times on our way back in. But we made it. The first thing most of us did when we reached our bunkers was sit down to catch our breath and chug some water from our canteens. I took off my gear and breathed a sigh of relief that we had safely made it back to Hunsley.

After Rick briefed the CO about the ambush, he learned that Lieutenant Fielding made it to the 12th Evac in Cu Chi alive, but he was in serious condition. While I settled into my bunker later that night, I thought about how lucky we had been. We had a firefight with over a dozen VC and our own claymores had caused our only casualty.

The next morning the Third Herd led the entire company back to the ambush site. As we neared the trail, Captain Dalton had the other platoons fan out around us while the third platoon walked through the ambush site and moved along the trail. It looked like we had won the battle. We spotted several dead VC on or near the trail and eventually found a total of ten bodies grotesquely lying on the ground. We had obviously surprised them before they had time to react and return any significant fire. We confiscated several weapons, ammunition, a few supplies and a map.

We expanded our search and followed a couple of blood trails that turned into dead ends. The surviving VC must have pulled back shortly after we opened up on them and didn't stay around for a long battle. We spent the rest of the day moving west along the trail trying to trace the route we believed the VC had followed, but we found no more signs of the enemy and didn't encounter any enemy troops.

Serving as an infantryman in Vietnam, I knew casualties were inevitable. Lieutenant Fielding had only been with us for two months, but I felt a big void without him. He had become a good friend to many of us. It took awhile for me to adjust to his absence. While there was a strong bond of comradeship among most of us in the Third Herd, I also saw a hesitation by some of the men to build a strong friendship with any one man because they knew on any day he could be gone. Five days later we learned Lieutenant Fielding had stabilized enough to be flown back to the world for further treatment and rehabilitation. We would probably never see him again.

Rick Shields would be our acting platoon leader until a new lieutenant was assigned. Jim Overbey and I informally shared platoon-sergeant duties in addition to leading our respective squads. We continued our daily RIFs and nightly ambushes out of Patrol Base Hunsley for a few more days without any significant encounters. We knew the VC had strongholds scattered across the area, but they were well concealed in areas with thick vegetation. They knew if their complexes were spotted from the air or by ground troops, they would be immediately destroyed by air strikes and artillery fire. Often those enemy fortresses were found simply by chance.

While my tour in Vietnam continued, I realized what a decided advantage we GIs had, simply because we were re-supplied almost daily. The NVA and VC normally had to live day-to-day and find food and water. They maintained some central supply locations, but more often food, ammunition and clothing were stored in tunnels, wells or other hiding spots, which they used when they came across their stashes. We often found small wire mesh cages with a spring-loaded door they used to trap rats to eat. I would have to be awfully hungry to eat one of those ugly black rats that were the size of a small cat. Whenever we found a trap we shot the rat, if there was one inside and destroyed the trap.

One day we found a bag of supplies in a tunnel and I dumped the contents on the ground. There were some clothes and a green hammock. I stuffed the hammock into one of the big pockets on the side of my fatigue pants. I thought it would be fun sleeping in the hammock knowing that the NVA or VC who hid it would return to find it missing. I slept in that hammock for a couple weeks until one of the ropes broke while I was sleeping one night. I dropped to the floor of our bunker with a thud, leaving me with a sore butt for a couple days. Maybe that enemy soldier got the last laugh after all.

We saw one good change in early November: the monsoon season that generally lasted from May to October was over. The daily rains had stopped, and the countryside was slowly drying out. We could go out on an ambush and not get soaked, and we didn't have to worry any longer about a bunker springing a leak. That was the good news. The bad news was the enemy would be planting more booby traps. Additionally, the skies were normally sunny all day long, making the afternoons hot and muggy and our daily RIFs a lot more uncomfortable. Most of the guys started carrying a second canteen of water.

One afternoon in mid-November we were working our way across a fairly open area on our way back to Patrol Base Delta. Agent Orange had been sprayed on much of the surrounding countryside, making it desolate and dry. It had been an uneventful day while the third platoon led the RIF through a grassy area. I was the third man walking in the right column when Rick Shields, who was right behind me, yelled,

"Everybody stop!" We all knelt down and looked around for signs of trouble.

Rick then said, "There's a booby trap here!" as he cautiously backed away from where he had been standing.

We all looked around for others. Where there was one booby trap, there could be more. Rick notified the CO by radio what he had found and wanted our demolitions man to move up. Rick had spotted a shiny reflection from something. When he looked closer he realized it was a booby-trapped mortar round. The men took watchful steps while we formed a defensive perimeter. After carefully surveying the device, our demolitions man placed a stick of C-4 explosive beside it. When the C-4 detonated, it would detonate the mortar round. While the C-4 was being set, Rick and I met to talk.

The booby trap was alongside the path our point man, Vic Ortega, the second man, Jim "Red" Mincey, and I had taken. Each of us had either stepped over or beside it without seeing it, and fortunately, without detonating it. My heart pounded when I thought about the disaster that could have happened. That mortar round probably would have killed anyone who detonated it and wounded others nearby. If Vic, Red and I were cats with nine lives, we had each used up one of those lives that afternoon. After the entire company moved forward, the fuse leading to the blasting cap was lit. A couple of minutes later a loud explosion sent a cloud of dust into the air behind us. I kept walking, trying to forget I could have died back there.

After we walked back into Delta later that afternoon, I took off my gear, feeling very thankful. I checked my M-16 before I hung it on a rack. It was still clean. Most of the guys were pretty diligent about keeping their weapons clean, but I periodically checked their rifles to be sure. I looked at the M-16 hanging next to mine. It was filthy. The bolt and firing chamber were covered with dirt and sand. The rifle could only have fired a few rounds before it would have jammed. I asked whose rifle it was. PFC Randal Johnson walked up and said it was his.

I said, "Look at your rifle, it's filthy. Clean it and keep it clean."

Johnson wasn't the most ambitious guy in the platoon and bordered on being lazy. Johnson, who was much bigger than I, said, "You can't make me clean it."

After my close encounter that afternoon, I was in no mood for his bullshit. If someone else's life had depended upon Johnson being able to fire his rifle that day, they would have been in trouble. I put my face close to his and said, "Listen, Johnson, if I can't make you clean it, I know twenty other guys who will. Understand?"

Johnson understood. He grabbed his rifle and began cleaning it. He knew all I had to do was show his filthy rifle to the rest of the guys. They would be all over him in an instant.

It had been nearly two weeks since we lost Lieutenant Fielding, and we still hadn't been assigned a new platoon leader, but that wasn't a big deal. Everyone was comfortable with Rick Shields leading the platoon, while Jim Overbey and I worked with him to manage the men. We knew that most every man could be relied upon to do his job when the bullets started flying without waiting for orders. The strong bond of comradeship that had developed among the men in Third Herd made the job of running the platoon much easier.

A few days later we again led the RIF on a hot and humid November afternoon as we walked along a path. A sudden BOOM erupted near the front of the columns. Everyone hit the ground and looked around holding weapons ready. I looked forward and saw a thick cloud of purple smoke rising from the ground in front of me. What the hell had happened?

I moved forward and saw Sergeant Matson lying wounded on the ground. The dense cloud of smoke was coming from a smoke grenade he was carrying. It had been hit by shrapnel and was spewing smoke into the air. Someone pulled the smoke grenade from Matson's gear and tossed it away. Doc Jackson ran forward and knelt at Matson's side. Doc was a gutsy medic who willingly put his butt on the line whenever one of the Third Herd went down. A booby trap had peppered Matson's body with shrapnel, but it looked like he would survive. Jim Overbey and I directed men forward to set up a perimeter and told them to keep a close eye out for other booby traps. Doc bandaged Matson's multiple wounds and gave him a shot of morphine to ease his pain while he waited for a medevac.

Bob Emery had also had a minor shrapnel wound in his right arm. Fortunately no one else had been wounded, because the men were well-spread-out when the booby trap exploded. From the sound of the blast I guessed it was a hand grenade. The VC liked to secure a hand grenade near the ground, attach a wire to the pin holding the handle, and then string the wire (trip wire) and attach it to another object. When someone snagged the trip wire, it would pull the pin from the grenade and in three or four seconds it would go off. One of the men in front of Matson had unknowingly tripped the wire, but Matson got the worst of it.

RTO Dennis Schultz talked with the medevac pilot and then yelled "pop smoke," to help guide the Huey into our position. We hadn't seen any signs of the enemy, but we knew the sound of the exploding booby trap would have drawn the attention of anyone in the area. Most medevac choppers had a big red cross painted on the nose and on each side and, theoretically, weren't to be fired upon by the enemy. But the NVA and VC fought with no rules; and they would shoot a medevac down if they had a chance.

We kept a watchful eye around us as the medevac landed and John Matson was swiftly carried aboard on a litter while Bob Emery stepped on board on his own. In less than a minute the chopper was off to Cu Chi. Just like that, we were down two men. I expected Emery to be back with us in a short while, but I doubted we would see Matson again. He had been in the field less than two weeks and was already going home. It wasn't an easy way to get a trip home, but he was going home alive. As the chopper flew off into the distance we gathered up Matson's and Emery's gear and cautiously moved on. Bob Emery was my machine gunner, which meant that his assistant Mike Stark instantly became my "gunner."

The following day we were flown from Patrol Base Delta and gladly landed on the LZ on the east side of Firebase Patton to work out of there for awhile. After we settled into our bunkers we were told we had to clean the place up because Vice President Agnew was coming out for a visit. He had traveled to Vietnam to discuss peace talk alternatives with the South Vietnamese government. The brass wanted to show him one of the newest state-of-the-art firebase, and Patton was it. The vice president would fly out the next morning.

We spent several hours picking up the trash (even cigarette butts) and fixing up anything that looked in need of repair. The brass wanted the firebase spick-and-span for the Vice President's arrival. Top was having a heyday, walking around barking out orders to fix this and pick up that and cussing up a storm at anyone who didn't move fast enough for his satisfaction.

Early on the morning of the Vice President's arrival we were each given a new helmet cover. We were told – no, ordered to put new covers on our helmets and to wear our helmets during Agnew's visit. A helmet cover was a camouflage-colored cloth cover that fit over our helmets to eliminate the glare from the metal. Most of us wore the original helmet cover that we had been issued with our helmets when we arrived in country. Our helmet covers had been dulled by constant exposure to the sun, and most of the men had written slogans or drawn designs on them, many of which were derogatory or offensive. We all removed our old helmet covers and put on the new ones to look presentable for the occasion. We were all to be clean-shaven and were told to wear the cleanest jungle fatigues we could find.

Just before eleven o'clock that morning one shiny OD-green Huey landed near the aid station and Vice President Agnew stepped out, dressed in a suit, white shirt and tie. Two Secret Service agents in suits and ties and a couple other officers in jungle fatigues accompanied him. I hadn't seen anyone in a suit and tie since I left the world.

Our battalion commander met the group near the landing pad and escorted them to the battalion headquarters bunker. While the Vice President was in the headquarters bunker, we gathered around a small platform that had been built for him to speak from. Fifteen minutes later the Vice President walked to the platform and was greeted by cheers and applause from us GIs. Although some of the men weren't particularly happy to see him, at least we weren't out on a RIF that morning. That was something to cheer about.

The Vice President spoke for a few minutes saying how proud he was of us and what a great job we were doing in fighting the war. He concluded his speech with a statement I will never forget. He said "... and I wish I could take you all home with me."

That statement earned him a loud cheer from us GIs, although we all knew most of us were a long way from going home. After his speech the Vice President shook hands with every man who wanted his handshake. I slowly moved along with the large group of men. When I reached the platform I too shook his hand. A short while later, the pilot of the shiny Huey started the engine and the chopper carrying the Vice President lifted off the pad. "Hey, where's he going?" someone yelled as the chopper flew away.

Vice President Agnew had taken a few minutes to walk around the interior of the firebase and check out one of the artillery pieces, but he hadn't come near any of the perimeter bunkers. We had worked for hours and he didn't even notice. After Agnew left many of the men took off the new helmet cover they were given that morning and put their old one back on. Most of the new helmet covers issued earlier that day ended up in the trash before nightfall, wasted for a politician's visit.

The next morning we put on our gear and headed out the east side of Patton and walked across the LZ to begin a fairly short and what turned out to be uneventful RIF. But we found a surprise when we returned. There had been a fire. One of the wooden latrines near our bunkers had burned down. The Army's way of dealing with the poop was to cut a metal drum in half and slide it under each hole in the latrine. Each morning one or two men would stay back in the firebase for latrine duty to pull out the drums filled with poop and burn it. They would mix in diesel fuel and light it. The poop would eventually burn down into a little pile that was buried near the outskirts of the perimeter. Although it wasn't pleasant duty, most guys figured latrine duty was safer than going out on a RIF.

One of the men who had latrine duty that day apparently hadn't pulled one barrel far enough away from the wooden latrine. After lighting the fuel he moved on to another latrine. When he returned he found the latrine in flames. There was no fire department to call out there, and the latrine burned until there was nothing left but a pile of rubble. Fortunately, a few days later a supply of lumber was delivered to build a new latrine.

During that stay at Patton, Alpha Company was assigned to a group of bunkers on the northeast side of Patton. In addition to entering and exiting through the main gate on the west side of Patton, we used two other paths. There was a path on the southeastern perimeter leading to the landing zone, and a second path in between two of our bunkers on the northeast perimeter used to leave or return from a RIF or ambush in that direction. The two paths went through sections of the concertina wire that were opened during the day to make our way in and out. At night, we pulled the concertina wire across the path.

Early one evening a group of us were standing outside our bunker near the northeast path when a group of men from another company walked by on their way to pull an ambush. We waved and said, "be careful," as they walked out along the path. Unexpectedly, an explosion near the edge of the perimeter destroyed the evening's peace and quiet. We were all startled and some of the men started running into our bunker when someone yelled, "Incoming!"

I then heard someone yelling, "Medic!" As some of the men from the other platoon walked back inside the perimeter one of them said it was a booby trap along the path. I couldn't believe it.

Doc Jackson pushed men aside, trying to get to the wounded men who were near the last row of concertina wire on the outskirts of our perimeter. The two wounded men were both screaming in pain while Doc Jackson and the ambush patrol's medic attended to them. The two men were soon carried back and placed on litters that had been brought over from the aid station. I helped carry one of the seriously injured men to the aid station and load him onto a medevac that landed a few minutes later. While walking back toward our bunkers Doc Jackson told me he thought one of the men might lose his right leg. A booby-trapped hand grenade had detonated right next to him.

Most of us didn't think about looking for booby traps close to the perimeter of Patton. We had all walked that same path many times and thought nothing of it. Normally the only non-GIs who came near Patton were kids, who sometimes wandered around the perimeter playing or looking for whatever they could find. It was unlikely an adult civilian could have walked up unnoticed. That meant one of the kids, whom we often tossed candy to, must have set it. Although I felt bad for the two wounded men, I also knew that if those men hadn't used the path that night, one of us would have gone out there later to pull the concertina wire across the path and would have detonated that hand grenade.

The following morning the company gathered on the landing zone outside the eastern perimeter at Patton to wait for choppers to take us up north for a RIF. I noticed a lone chopper flying from the north and then it turned east. I wasn't sure what the pilot was doing, but several of us watched him circle a cluster of trees 300 meters northeast of the LZ. Suddenly, a door gunner opened fire with his M-60 machine gun. The pilot radioed that two VC had been seen in those trees. While the lone chopper continued to circle the trees, the choppers scheduled to take us out on the RIF were arriving from the south. The CO yelled, "We're going over to those trees!"

The third platoon quickly boarded the first lift of choppers and in less than a minute was dropped near the cluster of trees. We quickly spread out to surround the trees, cautiously watching for any movement. If the VC were alive we didn't want them to escape. The rest of the company soon arrived to join us.

When we swept through the area we came upon two VC lying side-by-side near the center of the trees. They were both dead. One soldier had an AK-47, and the other had a .45 automatic pistol and two American-made hand grenades. They had apparently climbed up a tree in an attempt to take a few shots at us while we were on the LZ, or shoot at the choppers when they flew near that cluster of trees. The choppers often flew in directly from Cu Chi to pick us up, which was southeast of Patton. That meant they took off to the north close to those trees. The pistol wouldn't have had long-range capability, but AK-47 rounds could have reached the LZ or damaged a Huey. A Huey had been hit by rifle fire a couple of days earlier shortly after it took off from the LZ at Patton. Fortunately, the pilot was able to maintain enough control of the chopper to return and make a safe emergency landing. Maybe those two dead VC were the culprits.

When I looked closely at the soldier with the pistol, I noticed the long hair. One of the guys reached down and ripped open the soldier's shirt. It was a woman who appeared to be in her early twenties. She was wearing a white shirt, black slacks and sandals, and looked like many of the other women we saw walking up and down the roads and trails and in the villages. Except that woman would have tried to kill us if she had the chance.

We checked the bodies for anything that might provide useful information and swept the surrounding area for any other signs of enemy activity, finding nothing more. However, that little incident had messed up the plans for our scheduled RIF. Captain Dalton split up the company to conduct sweeps to the north, east and south of Patton. Although the area around Patton normally appeared peaceful, the booby trap in the concertina wire and the two gooks in the nearby trees proved the VC worked everywhere.

The third platoon was assigned the southern sweep. We walked south for three klicks and then turned west shortly after noon. As we moved through an open grassy area with a few scattered bushes, we began to smell a terrible odor. The odor became stronger and stronger as we moved west. There had to be something dead or rotten around there. We slowed our pace, searching more closely for the source of the odor. Finally, one of the guys yelled, "There's a body over here!"

And did it stink. Men were holding their towel or the sleeve of their fatigue shirt over their noses, trying to filter out the smell. When I walked closer I saw a Vietnamese man lying under a small bush. Maggots and other bugs were crawling over his skin that had turned almost black. There was no indication of a firefight; in fact, we didn't find a weapon anywhere nearby. We didn't take the time to closely examine the body because of the smell, but we thought he might have been wounded by harassment and interdiction mortar fire and crawled under the bush and died. We quickly moved out to get away from the smell. We turned north and returned to Patton without finding anything else interesting.

We walked past one of the artillery pieces on our way to our bunkers and waved at the artillerymen standing nearby. The artillerymen worked long hours to clean and maintain their guns and perform fire missions any time, day or night. We didn't spend much time with those guys and never really got to know them. That day one of the artillerymen asked what had happened that morning by the trees. A few of us stopped and told him about the two VC and that one was a woman.

The artilleryman then told us a story about one of his friends who had gotten involved with a Vietnamese woman. The man had somehow found a girlfriend in Trung Lap, the village directly north of Patton. He would leave Patton during the day to visit her and then return before dark. Two weeks earlier the man left to visit his girlfriend, but didn't return that evening. The next day there was still no sign of him. His buddies knew something had to be wrong. They finally told their CO their friend was missing in Trung Lap. A company of men was sent to search through the village for the missing GI. They eventually found him.

The artillerymen were told that their friend's body had been badly mutilated during what had to have been a painful and terrifying death. It was surmised the VC discovered the GI in the village and they tortured him to death. The VC knew we would ultimately find his body and that the brutality of his death would be demoralizing to every GI who heard about it. That story was another reminder that Firebase Patton and the nearby countryside really weren't as safe as we might have thought.

While we prepared for another air assault mission the following morning, someone asked me what date it was. I looked at the little calendar in my wallet and it was November 21st. We often lost track of the date because we didn't get weekends off, and holidays had been just another day. We had gone on a RIF on Labor Day, and although Veterans Day had become more meaningful for all of us, it also passed without fanfare. Each day became much like every other day as we continued our routine of RIFs and ambushes. Most of us simply hoped and prayed we would see the sun rise each morning.

We were to fly several klicks northeast of Patton for a RIF. Once again I was one of the last men to board the chopper after making sure everyone else was aboard before we lifted off. While I sat on the floor with my feet hanging out the door, I noticed most of the bomb craters that had been filled with water during the monsoon season were drying up. As we neared our remote LZ we were all startled by two "thuds" coming from the tail section of the Huey. We looked at each other thinking the chopper had been hit by enemy fire.

One of the pilots yelled, "Hold on!" as the chopper swayed back and forth a couple times and then continued smoothly on our flight path. The door gunners both immediately opened fire, spraying the countryside on both sides with M-60 fire. I quickly slid back toward the center of the chopper floor realizing I had made myself an easy target by sitting in the doorway. I guess it wasn't my time to go.

The huge main rotor blade of each Huey that swirled directly over our heads provided the lift to get the chopper in the air. The turbine-powered engine sat overhead, just behind the main body of the chopper. The tail section led to a smaller rotor blade that rotated vertically and guided the chopper in a straight path or through turns. Bullets striking the tail section could damage the controls leading to the tail rotor, impacting the pilot's ability to control the chopper. Fortunately, we descended into the LZ and landed without any difficulties.

Although we were in the boonies, the pilot kept the chopper on the ground while the door gunner behind me quickly stepped out to check the tail section of the Huey. I stayed near the chopper while the gunner walked along the tail section and then pointed at two bullet holes three feet back from the main section of the chopper. The door gunner gave a "thumbs-up" and quickly boarded the chopper. The chopper was soon back in the air with no apparent serious damage.

The Third Herd led the RIF while we searched an uninhabited area that was mostly grassland, abandoned rice paddies and small trees and scattered hedgerows. When we came upon a lone hootch in the middle of nowhere, we cautiously walked up to it. Two men each threw a hand grenade inside. Straw from the roof flew in the air and a cloud of dust was stirred up when the grenades exploded. When we checked inside the hootch it appeared to have been abandoned. We didn't find anything stored inside or anywhere nearby. A couple guys lit the straw roof afire with their cigarette lighters, and in a minute the entire roof was burning and soon collapsed, making the hootch much less useful to the enemy.

We had been scheduled to be flown back to Patton that afternoon, but when the CO radioed that we had finished our RIF early that afternoon without any enemy contact or finding any signs of enemy activity, the battalion commander decided we should walk back to Patton and search additional areas on our way in. "Damn," we all thought. It was a hot, sunny afternoon and we had all worked up a sweat, humping through the boonies for several hours. We weren't looking forward to walking another eight klicks back to Patton.

When we walked south and passed a group of bomb craters, we saw a partially decomposed body of an enemy soldier at the bottom of a dried up crater. The bodies of hundreds if not thousands of NVA and VC soldiers were surely buried under debris or lying unnoticed all across the countryside after the years of fighting in South Vietnam.

As we moved on, Vic Ortega was our point man for the right column, and James "Red" Mincey was the pace man behind him. Half of us, including Rick Shields and me, were behind them while the remainder of the Third Herd followed Ed Leberski, the point man for the left column. We were over halfway back when we came upon a long line of hedgerows with a clearing near the middle. The two point men led the columns closer together while slowly approaching the clearing. Vic Ortega passed through first with Red following several steps behind.

All of a sudden, Ed Leberski stopped and frantically yelled, "Hold up, Red!" Red looked at Ed just before an explosion directly in front of Red hurled him to the ground. The blast sent us all instinctively to the ground.

Ed yelled, "It's a booby trap!"

185

There was only that single explosion. No gunfire or other explosions. Rick Shields, who was still acting platoon leader said, "Set up a perimeter, Hound Dog. I'll check on Red."

Doc Jackson, who had been walking behind me, ran forward and knelt beside Red, who was the only man who had been wounded. With the perimeter in place, I walked to the center where Doc and Rick were kneeling beside Red. He didn't have any major visible wounds. I saw only a little blood around his face and neck.

But Red was having serious trouble breathing and was in a desperate panic as he gasped for air. Doc checked Red for other injuries while Rick tried to calm him down. I knelt down by Red's left side and lowered my head toward his and said, "Take a slow breath, Red, you'll be OK."

Red raised his left hand and I grabbed it to give him some moral support and comfort. Red couldn't speak but kept putting his right hand by his throat, indicating he couldn't breathe, desperately hoping we could help him. Shrapnel had hit Red in the front of his neck and must have damaged his airway. Although Doc was a great medic, he didn't have any tools to open Red's airway to help him breathe. All we could do was try to keep him calm and get him to Cu Chi as soon as possible!

Bill Casey had immediately radioed for a dustoff, and a Huey gunship that was near our position heard the call. The gunship pilot radioed to ask if we wanted them to drop in and evacuate our wounded man. Casey told Doc about the nearby gunship. Without hesitation Doc said, "Get that chopper in here now!"

I had never seen such a concerned look on Doc Jackson's face before. Captain Dalton had walked forward, but he stood back and let those of us in the third platoon continue to manage the situation. Doc was doing everything he could to save Red, but as the seconds passed, Red continued to frantically struggle for a breath of air while he tightly clutched my hand, desperate for help. While I talked to Red trying to keep him calm and give him encouragement, I saw a look of desperation in his eyes that I had never seen before, a look that I will never forget. Rick and I looked at each other helplessly but didn't say a word.

When I heard the familiar sound of the chopping blades, I said, "Hang in there, Red. The chopper's coming in."

Someone popped smoke, and the gunship landed within five minutes after Red had been hit. The gunship didn't have any litters on board, so we just picked up Red and rushed him to the waiting chopper and laid him on the floor. Doc and Rick Shields hopped aboard hoping to keep Red alive somehow until they reached the 12th Evac in Cu Chi, eight miles south of our location.

Rick yelled, "Hound Dog, you take the platoon." which meant he wanted me to take charge. I waved back in acknowledgement as the chopper lifted off. I knew the pilot would soon have the Huey at full throttle. Red would be at the hospital in a few minutes. As the chopper roared off in the distance, I said to myself, "Hold on, Red."

After the chopper left, we took a few minutes to carefully search the area but found no other booby traps. The detonation sounded like another hand grenade. It appeared Vic Ortega had unknowingly tripped a wire, pulling the pin from the grenade, and it exploded when Red walked up to it. It was nothing sophisticated, but it had wounded Red. Hopefully it hadn't killed him.

I talked with Ed Leberski while we searched the area. He said he had seen a reflection from something in front of Red and had called for him to stop, but it was too late and the grenade exploded. Ed was visibly shaken. I put my hand on Ed's shoulder and said, "Hey, Ed, you did all you could."

We gathered Red's gear and moved on toward Patton. I was somewhat surprised we had encountered a booby trap less than two klicks northeast of Trung Lap. However, that incident again reminded me not to take anything for granted, and to be prepared for the worst almost anywhere. We safely completed the remainder of the RIF and quietly walked to our bunkers at Patton late that afternoon. We didn't know if Red was dead or alive.

An hour later Captain Dalton walked up to me near my bunker and said, "Red didn't make it. Sorry." My heart sank. I stared into the distance for a moment, trying to comprehend what I had just heard.

I then said, "I'll tell the men sir. Thanks for coming over to tell me." Captain Dalton gave me a supportive pat on the back and walked away.

Red was only twenty years old. He had joined the platoon that past September along with several other men. I had told Captain Branch and Captain Dalton about Red's brother dying of malaria, and they both had said they would try to get Red out of the field. Unfortunately for Red, it didn't happen soon enough. I gathered the men together. By the solemn expression on my face, they knew I had bad news. I said, "The CO just told me that Red died." There was silence. Some of the men looked at each other and shook their heads while others dropped their heads and stared at the ground.

Someone yelled, "Those son-of-a-bitches!" The yelling was primarily aimed at the enemy troops who planted the booby trap. But the men were also angry with the battalion commander. They knew he had made the decision for us to walk back to Patton rather than be flown back. If we had flown back, Red would still be alive.

I saw Vic Ortega turn and walk away to be by himself. Vic knew he had tripped the wire on the booby-trapped grenade. I walked over and put my hand on Vic's shoulder. "Don't be too hard on yourself, Vic," I said,

"I know, Sarge, but Red is dead because of me."

I said, "Don't feel that way. The damn gooks who set the booby trap are to blame, not you." We all knew it was nearly impossible to see trip-wired booby traps out there. Although none of us blamed Vic, a sense of guilt would remain with him for a long time. I took Vic off point the next day and assigned Glenn Haywood to walk point for a while.

Doc Jackson and Rick Shields were flown back to Patton early that evening. Doc said Red died before they reached the hospital. They gave him mouth-to-mouth respiration on the way in, but they couldn't save him. Rick was very upset over losing Red. He said, "Red died in my arms."

The following week was Thanksgiving. Although the sadness of Red's passing remained, we were all thankful to still be alive. We didn't go out on a RIF on Thanksgiving Day because a one-day American truce was called. We enjoyed a delicious turkey dinner served at Firebase Patton. Thanksgiving Day passed with guys relaxing and writing letters home and I lost a few bucks in a poker game early that afternoon.

I took time later that afternoon to write a letter to Jan Griffin. I had normally received one or two letters a week from her since I had arrived in Vietnam, but I had only received two letters since the first of November. Jan and I hadn't made any commitments to each other, and since she was an attractive girl I assumed she would be asked out by other guys. That was fine; I didn't expect her to spend a year by herself waiting for me. But not hearing much from her lately, I thought she might have found someone else she liked and had forgotten about me on the other side of the world.

I tried not to get too concerned over what Jan was doing back in Omaha, because I couldn't do much about it anyway. It was like most everything else in my life at that time; I had to hope and pray for the best. Besides, I still had to survive eight more months in Vietnam before I could start thinking about going home. I finished my letter to Jan and signed it, "Love and Kisses, Dick." A couple of men in the Third Herd had gotten "Dear John" letters from their girlfriends. "Jody" was the nickname for the guy back home who hadn't been drafted and was chasing GIs' wives and girlfriends. Unfortunately, "Jody" took some girls away from men while they served in Vietnam. For many men in Vietnam, getting letters from that special girl back home was what kept them going during their tour.

During the last week of November we operated out of a little patrol base several miles west of Patton. One day the third platoon went on a short RIF by ourselves. We finished our RIF early that afternoon and stopped in a grove of trees outside a village. We planned to hold up there for a few hours and then move out to pull an ambush that night. Although the area had been relatively peaceful, we set up a perimeter around the edge of the grove and kept a few men on guard.

After we settled in, most of us enjoyed a surprise experience. If there was enough water at the remote patrol bases we would hang a canvas bucket with a little showerhead on the bottom from a pole and take a quick shower; or sometimes we took turns pouring water from a five-gallon container over our heads. But that afternoon someone found a rusty bucket lying next to a well in the middle of the grove. Since none of us had taken a shower for a few days, a few men worked together to make a tripod with tree branches, and attached the rusty bucket near the top of the tripod with a belt. A rope was tied to a couple of helmets and men began drawing water from the well to fill the bucket. The water flowing from the holes in the bottom of the rusty bucket made a great shower. We spent the next hour or so taking turns keeping the water flowing while one-by-one we stripped down and took a cool shower in the middle of that grove of trees.

➢ Corporal James "Red" Mincey was from Conway, S.C. He was twenty years old. Red arrived in Vietnam on September 8, 1969. He was killed by a booby trap on November 21, 1969. Red's older brother John had died of malaria in Vietnam in 1968. In 1999 I found Red's mother and sent pictures of Red in Vietnam along with details of his death. Ironically, two weeks after I contacted her, she passed away. It was as though she had waited to hear how Red died and was ready to join him.

The causes of combat fatalities among Army troops in Vietnam are as follows: Small Arms Fire 55%; Shelling Fragments 35%; Mines and Booby Traps 7%; Other and Undetermined 3%.

Dave Hardy (standing) and James "Red" Mincey.
The tower at Fire Support Base Patton is in the background.

Chapter 14

Christmas in Vietnam

December 1969 started on another sad note. Steve Robinson eventually got tired of taking care of the monkey and gave it to someone back in Cu Chi. But one of the men had found a lonely young puppy during a RIF the day after Thanksgiving and brought it back to Patton to become our new mascot. It was a cute little dog with a pug nose and dark brown fluffy fur. He loved to lick your face when you held him. One afternoon in early December, we returned to Patton and found the dog in convulsions and whining in pain. Someone found a piece of C-4 plastic explosive nearby with little teeth marks on it. The little dog must have eaten some of the C-4. We had no way to treat our suffering little friend. One of the men reluctantly fired an M-16 round into the puppy's head to put him out of his misery.

A couple of days later the Third Herd was assigned to Venice East, the little guard post southwest of Firebase Patton. It was a welcome relief from the hazardous daily RIFs and ambushes. It was hard for me to believe it was already December. I had been in the field for four months. Although some of the days and nights seemed like they would never end, in retrospect the time had gone by faster than I had imagined it would. Most importantly, I was alive. I still had a long way to go before I would be going home, but I had survived longer than many men.

The platoon also continued to undergo changes. Bob Emery had returned after recovering from his minor shrapnel wound and had been promoted to sergeant. Mike Stark, who had been Bob's assistant machine gunner, and Doc Jackson, were both reassigned back to Cu Chi, and Bill Casey moved to the CP group to become one of Captain Dalton's RTOs. PFC Mertis Snyder arrived to become our new medic, and PFCs Larry Sutton, Hugh Hearn and Chester Sampson had been assigned to us shortly after Thanksgiving. And finally, twenty-six year old Second Lieutenant John Foreman joined the Third Herd as our new platoon leader. I was no longer the oldest man in the platoon. Lieutenant Foreman was from New York and was a fairly quiet man, much different from Lieutenant Fielding. He kept a low profile while adjusting to field duty and relied on us NCOs to help him with his on-the-job-training. Several men reminded him that the duty at Venice East was far from the normal routine. I simply told him to enjoy it while he could.

During our second day at Venice East the focus for several of the guys was women. Obviously, serving as infantrymen in Vietnam we had no social life. We were either stomping through the boonies, on an ambush or confined inside a firebase or patrol base twenty-four-hours a day. Except during our previous stand downs in Cu Chi, we never had more than a few hours at any one time to relax. Venice East was the one place where we could semi-relax and have a little fun in the field. When the local adults and kids stopped by that morning, a couple of the guys asked for "boom-boom" (Vietnamese slang for sex). Most of the civilians didn't speak or understand much English, but they knew what boom-boom was. Two kids headed down the road toward the village of Bau Dieu and returned a short while later with an older woman and a young girl. The kids pointed toward the young girl and said, "boom-boom."

I was the acting platoon sergeant because Rick Shields and Jim Overbey were both back in Cu Chi. The men asked me if they could bring the woman and younger girl into Venice East. I thought for a few seconds, and then said, "OK." I knew there had been women inside Venice East before. Lieutenant Foreman had been inside his bunker most of the morning reading a book but happened to step out when the woman and young girl were standing outside another bunker. He asked me what was going on. I told our new 3-6 what the men were up to, and that they had searched the woman and girl before they came inside. I said it was an unofficially condoned practice to let women come inside Venice East.

Lieutenant Foreman hesitated for a brief moment and finally said, "OK, but you keep an eye on them."

"Yes sir," I said. 3-6 turned and walked back into his bunker.

The men soon learned the older woman was the young girl's mother. The mother was "pimping" her fourteen-year old daughter. Some of the men were "hot to trot," so to speak, and quickly negotiated a price (normally $3 to $5) with the mother and took their turn with the daughter in one of the bunkers. I didn't keep track of which men ultimately shared the pleasures the young girl offered, but a few men walked around with smiles on their faces after the young girl and her mother left after noon that day. While the mother and daughter walked toward Bau Dieu I thought about how desperate that mother must have been to turn her young daughter into a prostitute. The reality was, she could make much more money selling her daughter's body than she could doing anything else.

Early that afternoon a girl who looked to be in her early twenties stopped by Venice East with a girl who was only thirteen years old. The older girl told the guys the young girl was "available." Again the men asked me if they could bring the girls inside. I sighed and said, "You guys are going to get my butt in trouble." I didn't know how much frolicking Lieutenant Foreman would put up with.

"Oh, come on, Sarge," was the reply. I finally said OK and told the guys to keep a low profile and keep it quiet.

It was humorous watching some of the guys almost fall over themselves while they checked out the cute young girl, Chae, and then negotiated a price with the older girl for Chae's services. Most of those same men would have beat the crap out of any man who would have tried to have sex with their own thirteen-year-old sister back in the world. But thousands of miles away in Vietnam, the drive for female companionship overcame morality issues. Many men accepted whatever was offered to them, including thirteen and fourteen year old girls. Venereal disease (VD) was prevalent among Vietnamese prostitutes, but for infantrymen in the field, that was the least of their concerns. A shot of penicillin cured most anything they picked up. VD was simply one of the hazards of the "duty."

The older girl, named Sung, was attractive with long black hair. She was short and slender, like most Vietnamese women, and she spoke English fairly well. The men had told Sung I was in charge of the platoon and I talked with her for a while that afternoon. The two girls lived in Saigon and had traveled to Cu Chi. That morning they had moved on to Bau Dieu where she was told some GIs up the road were looking for girls, so, Sung and Chae walked to Venice East.

Late that afternoon I told the men the girls should leave pretty soon. But a few minutes later, I looked out to the road and saw a deuce-and-a-half and a jeep stop to deliver our mail and evening meal. Surprisingly, I saw our CO, Captain Dalton, sitting in the jeep. I thought, "What the hell is he doing here?"

I quickly turned and told the guys standing by one of the forward bunkers, "Keep the girls inside the bunker and out of sight. The CO's here!" Lieutenant Foreman stepped out from his bunker. I joined him and walked to the road to greet the CO. Captain Dalton had been told about Venice East but hadn't visited the compound. He had informed Lieutenant Foreman that he would stop by that afternoon. Unfortunately, Lieutenant Foreman failed to tell me the CO was paying us a visit. While we stood beside the road, I explained the layout of the compound to Captain Dalton and told him generally how we operated during the day and at night. The CO then wanted to walk inside and look around. I thought, "Oh no, I'm in trouble now."

Lieutenant Foreman, who didn't know the two girls were still there, led the CO through the gate and inside Venice East. As luck would have it, Captain Dalton walked right toward the bunker the girls were in. He kneeled down at the entrance and peeked inside. The CO spent a couple of minutes talking to the men inside while the two girls quietly lay under a poncho liner and gear inside the bunker. He then stood up and walked to the guard tower in the center of the compound. The CO climbed up to check out the view and talk with one of the radar operators sitting at the top of the tower.

A short while later the CO decided he had seen enough and walked back to his jeep. We waved at him and the other men in the jeep and the duce-and-a half when they turned around and drove towards Patton. WHEW! That was a close call. I didn't know how Captain Dalton would react to us having two Vietnamese girls inside Venice East. I could have become Corporal Hogue that day.

But quickly, I had another problem. It would be getting dark soon. The girls would have to walk nearly a mile to Bau Dieu. I could have kicked them out and have them make a run for it, but they would have had to pass the ARVN compound before they entered the village. If they didn't make it to Bau Dieu before dark they could be in trouble. The men wanted me to let the girls stay all night, but I was reluctant. It could be my butt if the CO found out. However, also I didn't want to kick them out and risk the girls getting killed if they didn't make it to Bau Dieu before dark. How would I explain that?

I finally decided to let the girls stay, but I reminded the guys we had to keep it quiet. I didn't want things to get any further out of hand than they already were. I told Bob Emery to make sure the blasting caps were set in the claymores and to set up the guard rotation for the night. Lieutenant Foremen had fallen asleep early and didn't know the girls were there for the night. I would get them out of there early the following morning.

When darkness fell we secured the perimeter and men began pulling guard in the tower. I peeked inside the bunker where Chae and Sung were talking with the guys while someone was fixing a place for the girls to sleep. I stepped outside and looked up at a starry sky and thought to myself, "What have I let happen?" The day started simply with guys looking for girls. We then had a mother pimping her four-teen-year-old daughter; a thirteen-year-old girl had sex with several of the men, and I had a conversation with Sung as though we were friends. And to top it off, two Vietnamese girls were spending the night inside Venice East. I chuckled to myself and shook my head in disbelief.

Later Sung stepped out from the bunker and walked up to me. She said Chae had fallen asleep. We talked for a while, and then Sung put her hand on my arm and said, "I want to spend the night with you."

I was speechless. But then I thought, "How could I refuse such an offer from an attractive young woman?" I put my arm around Sung while we stood beside the bunker and shared a few minutes of peace-fulness. Sung and I then crawled inside my bunker. We lay down on my air mattress and covered ourselves with my poncho liner. While Sung snuggled close to me, I couldn't believe what was happening. We kissed while I moved one hand under her blouse and felt her warm, firm breasts as I pulled her body close to mine. As our passions quickly rose, I removed her loosely-fitting slacks and caressed her soft, warm flesh. Surprisingly, Sung whispered near my ear, "I love you, tee tee." (Tee tee is Vietnamese meaning "a little" or "small").

The next morning started as normal at Venice East. I sent half the platoon out to escort the minesweeping team while the rest of us stayed around the compound to disarm the claymores and clean the place up. I told Sung that she and Chae would have to leave when the road was cleared. We all would have enjoyed having them stay longer, but I knew the girls should leave before the old sarge got in trouble. I walked with the girls to the road a short while later and gave Sung a little hug and said good-bye when they turned and began walking down the road toward Bau Dieu.

Later that day I talked with Willard Spivey, who had joined the platoon in mid-October. He showed me the picture of his wife and one-year-old daughter that he had recently received. He was proud of them both. He said he enjoyed staying back and watching what he called the "entertainment" of the past day, while he remained faithful to his wife in Kentucky.

We spent three more relatively uneventful days at Venice East before we joined with the rest of our company at Patrol Base Delta. During our first night at Delta we were asked to do another first. We were to pull a company-sized ambush. We normally took twelve men on an ambush and, now and then, used a full platoon of twenty to twenty-five men. But we had never used the entire company of almost ninety men for an ambush.

We moved fairly quickly toward the ambush site two klicks east of Delta and arrived well before dark. The company set up in a big circular perimeter near a tree line, and then moved into the site when the sun began to set. We formed a perimeter behind rice paddy dikes about sixty meters square. The site was on high ground, giving us great visibility. It looked like it would be a simple ambush. Each platoon had a designated area of responsibility where we set out our claymores and established fields of fire while the CO formed a command post in the center. We had just started guard duty when Lieutenant Foreman came over to me and said we were moving out.

I said, "What?"

The battalion commander who had planned the company-sized ambush had changed his mind. He had radioed the CO saying he wanted us to split up into three platoon-sized ambushes. It frankly made more sense to set up three separate ambush sites, but his timing was lousy. I told Lieutenant Foreman we were asking for trouble relocating in the dark. He didn't like it any better than I did, but we had orders to split up.

The second platoon would stay in place with Captain Dalton and his command post group while the first and third platoons moved to new sites. We quickly gathered up our claymores and gear while the men bitched and moaned about what we had to do. They knew how dangerous it was for us to be moving around in the boonies at night. It was nearly dark when we left our original ambush site and began walking 500 meters directly north to a new site along a trail. It was completely dark when we reached our new ambush site. We set up in another rice paddy with most of the men spread along a dike, facing a rise to the north toward what we believed was the trail. We set out our claymores and settled in again.

I was sleeping between guard shifts, when someone shook me and said, "Hound Dog, there's VC out there!" I quickly grabbed a starlight scope and saw three figures walking east in the distance well over fifty meters away. I almost told the men to fire some claymores, but the VC were beyond the effective range of our claymores. I whispered, "No claymores, don't fire."

We could have opened fire with our rifles and machine guns, but it would have been tough trying to hit anyone that far away in the dark. I hated to let the VC get away, but I knew we didn't have a very good chance of getting them. I wondered why the men hadn't popped the ambush sooner but didn't take time to ask. I quickly told Lieutenant Foreman what happened, and we called in a fire mission to have several artillery rounds fired northeast of our position where we believed the trail led, hoping to nail the VC.

I was on guard in one of the forward positions when daylight slowly began to appear on the eastern horizon. One of the men in the rear position crawled toward me and said there was movement to our back side. I crawled to the rear and looked out. I could see several figures and again almost told the men to open fire. But then I recognized a GI helmet in the dim light. It must have been the first platoon. Several men were sitting up and pointing their rifles toward the moving figures in the distance.

I said, "Hold your fire! Don't shoot!" I told Bob Ryken, who had become one of our RTOs, to get on the radio and tell the first platoon to hold their fire! We were directly north of them. I knew if we could see them, they could also see us and might open fire.

Fortunately, the first platoon received Bob's message, and we didn't fire on each other. When the sun rose we stood up and waved at men in the first platoon, wondering how we had managed to set up our ambushes less than 100 meters apart. If we had popped our ambush on the VC walking along the trail during the night, the first platoon could have thought we were enemy troops firing on them. The first platoon might have opened fire on us and we naturally would have fired back at them. It was scary to think that we could have annihilated each other before we knew what was happening.

A few nights later most of the company set up in a night laager position with Captain Dalton and his CP group west of Firebase Patton. I took a dozen men to set up an ambush 750 meters to the northwest while half of the second platoon moved southwest to set up an ambush. We set up a perimeter in a holding area surrounded by trees on three sides before moving to our site that was 100 meters south near some rice paddies. I placed my machine gun team facing east toward a small trail. We had only been there for a few minutes when Wop began firing his M-60 down the trail. I immediately crouched down and rushed beside Wop. Two other men on each side of Wop were firing their M-16s towards the trail.

Wop stopped firing for a few seconds and told me he had seen two gooks walking toward him as he pointed down the trail directly in front of him. "OK," I replied and patted Wop on the back.

"Open fire!" I yelled to the men on our eastern perimeter and pointed down the trail.

We covered the area to the east with M-16 fire and fired several M-79 grenades down the trail, while Wop's M-60 blasted rounds across the area. We had received only brief initial return fire that hadn't hit any of us. A minute later, RTO Bob Ryken scurried up to me and said we were hitting the CP group.

I immediately yelled, "Cease fire! Cease fire!" When all was quiet I asked Bob what was going on. He said the CP group radioed they were getting stray rounds from us. The CP group should have been nearly 800 meters south of us and beyond the range of our M-16s, which was 500 meters. But Wop might have sprayed some M-60 rounds to the south. An M-60 machine gun round could travel 1,000 meters. Fortunately, we hadn't hit any of our own men.

I told Captain Dalton over the radio that we had spotted two VC on a trail, and we talked briefly about moving down the trail to conduct a search. I told him there were thick hedgerows on both sides of the trail, limiting our visibility. Since it was getting dark, I didn't want to walk into an ambush if the two VC were still alive or if there were others we hadn't seen. The CO agreed and told me to work our way back to his location.

"Oh, great," I thought. Here we go stomping around in the dark again. But I didn't have time to worry about what else might happen. We had revealed ourselves to anyone in the area and needed to get out of there. I quickly told the men we were moving back to the CP group. I pointed straight south and told our point man Glenn Haywood that was where I wanted him to lead us. I then noticed a new guy named Ben Carlson. He hadn't been near the trail and I don't believe he had fired his M-16, but he was scared to death and wasn't moving. I shook him and said, "Hey, Carlson, we're moving out!"

He looked at me with a blank stare and then jumped up to join the rest of the men who were forming a column behind Haywood. Carlson had been carrying our starlight scope, but he walked away, leaving it on the ground. Rather than tell him to come back and get it, I grabbed the scope and carried it with me. I would talk with Carlson the next morning.

After I knew all the men had joined the column, I moved forward to help guide us away from the trail and trees and into an open area in the middle of some rice paddies. After we walked nearly 200 meters it was completely dark. I told Haywood to stop. I contacted Captain Dalton on the radio and asked him to call in some mortar fire along the trail hoping to hit anyone who might still be out there. We then slowly navigated our way toward the command post as the mortar rounds exploded in the distance behind us. After we reached the CP group we settled in with them for the remainder of what was an uneventful night.

Early the next morning the third platoon led the company back to the trail where we searched for bodies or signs of the VC. We found a sandal and a blood trail, but no bodies. If we had killed or wounded anyone their buddy or buddies must have carried them away. We walked back to Patton without finding any other signs of the VC.

That evening Dennis Schultz was talking with some guys near his bunker when he started waving his arms and yelling things like, "I've got to get out of here! I know I'm going to get killed! I can't leave Linda (his wife) and my kid alone!" Some of the guys tried to calm Schultz down, but he kept pushing them aside and continued walking around and yelling about getting killed. I thought to myself as I walked toward Schultz, "This place has gotten to him." Schultz had arrived in country that past summer and had been one of our RTOs since the time I joined the third platoon. Doc Snyder walked up to me and said, "We better get him out of here."

Doc Snyder and Larry Sutton each firmly grabbed Schultz by an arm and forced him to walk to the aid station. Schultz was flown back to Cu Chi and eventually assigned to duty there. He never returned to the Third Herd.

That evening Lieutenant Foreman gave us the news concerning our RIF the next day. We were flying to the Ho Bo Woods to sweep through an area of suspected enemy bunker complexes, and to make things worse, the area was known to be loaded with booby traps and land mines. Although we knew the NVA and VC planted booby traps and land mines all over South Vietnam, we were rarely told during our briefings that an area was specifically known to have booby traps and land mines.

The following morning, December 17th, I walked to the landing zone at Patton to wait for choppers. While I checked to be sure everyone was present, I noticed our Chieu Hoi, Hue, who served as our scout, wasn't there. The Chieu Hois were given a lot of latitude with their duties and often would come and go as they pleased. Hue sometimes left for a few days, saying he was going to visit his family. Some of us had also noticed Hue sometimes just didn't go out with us on a RIF. We finally figured out that if Hue knew we were going into a particularly hazardous area, like the Ho Bo Woods, he would simply disappear that morning. Knowing Hue wasn't on the LZ that morning wasn't comforting after learning his logic.

A short while later a lift of Hueys flew us to the west-central part of the Ho Bo Woods. We landed in an open LZ that remained peaceful while we organized ourselves and headed out on the RIF led by the third platoon. We first walked through an area of mostly tall grass that had dried out after the monsoon rains had stopped. There were scattered trees and bushes in the area, but it was pretty easy walking.

We then came upon the area of suspected bunker complexes. The terrain was covered with tall grass, thick hedgerows and bushes and trees. It looked like a solid eight-foot wall of vegetation with no identifiable trails into the area. It was an ideal hiding spot for enemy bunkers. We stopped and called the CO to get his OK to fire some M-79 grenades into the area hoping to detonate any booby traps that might be along our intended path. After two men fired over a dozen grenades without creating any secondary explosions, Captain Dalton said, "That's enough, let's move out."

Glenn Haywood led the right column, followed by Willard Spivey, who would have a difficult time trying to count paces walking through the heavy vegetation. Bob Emery fell in behind Spivey, and I followed Bob. Wop, my machine gunner, and FNG, Hugh Hearn, Wop's assistant gunner, fell in behind me. Carl Seals led a second column to our left that I could barely see through the trees and thick brush. We had to walk slowly and stay close together to maintain sight of each other while we wound through and around large hedgerows and trees.

We had struggled through the area for less than ten minutes when BOOM! A huge explosion directly in front of me shook the ground under my feet. I instinctively hit the ground and felt my heart pounding, not knowing what had happened. The explosion had made a tremendous sound and left my ears ringing. The large cloud of dirt and debris that had been thrown into the air by the force of the explosion rained down around me. We had hit something big.

There were no more explosions or gunfire. The sudden silence was almost ghostly. My sweaty face was covered with dirt as I raised my head and looked around. I only saw Bob Emery in front of me and Wop directly behind me. I heard someone behind me yell, "Medic!" I turned and motioned for Wop to move up toward me and told him to cover Bob and me as we moved forward to see what had happened. I stood up and walked forward beside Bob, and saw him wiping blood from a cut on his left cheek. Bob said he was OK. It looked like a piece of shrapnel must have hit him.

I said, "Let's go see what happened." Bob nodded his head and followed me.

I turned the lever on my M-16 from safety to automatic and cautiously moved forward with Bob Emery directly behind me. I soon found Willard Spivey. His fatigues were covered with blood, as he lay motionless on the ground. I motioned for Bob to stay and help Spivey. I walked forward by myself a few more feet and saw our point man Glenn Haywood.

Most of the heavy vegetation around Haywood had been completely blown away by the force of the explosion, creating a clearing ten feet in diameter. Haywood sat, motionless, near the center of a shallow crater. I didn't know if he was dead or alive. I held my finger on the trigger of my rifle while I looked around and slowly walked toward Haywood, expecting something else to happen. I didn't know where the rest of our men were. I was on my own.

I knelt beside Haywood who was sitting upright and looking forward with a blank stare. I put my hand on his arm and he turned his head slightly and looked at me. He was alive! I then looked down and saw in horror that both of his legs had been completely blown off at his knees. There was no sign of either leg anywhere. They were completely gone! Amazingly, the shredded stumps of his legs weren't bleeding severely but were caked with blood and dirt. The heat from the explosion had partially seared many of his blood vessels, but he was bleeding from his hands, face and arms. Haywood's entire body was covered with a layer of dirt stirred up by the explosion.

I immediately yelled, "Medic! I need some men up here!" I needed a medic to help treat Haywood and wanted to get a defensive perimeter set up around us until we could get him out of there.

Slowly a few men began to appear as they cautiously walked forward. I was directing them to set up around me, when Carl Seals, who was slowly walking from his point position in the left column suddenly yelled, "There's another booby trap over here."

I yelled, "Don't anyone go in front of me. And watch your step!"

Lieutenant Foreman, who had moved forward, then yelled, "There's a bunker just past that hedgerow!" as he pointed to the area in front of Haywood and me.

I thought, "What the hell did we get into?" Haywood and I were totally exposed, but we couldn't risk putting anyone in front of us for protection. We must have found a NVA bunker complex and were sitting in a series of booby traps and land mines. Haywood either stepped on a detonator or the NVA may have detonated the first land mine with a remote detonator from a nearby bunker.

Lieutenant Foreman and second platoon leader Lieutenant Higginson spread the word to watch closely for booby traps. I told them to set some men on line behind me for cover until we got Haywood out of there. Lieutenant Higgenson directed several men forward and organized them to stand guard over Haywood and me. Wop had moved up with his M-60 and had a couple hundred rounds of ammunition laid out, ready to fire if needed.

Doc Morrison, our company medic, had moved up and he knelt beside Haywood with a shocked look on his face when he saw Haywood's missing legs. Doc quickly opened the canvas bag containing his medical gear and started pulling out bandages and large field dressings. Doc first bandaged the bloody stumps of Haywood's legs and then put a tourniquet around each thigh, while I wrapped a large field dressing around each of Haywood's hands, which were bleeding badly. The explosion had blown Haywood's fatigue pants and the lower portion of his shirt completely off. He was naked up to his mid-section. He had been peppered with shrapnel all over his body, including his groin.

It was hot and dry as hell out there, and sweat was running down my face as Doc Morrison and I bandaged Haywood's wounds. Haywood didn't say a word as we treated him, but his body began shaking uncontrollably. He was going into shock. I don't believe he realized what had happened to him. Haywood's helmet was nowhere in sight, but I saw his M-16 a couple feet behind him and was amazed when I picked it up. The plastic handgrips attached to the barrel had been completely blown off and the flash suppressor at the end of the rifle barrel had also been ripped off.

Only a land mine could have caused that kind of destruction. Land mines contained enough explosives to destroy or immobilize military vehicles. I was frankly amazed that Haywood was still alive. I looked around the area again, but saw no sign of Haywood's legs, not even one of his boots. I kept giving Haywood words of encouragement, "Hang in there, Glenn. We'll get you out of here soon." That was what I was hoping for anyway.

After double-checking Haywood's bandages, Doc asked if I had seen his glasses. They had fallen off during all the commotion. We both glanced around for his glasses and then Doc said, "There they are," as he pointed over my left shoulder near a bush. Doc stood up and had taken three or four steps, when I heard Lieutenant Foreman forcefully shout, "Stop!"

Doc Morrison froze in place.

Lieutenant Foreman, who was standing behind me, pointed at Doc's feet and said, "Look, Doc, next to your right foot." I looked toward Doc, and my heart pounded when I stood up and saw a metal detonator the size of a silver dollar within an inch of Doc's right foot. Without moving his foot, he bent down to inspect the detonator that was barely visible amongst the grass and leaves covering the ground. It appeared another land mine was buried beneath the ground at Doc's feet. Doc looked at Lieutenant Foremen and calmly said, "Oh!"

Lieutenant Foreman and I looked at Doc Morrison in astonishment. We knew that if he made the wrong move we were all were dead. "Step back slowly, Doc," Lieutenant Foremen said as he turned his head and looked at me as though he was looking for my reassurance that he had given the right direction. I nodded my head and held my breath as Doc slowly lifted his right foot, making sure he didn't jar the detonator. Doc reached to his left and picked up his glasses from the ground and then slowly returned and knelt beside Haywood and breathed a huge sigh of relief.

I gave Doc Morrison a comforting pat on his shoulder and said, "Good job, Doc. Are you ready to get out of here?"

"Yes I am," He firmly replied. He knew he had just narrowly escaped death.

I turned to Lieutenant Foreman and told him I needed two men to help carry Haywood out of there. I wanted to get away from that second land mine that was less than ten feet behind me. Doc then looked at me and said, "Hey, Sarge, your head is bleeding," and pointed to the left side of my head.

I moved my hand along the side of my head and pulled it back. I saw a combination of sweat, dirt and blood. Doc took a quick look and said, "It looks like you took some shrapnel by your ear." He gave me a supportive nod and said, "You'll be OK." Though my ears were still ringing, I hadn't realized I had been hit. I wasn't concerned about myself at that point. I wanted to get Haywood out of there before something worse happened. While we waited briefly for some men to help carry Haywood, I asked Doc if he knew how Spivey was doing.

Doc hesitated a second and said, "I think he's dead." He had seen Doc Snyder working on Spivey on his way up, but he was getting no response. "Damn it," I said, "He's only been here two months." The force of the explosion had killed Spivey instantly and knocked him to the ground, where I had found him.

Carl Seals and Dave Hardy had cautiously walked forward to help carry Haywood. I noticed blood on Carl's fatigue shirt and asked if he was all right. He nodded his head and then leaned toward me and told me that parts of Haywood's legs fell right on him. It was Haywood's blood. Carl was visibly shaken. I put my hand on his shoulder and said, "Take it easy, Carl, you'll be fine."

Lieutenant Foreman then yelled, "They're bringing the medevac right in here."

I said, "No. We don't want to do that! What about that land mine?" as I pointed to the land mine that Lieutenant Foreman was fearlessly keeping watch over.

But it was too late. Someone "popped smoke" and one of the company RTOs was directing the pilot to the front side of the small clearing where we were sitting. I took a deep breath and hoped for the best. Doc and I leaned over Haywood to protect him from the torrent of dirt and debris that flew around as the chopper slowly dropped into the clearing and hovered a couple feet off the ground. The pilot couldn't drop any closer. The rotor blades were already clipping the top of nearby trees.

The medic onboard the chopper handed litters to some men and one litter was brought over near Haywood. Doc Morrison and I carefully lifted Haywood and laid him on the litter. Four of us carefully watched our steps as we carried him to the waiting chopper. There was so much dirt and debris being stirred up by the chopper I could barely keep my eyes open as I lifted the litter to the medic on board, who grabbed it and pulled Haywood onto the chopper. Men were yelling, but the roaring sound of the chopper blades swirling directly above us drowned out all other sounds as Willard Spivey's lifeless body was carried on a litter and placed aboard the chopper.

I then saw a third man being carried toward the chopper on a litter. I hadn't realized until that moment that anyone else had been seriously wounded. It was Larry Sutton, who had joined the Third Herd a few weeks earlier. He looked as if he was in agony. Large blood-soaked dressings covered Sutton's left shoulder and upper arm. After Sutton was loaded aboard, the pilot revved the engine and we all protected our faces from more dirt and debris stirred up when the medevac lifted off. Amazingly, no other booby traps were detonated during the commotion of loading the wounded men.

Dave Hardy had seen the blood on the side of my face and asked me if I was OK. I said, "Yeah, I'm fine. I quickly asked Dave what he knew about Sutton. He said Sutton's left arm was nearly torn off by shrapnel. Dave doubted the doctors would be able to save it. I shook my head in disbelief. We were organizing to pull back when Lieutenant Foreman came up to me and told me the medevac was coming back to pick up Bob Emery and me.

I said, "What for? We can stay out here."

"I know, but the CO wants you two evacuated," 3-6 replied. I'm sure the pilot wasn't too happy to get the call to drop into the Ho Bo Woods again.

We pulled back to another small clearing where the pilot dropped the chopper down long enough for Bob and me to hop aboard. Although Bob and I were willing to stay with the company and have our wounds treated later, we were frankly happy to get the hell out of there. There could easily be more casualties before the company got out of that mess we had walked into.

Bob and I squeezed on board the medevac and I was sitting on the floor with my feet hanging outside the left doorway when the pilot took off. After we were about fifty feet off the ground, the pilot veered to the left to turn south toward Cu Chi. I held on tightly to a metal pole that supported the litters to avoid sliding out of the chopper until the pilot leveled off. I slid a little further inside the chopper when we gained speed. I had survived that day on the ground; I sure didn't want to meet my death by falling out of the chopper.

Medevacs could carry up to six injured men on litters, but they often only carried four litters to give the onboard medic more room to maneuver and care for the wounded. Litters could be laid on the floor or attached to framework that held a litter midway between the floor and ceiling of the chopper. Spivey and Sutton were both lying on the floor. Haywood was suspended above Spivey and the medic on board was in the center of the chopper tending to him.

I leaned over and put my hand on Sutton's right arm and said into his ear, "Hang on, Sutton, we'll be at the hospital in a few minutes."

He nodded his head "yes." He was in a lot of pain from the traumatic wound in his left arm.

The pilot was flying just above treetop level for two reasons. First, Hueys could fly faster at a lower altitude. They could fly almost 100 miles per hour without a load, but with five wounded men and a medic on board, we were probably flying 70 MPH. And second, if there were any enemy troops in our path, we hopefully would fly past them before they could spot us.

The medic focused most of his attention on Haywood while we flew towards Cu Chi, fifteen miles south of the Ho Bo Woods. The medic looked at me once while he tended to Haywood and shrugged his shoulders. I assumed he didn't know if Haywood would make it. I looked at Spivey's body lying uncovered on the litter beside me. He had been a quiet but likeable man that I had just gotten to know. It was difficult to comprehend that he was dead.

I looked out over the countryside while we roared toward Cu Chi and took a moment to absorb the beautiful and peaceful view from the air. But unfortunately, right next to me was the tragic aftermath of what was really happening down there. I looked in the distance to the south and saw the big circular perimeter that surrounded Cu Chi and we were soon flying over the base camp. The pilot slowed the chopper when he neared the 12th Evac, and he glided it onto the landing pad outside the emergency room.

The medical staff rushed up and carried Haywood and Sutton into the emergency room. The litter holding Spivey's body was then lifted from the chopper. Bob Emery and I walked in a solemn procession behind our fallen comrade as he was carried into the hospital. I thought about Spivey's little girl who probably wouldn't understand what happened to her daddy, and his wife, who would soon endure the tragedy of the war in Vietnam by suffering the loss of her faithful husband.

When Bob and I walked into the emergency room carrying our rifles and wearing all of our gear, a corpsman met us and said, "Hey, hold up guys. You can't come in here with all that stuff." Bob and I were so accustomed to carrying our rifles and ammunition we didn't think anything about it. We turned around and left our weapons, ammunition and the rest of our gear in a little storage area surrounded by a wall of sand bags outside the entrance. We then walked back into the emergency room and saw doctors and nurses feverishly working at the examination tables where Haywood and Sutton were lying. I heard Larry Sutton screaming in pain while a corpsman quickly checked Bob's and my injuries and told us to wait in a nearby room until they had cared for our seriously wounded friends.

As we waited, Bob asked, "Why don't they bomb the hell out of the Ho Bo Woods rather then send us out to get blown to pieces?"

"I don't know, Bob. This war makes less sense every day I'm here. Spivey's life was wasted out there today." It was appearing that whole damn war was a waste.

Twenty minutes later Bob and I were taken into an examination room where they treated our wounds. An X-ray revealed a single piece of shrapnel imbedded under the skin just in front of my left ear. A corpsman injected Novocain to numb the area and then he removed a quarter inch jagged piece of shrapnel. The corpsman closed the wound with four stitches and put a small bandage over it. He gave me the shrapnel as my souvenir for being wounded, and then told me to return to the hospital in a week to have the stitches removed. As I was leaving the room, the corpsman said he would initiate the paperwork for my Purple Heart.

I said, "OK, thanks." Until that moment, I hadn't had time to realize I had earned a Purple Heart.

The Purple Heart was initially established by George Washington and was awarded to military personnel who were wounded in action. Unfortunately, Willard Spivey would never see his Purple Heart. It would be presented to his wife someday. I hoped Haywood and Sutton would live to receive their Purple Hearts.

The shrapnel that struck Bob Emery in his left cheek must have glanced off, because they didn't find any shrapnel in his cheek. He also received a few stitches and was soon on his way with a small bandage on his cheek. Sergeant Dave Holt met Bob and me at the 12th Evac. Dave had been in the Third Herd when I first arrived in country and had been rotated to Alpha Company in the rear. He had been notified that the third platoon hit a land mine and came over to see how everyone was doing. Dave told us Haywood and Sutton were still in surgery.

Holt had grabbed our weapons and gear from the storage space outside the emergency room and put everything in the back of his jeep. He drove Bob and I back to our company area on the southwest side of Cu Chi. Bob and I would remain in Cu Chi until our stitches were removed. We checked our rifles in with Tom Powers and then settled in to the little hootch in the company area that would be our home for a few days.

That evening I went to the little club next to our company area with a few of the guys assigned to Alpha Company in rear. Dave Holt bought me a fifteen-cent beer to commemorate my close scrape with death, while I shared the story of what had happened that day in the Ho Bo Woods.

Bob Emery stopped by the club later that night and shared a couple beers with us. There was an unwritten rule that if a man was wounded twice and survived to return to duty, they tried to get him reassigned to safer duty. The rationale was, if someone had been wounded twice and survived, he shouldn't press his luck any further. Bob Emery was now in that category. I told Bob I would talk with Lieutenant Foreman or Captain Dalton to see if they could reassign him. He said, "Oh, don't bother talking with anyone, Hound Dog, I'm happy staying with my friends."

I smiled and put my hand on his shoulder and said, "Bob, think about it. You might not be so lucky next time."

The following morning I walked over to our headquarters building and asked Tom Powers if he had any news concerning Glenn Haywood and Larry Sutton. Tom said Haywood had survived the surgery, but was in critical condition. He wouldn't be allowed visitors for a couple days. I was still amazed Haywood was alive. Sutton's left arm was amputated almost up to his shoulder, but he was in stable condition and would be allowed visitors that afternoon. Tom had also heard the rest of the company made it out of the Ho Bo woods OK. They found more booby traps, but the bunkers were unoccupied.

I asked Tom for my rifle and cleaned it. It was a mess from all the flying dirt and debris the previous day. I also asked Tom about getting a new set of dog tags. We had all had been issued a set of metal dog tags that listed our name, service number, religion and blood type. I had worn mine on a little chain around my neck like everyone else, but had lost them back in September and had never been issued a new set. If you were killed in action, they would take one of your dog tags to record your identity and leave the other one on your body.

Unable to find Bob Emery after lunch, I walked to the hospital by myself to see Larry Sutton. I found him in a recovery ward with a nurse by his bed checking the huge dressing that covered his left shoulder and chest. Sutton smiled when he saw me. I reached out and shook his right hand. It was difficult to know what to say. I had never known a friend who had been so seriously injured. I simply said, "Good to see you, Larry."

He was happy to see me and asked about the other injured men. Larry remembered other men lying on litters on the medevac but didn't know who they were or how badly they had been wounded. I first told him that Bob Emery and I both received minor shrapnel wounds and would be fine. I then said that Willard Spivey had been killed instantly. Sutton was shocked. I went on to say that Haywood lost both of his legs at his knees, but was still alive.

Sutton shook his head in astonishment and said, "Maybe I was the lucky one."

I replied, "No, you weren't lucky. But you're going home alive."

I talked with Sutton for awhile and then shook his hand when I left his bedside. He was evacuated from Vietnam the next day.

On Friday afternoon, December 19th, Bob and I walked to the hospital to visit Glenn Haywood. We had a letter from his parents and one from his girl friend that would, hopefully, lift his spirits. I almost didn't recognize Haywood when I walked up to his bed. He was nearly covered with bandages from his head to the stumps of what had been his legs. Both of his hands were wrapped in huge bandages that looked like white boxing gloves. Just looking at him was painful.

I stood beside his bed and quietly said, "Hey Glenn."

He slowly opened his eyes and turned his head to look at me but didn't utter a word. I said, "How are you doing?" It was a dumb question. He obviously was feeling lousy.

Haywood turned his head toward me and very quietly said, "Just let me die."

Bob and I looked at each other for an instant. I knew Haywood must have been in severe physical pain and emotional shock, having lost both legs, but I didn't expect to hear those words.

Bob put his hand on Haywood's shoulder and said, "Hey, man, don't talk like that. You're going to make it. You'll be back in the world in a few days."

Haywood looked at us with a solemn expression on his face, not saying a word. I told him we had two letters and asked if he wanted us to open them and he could read them, or we could read them to him.

He softly said, "No."

With the combination of pain and drugs, he was in no mood to talk. I told Haywood I would leave the letters on the bedside table and that we would stop back the next day to see him. As we left the ward, I asked a nurse how long he would stay in Cu Chi. She told me Haywood was in too serious condition to travel and would stay there for several days. I then told the nurse what he said about dying. Her reply was, "Oh, a lot of guys talk like that at first. He'll feel better in a few days."

Bob and I were both overcome by what we had seen and heard. We had both seen men seriously wounded in the field, but they were always evacuated to Cu Chi without us seeing the long-term suffering or consequences they endured. Seeing Haywood suffering in pain and then hearing him say, "Just let me die," was something neither Bob nor I were prepared for. Bob was so upset, he didn't know if he could go back to see him again. I had never seen anyone so depressed as Haywood was that day.

Some of the other guys in the rear also visited Haywood during the next couple of days. We all noticed the same thing. He didn't seem to enjoy seeing any of us. In fact, he hadn't read the letters Bob and I had left him or the other letters he had received since then. Haywood appeared to have lost his will to live. I couldn't imagine how difficult it would have been, both physically and emotionally to be in his situation, but I also knew many others had survived similar traumatic injuries and continued on to lead productive lives. I hoped Haywood would give himself that chance.

The following afternoon I learned Captain Dalton had recommended me for a Bronze Star medal for staying with Haywood until he was evacuated, and for my leaving myself exposed to the land mine and potential enemy fire. I thought I had simply done what was expected of me by helping a comrade who had been seriously wounded. I wasn't in Vietnam to earn medals but I had earned a Purple Heart and Bronze Star on December 17th.

Bob Emery and Lieutenant Kevin Higginson had also been recommended for the Bronze Star. Bob had immediately gone to the aid of Spivey. Unfortunately, it was too late. Bob and Lieutenant Higginson then organized the men to protect Haywood and me and kept everything under control while leaving themselves exposed to the second land mine and other booby traps.

It normally took several weeks to process the recommendation for a medal through Army channels. But they were trying a new process of presenting medals within days of when the action occurred. The official orders would be processed later. The next morning I shaved and found a clean pair of fatigues to make myself presentable for the one-star General who would arrive that afternoon to present the medals. A group of men from Alpha Company gathered in formation in our company area awaiting the general's arrival.

While we waited, Lieutenant Higginson told me what happened

after I was flown out on the 17th. Captain Dalton reorganized the company and they cautiously moved forward and swept through the enemy bunkers, but the NVA were gone. When they neared the bunkers, one of the men from the second platoon found a booby-trapped 105MM artillery round at his feet. It must have been wired to be command detonated from a bunker because it didn't go off. Lieutenant Higginson said they finally pulled back and called in an air strike and blew the hell out of the area before they flew back to Patton late that afternoon.

A few minutes later a jeep pulled up. It was the general. We were called to attention as he walked toward our formation. The ceremony began with the general standing in front of me while my citation was read as follows:

> "For heroism in connection with military operations against a hostile force: Sergeant Richard Hogue distinguished himself by his heroic actions on 17 December 1969, while serving with Company A, 2nd Battalion, 14th Infantry in the Republic of Vietnam. While conducting reconnaissance operations Sergeant Hogue went to the aid of a seriously wounded comrade and exposed himself to potential enemy fire and detonation from a land mine found near him. Despite being wounded, Sergeant Hogue ignored his personal safety and welfare and continued to aid and comfort his wounded comrade until he was safely evacuated from the area. Sergeant Hogue's valorous actions contributed immeasurably to the safe evacuation of the injured comrade. Sergeant Hogue's bravery and devotion to duty are in keeping with the highest traditions of the military services and reflect great credit upon himself, his unit, the 25th Infantry Division and the United States Army."

The general said, "Congratulations, Sergeant Hogue," and pinned the Bronze Star on my fatigue shirt. We shook hands and exchanged salutes. The general moved to Bob Emery and Lieutenant Higginson and awarded each of them their Bronze Star. The general gave us a brief pep talk, telling us how grateful he was for our willingness to serve our country and thanked us for doing a great job. He then walked to his jeep and rode off down the road. The guys who were there shook our hands to congratulate us and took a few pictures.

Rick Shields returned from a week of R & R in Hawaii with his wife on December 22nd. Rick quietly listened as I told him what had happened to us on the 17th. Rick thought we should chip in to buy Haywood a Christmas present. Haywood's watch had been blown off his arm by the land mine, so we decided to get him a new one and give it to him on Christmas Day. Several of us chipped in and Rick bought a watch at the PX. Although I had found a tough way to spend time in the rear, it was going to have a surprise fringe benefit. The Bob Hope Christmas show would perform in Cu Chi on December 23rd. I was scheduled to have my stitches taken out on the 24th; therefore, I would be in Cu Chi to see the show.

On December 23rd Rick and I visited Haywood before we went to the Bob Hope show. We talked with a nurse before we saw Haywood. She said he had developed pneumonia. She was also concerned about his emotional state. She said he had finally read a couple of the letters from his family and girl friend, but the other letters remained unopened. The nurse said Haywood had told her he would rather die than go home without legs.

Rick and I walked in to see Haywood and tried to give him positive encouragement, but he wasn't very receptive. The medications they were giving him kept him pretty drowsy. He could barely keep his eyes open. Rick and I stayed only a few minutes. I put my hand on Haywood's shoulder as we left and told him I would visit him in a couple days.

When Rick and I walked outside the hospital, choppers were flying in men from the field for the Bob Hope show. I had never seen so many men in Cu Chi. Many of them were still wearing dirty fatigues and muddy boots and had several days' growth of whiskers while they walked around the base camp before the show. They had flown in half the men from Alpha Company. Rick and I joined the guys from the Third Herd to see the show.

Before the show started, I talked with Jim Overbey regarding December 17th. Jim said he helped a medic bandage Larry Sutton's arm that was just hanging on by shreds of muscle and skin. After seeing several other guys in the Third Herd being wounded, Jim was getting worried about being nailed himself.

A large stage with Christmas decorations had been built and several thousand empty wooden ammunition crates were laid in rows to be used as seats. There were trucks, tanks, and APCs parked nearby with guys sitting all over them. There were several thousand men, and a few women, sitting or standing anywhere they could to watch the show. Santa Claus (Chaplain Wideman) walked around wishing everyone a "Merry Christmas" while playing Christmas songs on a tape player.

The show began at noon with a huge cheer when Bob Hope walked on stage and began telling his one-liners about the military and all of us serving in Vietnam. A large orchestra played while a line of good-looking girls danced and sang to the whistles and cheers of the thousands of GIs. When Ann-Margret walked on stage wearing a bright red dress, she drew a standing ovation from those of us who had quickly forgotten about the war and were enjoying our brief escape from fighting in the rice paddies and jungles. Hospital patients sat near the stage and two of them joined Ann-Margret on stage in their blue hospital pajamas to dance and sing a song along with her. It was a great show that ended way too soon. I had seen Bob Hope's Christmas shows on television many times, but it was a hundred times better being there in person. I took over a dozen pictures and shot some 8MM movies to have a lasting memory of two of the best hours of my tour in Vietnam.

It was a madhouse after the show as guys scattered in every direction. Most of the men who had been flown in from the field had to return. I waved good-bye to the guys from the Third Herd when they headed for the chopper pad and told them I would see them in a few days.

The next day was Christmas Eve. I didn't visit Haywood. I planned to wait until Christmas Day and join some of the other men to give him the watch. I visited the outpatient clinic that morning where a corpsman removed my stitches. A doctor gave me a clean bill of health and sent me on my way.

It was a hot and quiet afternoon when I walked into our little hootch and found no one there. I sat down at a small table inside and thought about my family and friends back home. They all knew I was in the field most of the time, but I hadn't told most of them about the men in the Third Herd who had been wounded or killed. After my close call in the Ho Bo Woods, I thought I should tell someone back in Schaller, Iowa what I was really experiencing in case I didn't survive. I wrote a letter to Reverend Guy Nusbaum, the minister of our

Presbyterian church. He had served in the Navy during World War II. I thought he would understand what I was going through.

The letter follows:

December 24, 1969

Dear Reverend Nusbaum,

I am writing this letter to provide some details about my tour of duty in Vietnam that I have not shared with my family. Only a few college friends know any of these details so I request you keep this letter in confidence. Should I not survive my tour in Vietnam you may then share this letter with my family.

I have been serving in an infantry platoon since August. We have experienced firefights with the enemy, have received incoming mortar fire at firebases and have encountered several booby traps. Several men in my Company have been wounded during that time and three men in my platoon have been killed.

Today I am in Cu Chi, our Division Base Camp. I received a minor shrapnel wound when a land mine detonated near me on December 17th. I am fine, but one man was killed; one man lost his arm and one man remains in critical condition having lost both legs.

Things seem to be getting worse since the monsoon season ended. We are seeing more enemy action and encountering more booby traps.

Although I am concerned about my fate and there is certainly the possibility I could be killed on any given day, I try to keep a positive outlook. My fellow platoon members and I accept our daily challenges and have learned to deal with our losses.

This is obviously the most frightening and dangerous experience of my life. I ask for your thoughts and prayers for my safety while I am in Vietnam.

Sincerely,
Dick Hogue

Being so far away from home on Christmas Eve and writing that letter to Reverend Nusbaum put me in a somber mood on a day that should have been happy and cheerful. I mailed the letter and then joined several guys who had begun a Christmas Eve celebration at the club. It was a little difficult to get into the Christmas spirit. There weren't many Christmas decorations or lights around and the weather was hot and humid. There definitely wouldn't be a "white" Christmas in Vietnam, but fortunately I was in the rear and wouldn't have to pull guard or go out on an ambush on Christmas Eve.

That evening some of us went to the Special Services Club, where we sang Christmas songs and enjoyed Christmas goodies. When we returned to the company area, one of the guys found a dozen flares near the headquarters building. The flares were foot-long silver metal tubes with a cap on one end. You pulled the cap off the top which had a firing pin built into it, placed the cap over the bottom end, and then hit the bottom of the flare on something solid to fire the colored flare 100 feet into the air. We used them in the field to identify our location to other friendly troops.

Whitey, who had stayed in the rear after the Bob Hope show to see a doctor concerning a case of gout, a couple other guys and I fired the flares from the road in front of our hootch and celebrated Christmas Eve by lighting up the sky in red and green.

After we fired the last flare Tom Powers walked up to me. Tom put his hand on my shoulder and said, "I hate to deliver bad news on Christmas Eve, but Haywood died."

Tom had been in the headquarters building when a nurse from the 12th Evac called. She said that Haywood died from pneumonia an hour earlier. Our Christmas Eve celebration turned to silence. I looked at Whitey who was shaking his head in disbelief.

Rick Shields then walked up to the group. I told him about Haywood. We put an arm on each other's shoulder and stood there for a moment in silence. Hearing that Haywood had died was a shock, but it wasn't a total surprise. I had hoped reading the letters from his family and the visits by me and other men would help him pull through his ordeal. But that wasn't to be. Christmas Eve suddenly became another sad evening of my tour in Vietnam.

Some of the men who had joined the little group on the road didn't know Haywood personally, but they each extended their condolences.

Someone asked what kind of man Haywood had been in the field. I said he was a good man and didn't cause any problems. I went on to tell a funny story concerning him.

We were on a RIF and had stopped to take a break one afternoon. We told Haywood to walk up to a small rise to our north and watch over the countryside to prevent anyone from sneaking up on us. All of a sudden he stood up and began trotting back toward the rest of us while turning sideways and holding his arm out and firing his M-16 behind him with one hand. We thought he looked like John Wayne running and firing his rifle with one hand. Haywood said he opened fire when he saw someone moving through a hedgerow. We moved up the hill and searched the area, but didn't have any enemy contact. Haywood had scared off whoever had been out there with his initial gunfire. He earned the nickname "John Wayne" that day.

We all chuckled after I told the story. It helped ease the pain of losing another friend. Some of the guys were going to the club, but I wasn't in the mood. I walked toward the hootch by myself and stood outside to enjoy a little peace and quiet. I felt bad that I hadn't visited Haywood on Christmas Eve. I looked skyward and saw stars shining and kept hearing Tom Powers' words, "Haywood died," over and over in my head. The good Lord had taken control of Glenn Haywood's destiny. I crawled in my bunk and fell asleep.

I slept in on Christmas morning, along with most of the other guys who had partied at the club well into the morning. I passed on breakfast to save room for a big dinner at the mess hall. I had gotten some Christmas cards from my family and friends, but I had told them not to send any presents. I didn't need anything. My mom had sent me some of the homemade peanut brittle she always made during the holidays. It was great stuff that disappeared instantly when I shared with some of the guys.

Jan Griffin had thoughtfully sent me a bottle of whiskey. Unfortunately, when it arrived a couple days before Christmas, all I received was a soggy package with a broken bottle of Seagram 7 inside. I also received a letter from her. Jan apologized for not writing regularly. She had been busy studying for final exams and working extra training hours in the hospital during the past month. It was comforting to read Jan's letter.

I didn't think too much about Haywood until I thought of the

217

watch we had bought for him as a Christmas present. We hoped it would make Christmas a little more joyful for Haywood. I walked to the PX with Rick later on Christmas morning to return the watch.

Bob Emery and Whitey joined Rick and me for Christmas dinner in the mess hall early that afternoon. Rick talked about missing his wife and family back in California. Bob said his family was gathered at his mom's house in Marine City, Michigan. Whitey had a big family which was gathering at his brother's house. My mom said in a recent letter that my two sisters were spending Christmas with my folks in Schaller. The Christmas dinner was great, not exactly like Mom's home cooking, but pretty good for Army food in Vietnam.

With our wounds healed, Bob and I were scheduled to return to the field the day after Christmas. Whitey had been given medication for his gout and planned to go back out with us. Rick had been reassigned to the rear and was staying in Cu Chi. After the Christmas dinner I organized my gear, preparing to return to the field.

Late Christmas afternoon I returned to our hootch in the company area and met Sergeant Richard Benson. He was a new shake'n bake who had just been assigned to Alpha Company. After I told Sergeant Benson about some of my experiences in the field, he was full of questions. We drank a couple of beers at the club that evening while I continued to answer his steady stream of questions about serving as an infantryman in Vietnam. Richard Benson was a likable guy, and it appeared he would be a quick learner once he arrived in the field.

During the early afternoon of December 26, 1969, Bob Emery, Whitey and I left the comforts of Cu Chi on a convoy and returned to Firebase Patton.

➤ Private First Class Willard Spivey was from Franklin, KY. He was twenty years old. He arrived in Vietnam on October 13, 1969. Willard was killed instantly by a land mine explosion on December 17, 1969. He was married and had a daughter.

➤ Private First Class Glennon Haywood was from Monroe, LA. He was twenty-one years old. He arrived in Vietnam on September 1, 1969. Glenn was seriously wounded by a land mine explosion on December 17, 1969. He survived his initial injuries but died in Cu Chi on Christmas Eve, 1969.

An estimated 8.7 million Americans served in the armed forces during the Vietnam War. Approximately 2.8 million of them served in Vietnam, but less than 300,000 faced combat as infantrymen.

Sergeant Richard Hogue standing in a bomb crater during
the dry season.

Chapter 15

I Thought You Were Dead

After arriving back at Patton, Bob Emery, Whitey and I walked along the perimeter road until we saw familiar faces and were greeted by the guys in the Third Herd. I had seen some of the guys when they were in Cu Chi for the Bob Hope show, but I hadn't seen the rest of the men since I had been flown out of the Ho Bo Woods on December 17th. It was good to see them again. We were told the company had been given the day off to get ready for a special mission the following morning called a "bushmaster."

Unfortunately, my friendly welcome back to the platoon was over-shadowed by the sadness of losing Willard Spivey and then Glenn Haywood. The men at Patton had received the news about Haywood the previous morning, Christmas Day. I told some of the guys how very depressed Haywood was in the hospital. I shared my opinion that he lost his will to live.

Lieutenant Foreman came up and welcomed Bob and me back with a smile and handshake. I thanked him for having a good eye on the 17th and spotting the second land mine. We both felt lucky to have survived that day. I then asked what the bushmaster was all about. Lieutenant Foreman said, "Let's get Sergeant Overbey over here. I'll go over the plan with you guys."

Lieutenant Foreman and Jim Overbey had been running the platoon while Bob and I were gone. With Bob Emery and me back, Jim would continue as platoon sergeant having had a week's seniority in country over me. Bob would be the second squad leader and I would continue to lead the first squad.

Lieutenant Foreman began his briefing by saying that we would be flown the following morning to an abandoned hard spot in the middle of the Ho Bo Woods where we would set up a defensive perimeter and dig in to stay for two or three days. Jim Overbey and I looked at each other without saying a word. We both knew this wouldn't be good.

The entire company, including our mortar platoon, would be

going. They would fly out concertina wire, sand bags and whatever else we would need to fortify the position. One platoon would set up an ambush while the rest of the company remained inside the perimeter each night. It sounded like a pretty lousy idea to me. I asked, "Who came up with this bushmaster idea?"

Lieutenant Foreman explained that enemy activity in the Ho Bo Woods continued to increase. The brass in Cu Chi wanted a company to set up what they termed a bushmaster in the hopes of catching the VC off guard when they were moving at night. Colonel Crutchley (our battalion commander) came to Captain Dalton with this new plan and the CO volunteered us to be the first company to set one up. "Maybe you can ask the CO to volunteer another company," I said jokingly. We all chuckled for a second, but none of us liked what we had been volunteered to do.

Lieutenant Foreman replied, "I don't like this new idea either, but the decision has been made. We better get ready."

Lieutenant Foreman asked me to stay with him for a minute as Bob and Jim got up to walk away. He had talked with the CO about reassigning Bob Emery. The CO offered to move Bob to the mortar platoon because they normally didn't go out on RIFs. I said, "That's great. I'll tell Bob." I walked to the next bunker and told Bob he could move to the mortar platoon since he had been wounded twice.

Bob thought for a brief moment and then said, "No, thanks, Hound Dog. Like I told you back in Cu Chi, I'd rather stay here with my friends."

I said, "Are you sure? It's a lot safer in the mortar platoon." Bob said he was sure and wanted to stay. When I told Lieutenant Foreman that Bob wanted to stay with us, he said that was fine with him. He would pass the word back to the CO. I was frankly glad to have Bob stay with us. Bob was only eighteen years old, but he was a reliable man. I also admired his courage. First he had volunteered to come to Vietnam from non-combat duty in Germany, and then he declined a transfer to safer duty in the mortar platoon. I hoped he wouldn't regret his decision.

Four new men had been assigned to the platoon while I was in Cu Chi. Three FNGs: Allan Rader, Otis Carthage and Roger Cox, and Randal Collins, who had been reassigned from the first platoon just before Christmas. I introduced myself and welcomed the new men to the platoon. I would get to know them better in the next few days. I then gathered my squad together and gave them the details regarding the bushmaster. The first response was from Ed Leberski, "Oh, bull shit, Sarge."

Some of the other guys chimed in and said, "Yeah, you're kidding."

I smiled for an instant and then seriously said, "No, this is for real." Everyone was quiet.

I told the men to double check their gear, load up extra ammunition and make sure their weapons were clean. I wasn't sure how long we would be gone, but I said to plan for three days and to take their claymores and poncho liners. I told the new guys that I would be around later to make sure they had everything they needed.

Jim Overbey and I sat down later and talked for a while. He told me the third platoon was leading a RIF the day before Christmas when they ran into six VC in a tunnel complex. Jim said Hue (our Chieu Hoi) yelled for them to surrender but the VC refused and returned fire. After a short firefight and then throwing several hand grenades down the tunnel, all six VC were killed. Fortunately, the Third Herd survived the day without a single casualty.

Jim was also very concerned about taking so many FNGs out on the bushmaster. We had nine men who had been in the field for less than a month. Jim looked at me and said, "They can get you and me killed, you know." Jim and I had learned a lot during our few months in the field and, we knew the Ho Bo Woods was the most hazardous place they could send us. Although we had to accept each new assignment, the stress of combat and seeing friends wounded and killed had taken an emotional toll on all of us. I had never seen Jim so worried before. Maybe it was becoming too much for him. John Potts had "lost it" after his first and only firefight, and the stress had gotten to Dennis Schultz a couple weeks earlier. It was amazing that the constant combat exposure didn't crack more of us.

After a peaceful night at Patton, I got up early the next morning, December 27, 1969, and wrote Jan a quick letter. I doubted I would have a lot of spare time the next few days to write. I dropped the letter in the mailbox at Patton and headed to the mess hall for breakfast. As I finished my breakfast Doc Snyder walked up and told me that Whitey's gout was still bothering him. I asked Doc if he should go back to Cu Chi.

223

"No, I don't think so." Doc said. "He's taking his medication, but it's not clearing up very fast." We found Whitey standing outside his bunker and I asked him if he felt well enough to go out with us. Without hesitation Whitey said he felt well enough to go. Doc Snyder nodded his head indicating that was fine with him.

I said, "OK, Whitey, grab your gear."

I joined the men who were reluctantly gathered on the LZ on the east side of Firebase Patton shortly before ten o'clock that morning, just as I had done dozens of times before. I saw Chuck Merritt sitting on the ground and walked over to talk with him while we waited. Chuck had become our new radio/telephone operator (RTO) after Schultz went to the rear. Chuck was from Runnells, Iowa, a small town southeast of Des Moines. We talked about the snow and cold winter weather back in Iowa and chuckled while we enjoyed the warm, sunny December morning on the LZ. Chuck was normally a quiet guy who kept to himself a lot. He was the only man in the platoon who regularly read his Bible.

After relaxing on the LZ for half an hour, we finally heard the choppers coming from the south. Someone popped smoke for the lead chopper and we aligned ourselves to board. We flew northeast from Patton into clear skies and bright sunshine. I expected hot and dry weather while we were out in the Woods. It had rarely rained during the past month.

Once aboard, I relaxed on the floor of the chopper. Those flights became a brief escape from the realities of the war far below. The noise from the engine and rotor blades drowned out all other sounds, and the vibrations from the swirling blades were relaxing as we flew several hundred feet above the ground. I enjoyed what beauty remained of the countryside that was scarred from years of exploding bombs and artillery shells and decimated by Agent Orange. As we flew toward the Ho Bo Woods, I looked at the other men who were quietly enjoying the peaceful ride. Although all was quiet at the moment, I knew the dangers that lay ahead of us. I hoped we all would safely return to Firebase Patton.

We flew around for half an hour while Captain Dalton in the lead chopper scouted out the area. We were finally dropped off in the middle of the Ho Bo Woods. After the last lift of choppers arrived, we walked a short distance and then the CO said, "This is it men."

224

To our surprise we weren't at the abandoned hard spot, but the CO told the platoon leaders that was where he wanted to set up the bushmaster. The first thing we did was cautiously sweep the area checking for booby traps. We found none. Captain Dalton and the platoon leaders lined out a circular perimeter roughly 150 feet in diameter. The first and third platoons then identified individual positions to dig foxholes and assigned four or five men to each position. The second platoon would set up an ambush a few hundred meters outside the perimeter that night.

The foxholes were spaced about twenty feet apart to maintain visibility between each position after dark and to minimize the possibility of the VC sneaking in between any two foxholes. We then began the laborious task of digging foxholes and filling sand bags to build a wall of protection in front of each foxhole. Our mortar platoon set up 81MM mortar tubes near the center of the site. If necessary, they could initiate return mortar fire much faster than calling in artillery support from miles away. The CO also established his command post in the center of the site.

We stationed six men around the perimeter to stand guard while everyone else dug in. If there were any VC out there, and there were, they easily could have seen or heard the choppers flying in to drop off supplies and equipment after we arrived. If they were looking for action, they would be headed our way. The tall grass, bushes and small trees limited our visibility in every direction around the perimeter. Some of the men spent most of their time chopping down bushes and clearing as much vegetation as possible to improve our visibility.

I positioned my squad along the part of southern and southwest perimeter. Robert Draughn, Dave Hardy, Carlton Quick and I took a position near the center of the southern perimeter. We placed an M-60 at our foxhole to cover most of the south side with machine-gun fire. Bob Emery's squad was positioned to cover the northwest and part of the northern perimeter, along with Lieutenant Foreman. Jim Overbey joined three other men in a foxhole on the western perimeter. There was a huge pile of sand bags, rolls of chain link wire, coils of concertina wire, steel posts and tools in the center of the compound. The men took whatever they needed to set up each position.

Bushmaster Site - December 27, 1969

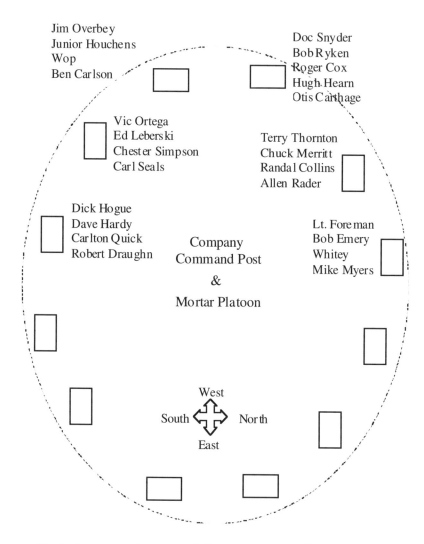

Jim Overbey
Junior Houchens
Wop
Ben Carlson

Doc Snyder
Bob Ryken
Roger Cox
Hugh Hearn
Otis Carthage

Vic Ortega
Ed Leberski
Chester Simpson
Carl Seals

Terry Thornton
Chuck Merritt
Randal Collins
Allen Rader

Dick Hogue
Dave Hardy
Carlton Quick
Robert Draughn

Lt. Foreman
Bob Emery
Whitey
Mike Myers

Company
Command Post
&
Mortar Platoon

West

South ◁▷ North

East

Foxholes were dug around the perimeter and the site was surrounded by concertina wire. First platoon manned the foxholes on
the southeast and northeast perimeter.

Choppers arrived periodically, bringing in more equipment, C-rations and water. We pounded steel posts into the ground and attached the chain link wire to form an eight-foot-high wire wall of protection from incoming rockets or grenades in front of each foxhole. When we began stretching the coils of concertina wire around the perimeter, we found a problem. There wasn't enough wire.

I told Lieutenant Foreman that we needed more concertina wire. With the wire we had we would have to stretch it too tight to surround the entire site. I said, "If we don't get more wire, we're going to end up with a half-assed perimeter." Lieutenant Foreman came by a short while later to tell me that the CO had requested more concertina wire, but it wouldn't be delivered until the following morning.

I said, "Tomorrow? We need it today!"

The multiple rows of concertina wire surrounding our firebases and patrol bases allowed only a few inches between the coils of wire and made it nearly impossible for anyone to crawl through without getting tangled in the wire. Unfortunately, we had to settle for one row of concertina wire that was stretched so tight there were spaces more than a foot wide between many of the coils. As I had told Lieutenant Foreman, it was a half-assed defensive perimeter.

Fortunately, they had delivered trip flares that we could set out in front of us, along with a huge supply of claymore mines. If the NVA or VC tried to sneak through the concertina wire, they would hopefully trip a flare. The NVA and VC used what were called sappers to sneak into an American position and inflict as many casualties as they could. It was normally a suicide mission for a sapper, like the Japanese "kamikaze" pilots diving their planes into American war ships during World War II.

By late afternoon we were all hot, sweaty and dirty from working our butts off in the heat and humidity to clear the vegetation, dig foxholes and fill hundreds of sandbags. Finally, each position had a two-foot high sandbag wall that curved around the front side of each two-foot-deep foxhole.

Jim Overbey and I took a short break while we looked over the site Captain Dalton had chosen. Jim said he had talked with the CO about moving to the hard spot before we started setting up, but he wanted to stay right where we were. Captain Dalton believed the NVA and VC surely knew about the hard spot, he hoped to surprise them by setting up elsewhere. I agreed with Jim that it was a lousy site, but we had a lot of firepower. I said, "It'll take a lot of gooks with lots of guts to come after us."

"Yeah, maybe so," Jim said, "but I can't wait to get out of here."

We put additional men on guard as the afternoon passed. There hadn't been any sign of enemy activity, but each chopper that arrived with supplies and equipment helped pinpoint our location. The last chopper arriving that afternoon dropped off a Night Pack containing a supply of M-16 and M-60 ammunition, mortar rounds, claymore mines and hand grenades. Although we had a lot of firepower, my biggest concern was that if the NVA or VC happened to have a mortar tube out there, they could tear us up with a few well-placed mortar rounds. We didn't have any bunkers to scurry into for protection. Our final defensive measure was to set out several claymore mines in front of each foxhole and run the electric wires back to the detonators.

Jim Overbey and I walked around to double check the third platoon's positions. The more I looked over the perimeter the more I didn't like it. At best we could not see more than twenty-five meters in any direction. And when it was dark, we wouldn't be able to see much of anything. Finally, Jim and I decided there was nothing more we could do and we began walking to our separate foxholes. I took a couple steps and stopped. I turned to Jim and asked, "Hey Jim, I haven't seen Hue. Did he show up this morning?

"No," Jim replied, "he disappeared early this morning."

I didn't say anything. We both knew Hue didn't want any part of that bushmaster. I walked back to my foxhole and opened a can of spaghetti and meatballs for a quick dinner. Unexpectedly, I heard the rumbling sound of our .50-caliber machine gun firing from the northeast perimeter. I threw my half eaten can of spaghetti on the ground, grabbed my M-16 and jumped inside our foxhole. We all looked out over the perimeter with our weapons ready, but saw nothing. The firing soon stopped, and someone yelled, "That was just a test fire."

The men in the mortar platoon had decided to test fire the "50" and had scared the hell out of everyone for nothing. I said to the guys in my foxhole, "What the hell are those guys doing? They just told Charlie where our '50' was." It wasn't a smart move.

When the sun started to set in the western sky I walked over to talk with Lieutenant Foremen. On my way, I saw Lieutenant Higginson and his second platoon leaving to set up their ambush.

When I reached the northern perimeter, I knelt down by Lieutenant Foreman who was sitting on the ground with his feet in his foxhole. There was even less visibility on the northern perimeter than we had along the southern perimeter. I told Lieutenant Foreman to make sure his men used a starlight scope. I knew after dark none of us would be able to see much without one. Lieutenant Foreman shared his foxhole with Mike Myers, Bob Emery and Whitey. I asked Whitey how he was doing. He said he was feeling better.

I said, "Great. I'll see you guys in the morning," and gave Bob a pat on the back.

I walked to the next foxhole where Terry Thornton, Chuck Merritt, Randal Collins and Allen Rader were settled in and told them I would see them in the morning. I continued to move along and talk briefly with the men in other foxholes to make sure they were prepared for what I expected to be a long night.

Quick had the M-60 resting on top of our sand bag wall. We could easily spray the area in front of our position and most of the southern perimeter if we needed to. We had over 3,000 rounds of M-60 ammunition laid out and ready to fire. Robert Draughn and I had our ammunition magazines laid out in bandoleers beside the foxhole, and over a dozen hand grenades lay behind us. It would soon be getting dark. We would shortly settle in and wait to see what would happen.

Unfortunately, I had a personal problem to deal with before it was completely dark. I had felt a case of diarrhea coming on during the afternoon. I didn't think I would make it through the night without making a "mother nature" call. I told the guys I was going to walk toward the concertina wire to take a quick dump. I picked up a shovel lying next to our foxhole to dig a little hole to bury my "duty." I had grabbed a packet of toilet paper from a case of C-rations and was prepared for my personal mission.

I also told the men in the foxhole to our left that I was walking forward in between our foxholes. I quickly dug a small hole amongst the grass, dropped my pants and squatted down with my backside facing outward toward the perimeter. I had been squatted down for only a few seconds when a loud "BOOM!" sounded behind me and my bare butt stung as something hit it. Instinctively, I fell belly first on the ground. Without hesitating I began low-crawling towards our foxhole with my fatigue pants down around my knees, while the men from the foxholes on either side of me opened fire over my head. Dave Hardy looked at me after I dove into our foxhole and asked, "Are you OK?"

I hesitated an instant and then said, "I think so." I really wasn't sure at that moment.

My heart was pounding, and I took a deep breath while I tried to figure out what happened to me. I quickly rubbed one hand over the cheeks of my butt. I felt no pain and saw no blood. I pulled my pants up while Quick sprayed M-60 rounds across the area in front of us.

I then heard "Cease fire! Cease fire!" I tapped Quick on his shoulder and motioned to stop firing. There were no other explosions after the one that had peppered me. I looked at the foxholes on each side of us. They both gave a "thumbs-up" that they were OK. Captain Dalton sent Tom Arcter, one of his RTOs, over to our foxhole to learn what happened. Tom knelt by me and said, "What the hell happened, Hound Dog?"

I explained that I had walked between our foxholes to take a dump and a gook must have thrown a hand grenade at me. I told Tom I was all right. Tom said he would brief the CO and then smiled and added, "I hope he believes me." Tom quickly walked back to the command post.

Fortunately for me, the enemy soldier's throw was too short. I was hit only by dirt and debris blown toward me by the exploding grenade. A little longer toss, and I might have been dead. "Damn," I thought. "It was my first day back in the field, and a gook already tried to kill me."

I then realized my case of diarrhea had disappeared. As the saying goes, that exploding grenade must have literally scared the shit right out of me. After things quieted down again, the guys in the foxhole chuckled as they told me I looked really funny crawling back to the foxhole with my pants down around my knees. I'm sure I did, but I wasn't going to stop to pull them up. I expected more grenades.

Although I had survived my little excursion, we definitely knew there were enemy troops close by. They probably worked their way toward us that afternoon and were waiting for the cover of darkness to make a move. It remained quiet for several hours after dark while we pulled guard with two men awake at each foxhole. I had finished an hour on guard and was wrapped up in my poncho liner sleeping behind our foxhole when it sounded like all hell was breaking loose on our northern perimeter.

It started with two large explosions followed with repeated blasts and gunfire. I grabbed my helmet and rifle and joined the three other men in our foxhole. We weren't taking any direct enemy fire but explosions and gunfire continued on the north and west perimeters. Gunfire then began erupting from several other positions. I then heard several claymores being fired. I didn't know for sure what was happening, but as a precaution I yelled, "Quick, open fire with the '60'!"

Hardy fed the string of rounds into the M-60, and orange tracers glowed in the dark while Quick sprayed hundreds of rounds back and forth along the southern perimeter. Draughn fired two of our claymores, and we both threw several hand grenades into the darkness in front of our foxhole in case enemy sappers were trying to work their way in.

The entire bushmaster had erupted with rifle and machine gun fire. Hand grenades were flying out from every foxhole. The continuous rifle and machine fire, combined with the hand grenade and claymore mine explosions, was as loud as I had ever heard. The flurry of action was so overwhelming I couldn't tell if it was friendly fire or enemy fire directed back at us. I only knew that the four of us in my foxhole were uninjured. If there were enemy troops outside the perimeter, they would have to be damned lucky to survive the barrage of firepower we were unleashing. Robert Draughn nervously yelled, "You guys see anything out there?"

I yelled, "No, keep firing!" I couldn't see anything to the left side of our foxhole, but I sprayed several magazines of ammunition from my M-16 into the darkness anyway. I could hear the "pops" as the mortar platoon began firing outgoing rounds and could hear the explosions when they landed a short distance outside the perimeter.

After several minutes we heard, "Cease fire! Cease fire!" coming from the command post.

Captain Dalton wanted everyone to stop firing so that he could determine exactly what had happened and what we should do next. Something had obviously initiated the action on the northern perimeter, but those of us on the south side still had no idea what had occurred. When the firing eventually stopped, Quick, Hardy, Draughn and I huddled in our foxhole. The barrel of Quick's machine gun spewed off white smoke as he poured silicone oil on it to cool it down. I scanned over the southern perimeter with our starlight scope, looking for any movement, but I saw nothing.

I then heard shouts for help and screams of extreme pain along the north and western perimeter. Someone yelled, "We need a medic over here, Doc Snyder is hit." Doc Snyder was the third platoon's medic. I could hear the voices of other men who were aiding the wounded and trying to gain control of the situation. I hesitated briefly and then told the guys in my foxhole that I was going over to help.

I stepped from the rear of our foxhole and had only taken a couple steps when someone from the CP group yelled, "Don't anyone move! There's a live gook inside the wire!"

I immediately stopped and hit the ground. I looked around while I slowly crawled back to our foxhole. Robert Draughn and I watched inward from the foxhole with our fingers on the triggers of our M-16s, while Quick and Hardy watched outward along the perimeter. Although I was ready to fire at any movement, I also had to be careful not to shoot any of our own men. Sitting in our foxhole was helplessly frustrating. Men were still screaming in pain, but I couldn't go help them. We had to find that gook!

A minute later the bright light from a trip flare lit up the eastern perimeter. Immediately, there was machine gun and rifle fire, claymore mines detonated and hand grenades were thrown in the direction of the flare. I guessed the enemy soldier who had been inside the wire had somehow made it to the perimeter and tripped a flare trying to escape. Robert Draughn yelled, "I hope they killed the son-of-a-bitch." The firing along the eastern perimeter soon stopped. It was again relatively quiet.

Word then came from the command post that sappers attacked the northern perimeter. We were to search the area around our foxholes to be sure there weren't other sappers still alive inside the perimeter. I told Robert Draughn to keep a watch over me while I searched the area around our foxhole.

I slowly moved from our foxhole in a low crouch toward my right with my left index finger on the trigger of my M-16. I soon met up with a man from the first platoon who had been in the foxhole to our east. We both shook our heads, indicating we hadn't seen anything. When I circled to my left and toward the CP group, I ran into Sam Ryan from the mortar platoon. We knelt down for a moment, and I asked, "What the hell happened?"

He told me sappers sneaked through the northern perimeter and threw satchel charges and hand grenades into several foxholes. Ryan then said, "You've lost several men, Hound Dog. I think 3-6 and the guys in his foxhole are gone."

"Son-of-a-bitch!" I said in frustration, "Who else?"

"I don't know. But there're a lot of guys down."

I asked if they needed more help on the north side. Ryan said no. The CO wanted us to stay in place in case they launched an attack on the southern perimeter. He said men from the CP group and the mortar platoon were treating the injured men and were standing guard along the northern perimeter where the third platoon had suffered heavy casualties.

I circled around to my left and met Vic Ortega who had been in the foxhole to my right. I quickly told him what I knew and then moved back to my foxhole without seeing anything. I told the guys that sappers had gotten through the northern perimeter and hit some of the third platoon's positions. I said, "3-6 and the guys in his foxhole may be dead." Hardy, Quick and Draughn were silent.

I looked at my watch. It was 12:30 a.m., December 28, 1969. Although it remained quiet along the southern and eastern perimeter, every man held his weapon ready while watching in the darkness for any signs of movement. I sat in the relative silence and thought about who was in the foxhole with Lieutenant Foreman – Bob Emery, Whitey and Mike Myers.

"No, not those guys," I said to myself. I wondered how many of the men I had spoken with before darkness were still alive.

After a short while I heard the sound of choppers in the distance. Two Cobra gunships were on the way. We were told to mark the perimeter with our strobe lights. I laid mine in my upside down helmet beside our foxhole to mark the southern perimeter. The gunships soon began peppering the surrounding area with rockets and unleashed a hail of Minigun fire before the dustoffs came in to evacuate the wounded and dead.

As the first dustoff neared we heard rifle fire in the distance to the southwest. Somehow enemy troops were still alive out there and were firing at the chopper. We immediately laid down another barrage of machine gun and rifle fire to protect the dustoff as it descended from the south into the western perimeter. The swirling blades pelted us with dirt and debris when the chopper landed, and again, when it lifted off a couple minutes later with a load of wounded men. The first dustoff was followed by two more. "We must have suffered a lot of casualties," I thought.

After the last dustoff disappeared into the darkness it was again quiet inside the perimeter. Robert Draughn then looked to his right and quickly raised his M-16 while saying, "Something's moving!"

I said, "Don't shoot!"

It was Jim Overbey. I immediately asked him how bad we had been hit. "We got the hell shot out of us," Jim anxiously replied. "Most of the guys on the north side are gone." Jim told us they were flying in more ammo that should arrive any minute.

Choppers soon arrived, bringing the much-needed ammunition and also two platoons of men from Firebase Patton. I'm sure those reinforcements were awfully apprehensive about being pulled from the relative comfort of Patton and dropped in the Ho Bo Woods during the middle of the night to help us.

The additional men were primarily used to fill in along the northern perimeter and also to quickly dig a few foxholes in between some of our existing foxholes to strengthen the entire perimeter. Additional ammunition and hand grenades were distributed to every foxhole. We had fired thousands of rounds after the initial sapper attack and had been re-supplied with thousands more M-60 and M-16 rounds and hundreds of hand grenades that hopefully would help us survive the remainder of what was becoming the longest night of my tour. Every man in each foxhole stayed on guard the rest of the night. I doubt if any of us could have slept anyway. Our strategy was to continue sporadic gunfire and throw hand grenades whether we spotted anything or not. The enemy knew where we were, but we would make it harder than hell for them to get close to us.

Every few minutes, rifle or machine gun fire erupted from a foxhole. Men threw out hand grenades all night long. I fired more rounds through my M-16 that night than I had during the rest of my time in Vietnam. Fortunately, our M-60 held up and fired thousands of rounds throughout the night. After what seemed like an eternity, I saw the eastern horizon begin to brighten and the sun slowly rose over our site. We stayed in our foxholes while two gunships arrived to survey the surrounding countryside in the daylight.

The second platoon had survived their night on ambush. I stood by our foxhole while they cautiously swept the perimeter looking for enemy bodies or weapons or whatever might be out there. Inside the perimeter, men slowly started stepping out of their foxholes, still tentative about moving around too much or relaxing their guard. We kept one man on guard at each foxhole. I told the guys I was going over to the command post to learn exactly what had happened and whom we lost during the night. When I walked toward the middle of the perimeter I ran into first platoon leader, Lieutenant Cartwright.

He looked at me in shock and said, "What are you doing here? I thought you were dead."

I said, "What?"

"Really," Lieutenant Cartwright said, "I was told you were killed last night." He said I should find Captain Dalton who had the names of the KIAs. Captain Dalton had seen me talking with Lieutenant Cartwright. He walked up and put his hand on my shoulder.

"I have some bad news for you, Sarge."

"Who did we lose?" I asked. Captain Dalton handed me a list of the men who had been killed. I read their names: "John Foreman (3-6); Robert Emery; Terry Thornton; Charles Merritt; Daniel Heiderich (Whitey); Allen Rader; Otis Carthage; Jr. and Roger Cox."

I couldn't believe it. I read the names a second time to be sure. I then asked about the wounded. Doc Snyder had been shot twice in the chest and Bob Ryken had a serious leg wound. Randal Collins, who had been reassigned from the first platoon, had his lower left leg completely severed. And Ben Carlson, who had joined the third platoon earlier that month, had serious multiple shrapnel wounds. As far as Captain Dalton knew, those four men were still alive.

I quietly stood there trying to comprehend what I had just learned when Bill Casey came up to me and put his hand on my shoulder. I looked at him and dejectedly said, "I can't believe they're all gone Casey."

"I know, Sarge."

"What happened, Casey?"

Casey explained that three sappers slipped in by 3-6's position and threw satchel charges and hand grenades and fired RPGs into Lieutenant Foreman's foxhole and the foxholes to the west. They then opened up with AKs. Casey hesitated for a second and then went on by saying that after the action started, he grabbed his M-16 and saw three men who were walking toward him in the CP group. He first thought they were GIs, but when they got closer, he was face-to-face with the three sappers. They apparently were planning to attack the CP group.

I said, "You're kidding."

"No, it's the God's honest truth," Casey replied and then went on, "I fired a burst of rounds into a gook carrying an RPG launcher," Casey raised his arms simulating firing. "He dropped to the ground."

He then said, "The second sapper with an AK-47 started moving to my left, and I squeezed a burst into him that spun him completely around and into the ground. The third sapper began running east toward the first platoon," Casey pointed to our right, showing me where the third sapper headed, and then continued, "I turned and knelt down and fired at his back. The gook hit the ground and crawled into some high grass. He was the one who tripped a flare when he tried to crawl out the eastern perimeter."

"Damn, Casey," I said, "You saved a lot of our butts."

"Well, that's not all," Casey said, "When I turned back to the first two sappers, one of them was raising his AK toward me. I put a few more rounds in him and put a couple more rounds in the other sapper to make sure they were both dead."

I patted him on the back and said, "You did one hell of a job, Casey."

"Maybe so, Sarge, but it was too late for those men in the foxholes," he sadly said. It was hard to believe that the sappers could have slipped in like they did. But in the darkness, and with all of the vegetation, our guys likely didn't see anything until it was too late.

Casey then told me about Randal Collins, who lost his leg. Collins was apparently so frightened he started hopping on one leg toward the medevac until two men came to carry him on board. He then yelled from the chopper, "Bring me my leg! Bring me my leg!" Someone picked up his left leg that had been blown off below his knee and handed it to him before the dustoff left.

"Son-of-a-bitch, Casey," I said while shaking my head, "We lost half of the platoon last night." The Third Herd had arrived with twenty-five men. Eight men had been killed, and four were seriously wounded. Only thirteen of us were left when the sun rose on December 28th.

Casey pointed toward the western perimeter and said, "The two dead gooks are still over there."

The body of the third sapper that had tried to crawl out the east side was found by the second platoon by the wire that morning.

I slowly walked over to see the bodies of the two sappers who had killed and wounded a dozen of my friends. The bodies were lying face up on the ground with their black shirts covered with blood. One sapper had a bullet hole in his forehead and the back of his head had been nearly blown away by the force of one of Casey's M-16 rounds. I felt like kicking the bodies or reaching down and beating the hell out of both of them in retaliation for what they had done. But that would have been a useless gesture of frustration. I stared at the two bodies for a moment and walked away in silence. We had set ourselves up for a butt-kicking in the middle of "Charlie's" country, and he had literally kicked our butts.

I then walked over by Lieutenant Foreman's foxhole and saw bloodstained gear lying nearby. I recognized Lieutenant Foreman's helmet by the purple smoke stain on his helmet cover. We had dropped a smoke grenade down a tunnel one day and he had placed his helmet over the entrance, trying to keep the purple smoke from rising up out of the opening. I picked up another helmet. "Whitey" was written across the front. I looked in disbelief at a bullet hole in the front of the helmet. Half of those men had been sleeping near their foxholes and probably never knew what hit them. Wop was sitting on the edge of the foxhole with Mike Myers. Mike had been in that foxhole with Bob, Whitey and Lieutenant Foreman. Amazingly, he had received only a minor shrapnel wound in his arm, and had remained with the rest of us during the night.

Mike and Wop were both in shock over losing their best friend, Bob Emery. "Those fucking gooks killed my friends!" Wop said in frustration. I put my hand on Wop's shoulder as he looked up at me with watery eyes. Mike then told me that he and Bob had formed a pact. If either of them were wounded, they would tell the other man what it was like. Mike said, "After Bob was hit, I held him in my arms, but he died before he could say anything." Wop put his arm around Mike as they both cried. Those men knew Bob had turned down a reassignment to the mortar platoon, a decision that had cost him his life.

Several men quietly walked past the foxholes along the north side to survey the remains of our fallen comrades. The men were speechless when they saw the bloody towels and fatigue shirts and other gear covered with blood. I then saw Hugh Hearn standing guard at the foxhole he had shared with Doc Snyder and Bob Ryken, who had been seriously wounded, and Roger Cox and Otis Carthage, who had been killed.

I walked beside him and asked if he was OK. Hugh looked at me and shook his head as he said, "I can't believe I'm still hear, Sarge."

I said, "We're all lucky to be here."

Hugh went on to explain that he was on guard with Roger Cox when the sappers hit the two foxholes to their right. The other three men (Snyder, Ryken and Carthage) started piling into the foxhole with their weapons. Before he knew it, he was lying on the bottom of the foxhole with the other guys on top of him. Savagely, one of the sappers opened up on them with an AK-47 hitting the other four men. Hugh said in a quivering voice, "Those other guys took all the rounds and saved me."

I put my hand on his shoulder and said, "Hey, Doc Snyder and Ryken are still alive. Be thankful you survived."

In addition to the body of the sapper that tried to sneak back out through the eastern perimeter, the men in the second platoon also found three more enemy bodies along the southern perimeter. One of them probably was the son-of-a-bitch who had thrown the hand grenade at me early the past evening.

The morning of December 28th was a terribly sad day for the thirteen remaining members of the Third Herd. Although we were all thankful for being alive, we knew that the emotional distress of losing eight of our friends would change our lives forever.

I stopped to talk with several remaining members of the third platoon as I walked back toward my foxhole on the southern perimeter. Those men were quietly milling around their foxholes trying to absorb the fact that half of the Third Herd was gone. When I asked how they were doing, they all said they were fine. But I knew they weren't doing fine. They just didn't feel like talking about it. I then found Jim Overbey sitting on the sand bag wall in front of his foxhole staring out over the perimeter smoking a cigarette.

"Jim," I said, "are you OK?"

He quietly said, "Not really. I knew this was going to happen. I thought for sure they would get me."

"The rest of us were lucky," I said.

"I had to load their bodies on the choppers last night," Jim said. "I don't know if I can take any more of this."

I put my right hand on his shoulder and said, "It's been one hell of a month for us, but we have to hang in there and move on."

"Maybe last night was my fault," Jim said, "I should have tried harder to get the CO to move to the hard spot."

"Don't feel guilty, Jim. They could have hit us anywhere out here." Jim then asked if I knew what we were going to do. I didn't know, but I told him I would find out. I gave Jim a pat on his shoulder and then walked toward the command post in the center of the site. When I found Captain Dalton I asked him what he wanted us to do. He said the battalion commander, Colonel Crutchley and General Watkins from Division Headquarters were on the way out to talk to him and then decide what to do.

A lone chopper soon circled overhead and then landed near the western perimeter. Captain Dalton walked over and greeted Colonel Crutchley and the one-star general. The division commander had been informed about what had happened and wanted one of his staff to fly out and talk with Captain Dalton and some men in the company. But most of us weren't too excited to see anyone who might have played a role in sending us out on the bushmaster. A few minutes later Colonel Crutchley and General Watkins walked around with Captain Dalton to talk with some of us. When they stopped near our foxhole Captain Dalton introduced me to the general.

"Good morning, Sergeant," General Watkins said as he reached out to shake my hand.

I replied with a solemn, "Good morning, sir."

"I'm sorry to hear you lost some good men last night. We are going to step up our activity out here and stop those VC bastards," the General said.

"That's fine, sir, but that will be too late for the twelve men we lost last night."

General Watkins then said, "It doesn't sound like you agree with using bushmasters."

"This operation was a big mistake," I said, "We played right into Charlie's hand." I turned and walked away. The general moved on without saying anything else to me. Captain Dalton probably didn't like my comment to General Watkins, but it was true. They could kill every damn gook left in the country, but it wouldn't bring those men back. What had been a desolate spot in the Ho Bo Woods twenty-four hours before had become a deathtrap for eight men. We had basically flown in and waved a big flag in front of the enemy and said, "Here we are, come get us." And they did.

A short while later Colonel Crutchley and General Watkins flew off. Captain Dalton stood in the middle of the site and yelled, "Tear everything down. We're going back to Patton."

With a big sigh of relief, I said, "Let's get out of this hellhole." We kept several men on guard while the rest of us began dismantling the site. When I walked in front of the wall at our foxhole I noticed holes in the sand bags. None of us on the southern perimeter had been wounded but those sandbags had taken some hits from shrapnel or bullets during the night.

Abruptly, there was an explosion east of our foxhole. We all grabbed our weapons thinking, "Hear we go again."

One of the men in the first platoon had seen a dud Chinese-made hand grenade. It exploded when he walked toward it. Amazingly, he wasn't injured. The NVA and VC used those grenades with a wooden throwing handle, but they were old and had a reputation for often not detonating.

We cautiously searched the entire site and marked nearly a dozen dud grenades with steel posts to be sure everyone stayed clear of them. Ironically, we found one of those dud grenades not far from the little hole I had dug in front of our foxhole early the past evening. Again, it must not have been my time to go.

We pulled the concertina wire out of the grass and took down the chain link wire and rolled it up to be hauled out. We didn't want to leave anything useful for the enemy. We piled the wire, the steel posts and anything else worthwhile near the southern perimeter to be loaded onto choppers. We worked into the afternoon emptying the dirt from the sand bags back into the foxholes, and tearing down everything we had worked so hard to build the previous afternoon. As the choppers landed, we quickly loaded them up with the wire and other supplies and ammunition we hadn't used. We also sadly took the gear belonging to the men who had been killed and wounded and loaded the remaining signs of their existence onto a chopper. We threw the remaining trash, empty C-ration cans and wooden ammunition boxes in a pile that covered the bodies of the two sappers near the western perimeter.

We were all hot, dirty, hungry and tired. We had busted our butts to set up the site, none of us had gotten much sleep, and then we had been working for hours to dismantle the site. But we all kept pushing on because we wanted to get the hell out of there. During the afternoon a couple of the men asked me what was wrong with Jim Overbey. They were concerned about his being so quiet. I told the guys that Jim was taking it pretty hard, and maybe he needed a break.

After all the supplies and equipment had been flown out, we gathered up our personal gear, ammunition and weapons and made a final sweep of the site to be sure there was nothing useful left behind. We waited for over an hour for the first lift of choppers to arrive and then the mortar platoon loaded their mortar tubes and flew out. The first and second platoons followed, and the CO's staff and the remainder of the third platoon would be the last to be flown out. While we waited, Captain Dalton told his demolitions man to set two sticks of C-4 in the pile of trash.

I heard him say, "We will blow the trash and those two gooks straight to hell!"

When the final lift of choppers landed after three o'clock that afternoon, the fuses to the C-4 were lit. I was on the last chopper that lifted off. We asked the pilot to circle the site until the C-4 exploded, consuming the pile of trash and the two dead bodies in a fiery blast throwing a huge cloud of smoke and debris into the air. Then the pilot turned the chopper southwest toward Firebase Patton.

The following members of the third platoon were killed on December 28, 1969.

➤ Sergeant Robert Emery was from Marine City, MI. He was eighteen years old. He arrived in Vietnam on July 26, 1969. I have been in touch with his mother and shared with her pictures of Bob while he was in Vietnam and the details surrounding his death. Robert Emery is buried in Holy Cross Cemetery in Marine City, Michigan.

➤ Private First Class Terry Thornton was from Tulsa, OK. He was nineteen years old. He arrived in Vietnam on July 30, 1969. He was married and had a daughter.

➤ Second Lieutenant John Foreman was from Manlius, NY. He was twenty-six years old. He arrived in Vietnam on November 24, 1969. He served as our platoon leader for less than one month. John Foreman is buried in Clinton, New York. I have been in touch with his sister Susan. As of the writing of this book, I am pursuing the posthumous award of a Bronze Star to Lieutenant Foreman for his actions in spotting the second land mine on December 17, 1969 that undoubtedly saved several lives, including my own.

➤ Private First Class Charles Merritt was from Runnells, IA. He was twenty years old. He arrived in Vietnam on October 12, 1969 and served as one of our RTOs. I later learned his dad and mine had grown up together in the small town of Kellerton, Iowa. I met with his family in 1970 and visited his grave in a small country cemetery near Kellerton.

➤ Specialist 4th Class Daniel "Whitey" Heiderich was from Overbrook, OK. He was twenty years old. He arrived in Vietnam on August 27, 1969. He was a good ole boy who died too young. Danial Heiderich is buried in Leon, Oklahoma.

➤ Private First Class Allan Rader was from Fostoria, OH. He was twenty years old. He arrived in Vietnam on December 7, 1969. He had been in the field approximately one week when he was killed.

➤ Private First Class Otis Carthage, Jr. was from Northport, AL. He was twenty-one years old. He arrived in Vietnam on December 9, 1969. He had been in the field approximately one week when he was killed.

➤ Private First Class Roger Cox was from Marietta, SC. He was twenty years old. He arrived in Vietnam on December 11, 1969. He had been in the field approximately one week when he was killed.

Visit the web site (www.thevirtualwall.org) to view additional information regarding these men and all others killed in Vietnam.

96 members of Alpha Company, 2nd Battalion, 14th Infantry Regiment were killed in action while the unit served in Vietnam from 1966 through 1970. The loss of the eight men in Alpha Company, Third Platoon, on the night of December 28, 1969, was the largest single-day casualty loss suffered by any of the five companies in the 2nd Battalion, 14th Infantry Regiment.

The Army UH-1 (Huey) helicopters accumulated over 7.5 million flight hours in Vietnam. The Army reported 4,643 helicopters lost in action in Vietnam.

Daniel "Whitey" Heiderich cleaning his weapon at Fire Support Base Patton. A 155MM howitzer is in the background.

243

In the foreground is Lieutenant John Foreman.
The first man behind John is Glenn Haywood, who died on
Christmas Eve 1969. The third man is Robert Draughn.

Chapter 16

Rebuilding the Third Herd

I normally loved flying in choppers, but the flight back to Firebase Patton the afternoon of December 28th was a depressing ride. Although it was a clear, sunny day, and the scenery of the countryside below was clearly visible, I could only think about my friends who weren't returning with us. When I had talked with every one of those men along the northern perimeter that past evening, I had expected to see them in the morning. I sat on the floor of the chopper staring into the distant countryside, sadly realizing that I would never talk with or see those eight men again. December 28, 1969 was the saddest day of my life.

After we landed at Patton I quietly walked along the path through the perimeter into the firebase. I walked with Captain Dalton part of the way along the interior road. I thought it was time to say something concerning Jim Overbey. I summarized my conversations with Jim and told the CO that some of the other men were also concerned about him. Captain Dalton told me to come see him after I settled in.

Although most of the men remaining in the Third Herd had been in country for a while and knew what they were doing, I didn't know what the CO expected from us. We were again without a platoon leader and didn't have a medic. Jim Overbey was next in line to be acting platoon leader, but I didn't think he should stay in the field. Seeing ten friends in the Third Herd killed and five others seriously wounded in less than two weeks had taken its toll on Jim. He had assumed a personal guilt regarding what happened at the bushmaster. Although everyone knew there was little more any of us could have done to save our friends, Jim felt responsible.

When we reached our two assigned bunkers I dropped my gear outside one bunker and breathed a sigh of relief. We had all worked our butts off the past two days and had only gotten a couple of hours of sleep before the sappers hit us. We were all in need of a good night's sleep, but with only five or six men in each bunker, we wouldn't be getting too much sleep between guard shifts. I had never seen the men so quiet as they settled in that day. Obviously the loss of our friends was still sinking into everyone's mind and was taking its emotional toll as we finally had a chance to relax. I could have easily walked off by myself and cried.

A short while later I walked over to the Alpha Company Command Post and found Captain Dalton inside his bunker. His bunker was high enough to stand up in so I walked in and I sat on one of the two bunks inside. The CO asked me how the guys were doing, and I replied, "Not too well. Most of those men were good friends to many of us." The CO said he expected us to be a pretty sad group for a while. He then asked about Jim Overbey.

I told Captain Dalton that Jim had admitted to me that the past night had gotten to him. Jim had lost his confidence and felt guilty about losing so many men. He needed a break. The CO said he hated to load everything on me, but he agreed that it sounded like Jim should go back to Cu Chi for a while. But the CO wanted to talk with him personally before he made a final decision. I also reminded the CO that without Jim Overbey, we only had twelve men. Captain Dalton said he would ask the battalion CO to send us to Venice East until we got some new men and to give us a few days to recover.

"That would be great." I said, "We can't do much else right now."

When I stood up, Captain Dalton put his hand on my shoulder to offer a little comfort while we walked outside his bunker. He then said, "Have Overbey come over in half an hour."

When I returned to our bunkers, I found Jim standing outside his bunker smoking a cigarette. I told him the CO wanted to see him in half an hour and summarized my conversation with Captain Dalton. I said, "You might get out of here, Jim."

Jim looked at me seriously and said, "I need to. I'm not worth a damn out here."

I told the men we were probably going to Venice East for a little breather. I also sensed a new feeling of uneasiness among the men that afternoon. Losing eight men in a matter of a minute made the rest of us start thinking more about our own chances of survival.

When I returned from the mess hall with some chow, Jim was waiting for me near my bunker. We walked away from the bunker to talk in privacy. Jim told me the CO was sending him back to Cu Chi.

Jim then said, "I don't want to let you guys down, but I can't handle it out here, last night scared the hell out of me."

I replied, "Last night scared the hell out of all of us, Jim. Some time in the rear will be good for you."

A short while later, Captain Dalton stopped by our bunkers and asked the men to gather around. He started by expressing his sorrow regarding the men we had lost. He said he had talked with the battalion CO concerning the bushmaster and that they might have miscalculated how smart "Charlie" was. He reluctantly admitted that things could have been handled differently out there. The CO then said that he was reassigning Sergeant Overbey to Alpha Company Headquarters in Cu Chi and that I would be acting platoon leader until we got a new 3-6. He was also sending us to Venice East for a few days. He then asked if there were any questions.

I knew the men had a lot of questions about the bushmaster, but no one asked any. However, after losing half a platoon, some questions needed to be raised before the matter was closed.

Captain Dalton looked at me and said, "They're all yours."

I said, "Thank you, sir," and we exchanged casual salutes before he walked away. In one day I had gone from being a squad leader to acting platoon leader, except I still only had three stripes on my fatigue shirt. But I was ready for the challenge. Lieutenant Fielding and Lieutenant Foreman had relied upon us NCOs during their short tours of duty with the platoon. I had often assumed much more responsibility than that of a squad leader simply because we lacked an experienced platoon leader.

Wop was standing outside our bunker when I walked up. He was normally a pretty happy-go-lucky guy, and while I didn't expect any of the guys to be too cheerful, Wop look dejected. I asked if he was OK. He said, "I'm not doing worth a shit. My best friend is dead." He was taking the loss of Bob Emery very hard.

Shortly before dark that evening "Top" Seavey quietly walked up to a group of us while we were standing outside our bunker. He had been in three wars and told us that the past night was as bad as he had ever seen. Top chatted with us for a few minutes to express his personal regret about the men we lost and gave several of us reassuring pats on the back before he walked toward his bunker as darkness settled over Patton.

I took the first guard at our bunker, wearing my helmet and flak jacket. The firebase had become quiet. I finally had a few peaceful moments to myself while I scanned the darkness along the perimeter. I couldn't get thoughts of the past night out of my mind and grappled to comprehend that those eight men were truly gone. I also thought about the four wounded men and hoped they were all still alive. Standing in the darkness under a clear sky with stars shining above, I solemnly said a silent prayer of thankfulness for being alive and asked the Lord to be with the families of the men who were killed. I then shed a few tears for my departed friends.

After my first hour on guard I crawled into my hammock, covered myself with my poncho liner, and fell asleep. We rotated guard duty at Patton through a quiet and uneventful night. The next morning we all cleaned our weapons. After firing thousands of rounds during the bushmaster, everyone's weapon needed cleaning.

With Jim Overbey going back to the rear, only twelve men remained with the third platoon on December 29, 1969. They were David Hardy, Carlton Quick, David "Wop" DiBiasio, Ed Leberski, Hugh Hearn, Robert Draughn, Mike Myers, Vic Ortega, Junior "Hough" Houchens, Carl Seals, Chester Sampson and myself.

Before we left for Venice East, we had one more difficult task to complete. We gathered up the personal gear of the men who were killed or wounded and sat it out to be taken back to Cu Chi on the supply convoy that afternoon. The guys in the rear would sort through it and send whatever they determined to be appropriate back to the families of our eight dead comrades and on to wherever the four wounded men would be sent.

Captain Dalton had asked for volunteers from the first and second platoon to transfer to the third platoon to give us a few more guys to defend Venice East, and also so that all of our replacements wouldn't be FNGs. Later that morning three volunteers walked up to join the third platoon: Tom Anderson, Randy Butler and John Bergen, nicknamed Bugsy.

I knew Bugsy because of a case of VD he got from a Vietnamese hooker a couple of months earlier, which landed him in the 12th Evac in Cu Chi for a few days. Several men in the company had picked up a case of VD along the way, but Bugsy was the only one whose condition couldn't be cured simply with a shot of penicillin.

After we shook hands, Bugsy told me he volunteered to join us because he wanted a Purple Heart. Since the third platoon seemed to be in the middle of the action, he thought he would have a better chance of earning one. He then said. "And one more thing, Hound Dog; I'll walk point for you guys."

I said, "What? Are you sure?" He said yes. I told him I would let him know. I thought to myself, "Bugsy, you crazy son-of-a-gun." Bugsy reminded me of Lieutenant Fielding, who had nearly gotten himself killed with his gung-ho attitude. We certainly didn't want cowards in the field, but I also had to wonder a little concerning guys who were too gung-ho about being out there.

That afternoon the Alpha Company supply convoy arrived from Cu Chi. After the supplies were unloaded, one of the deuce-and-a-halfs stopped in front of our bunkers. The driver yelled, "Load'em up." After we loaded the personal gear of our fallen comrades I threw on my backpack and climbed aboard for the short trip to Venice East. Jim Overbey joined us, however, he would continue on back to Cu Chi. Most of the men knew why Jim was being reassigned and had talked with him during the day. Although the rest of us could have argued he was getting off the hook, I think everyone knew he had put in his time and legitimately needed some time in the rear.

When our mail was delivered on December 30th, someone said there was a package for Lieutenant Foreman and brought it over to me. When I felt the package and shook it, I guessed it was a bottle of booze. I opened the package and sure enough, it was a bottle of Jim Beam Whiskey from Lieutenant Foreman's sister Susan. I initially considered sending it back, but then doubted his sister cared to have the bottle returned under the circumstances. I told the guys I would keep the bottle but didn't tell them what I planned to do with it.

We also heard news regarding our four friends who had been wounded. Doc Snyder had been shot twice in the chest, but amazingly survived. Bob Ryken's leg had been injured badly, but doctors were able to save it. Randal Collins, who lost his left leg below his knee and had other shrapnel wounds, was in serious but stable condition, and Ben Carlson was in serious condition with multiple shrapnel wounds. They would all be evacuated from Vietnam when they were stable enough to travel.

On New Year's Eve morning, we were up early as usual at Venice

249

East to clear the road, and after breakfast we settled in for the day. I spent a couple of hours writing my parents, Jan and other friends and family I had heard from recently. During the day I walked around to see how the rest of the men were doing in the peace and quiet. A few guys were writing letters, while several were catching up on their sleep. I saw Vic Ortega and Ed Leberski standing outside the front gate watching the local civilians as they passed by along the road.

I walked out to the road where we talked about the bushmaster. Vic had been in the foxhole just west of me, and said he saw shadows of movement on the north side, but he didn't want to fire. He didn't know if it was our guys or the gooks. Although reliving that night was painful for all of us, we also knew that if more of us had immediately started running to the northern perimeter, we could have easily shot each other. We sadly realized the action happened so fast, that none of us could have stopped it.

The three of us wandered back inside the compound and found a few other guys stirring around. Normally during the day at Venice East someone would be trying to get a poker game together, or guys might be out on the road hustling up some girls. Obviously, the men weren't in that kind of mood. I talked with several of the men during the afternoon and listened to their frustration about the bushmaster. We had been used as bait to draw out the VC. Unfortunately, it resulted in the death of eight friends. It would be much different going on without them.

Around four o'clock that afternoon a convoy of trucks stopped at Venice East and delivered the mail, C-rations, some ammunition that we had requested, sodas and our evening meal. Shortly after the convoy left I asked the men to gather around my bunker. I started by saying that the past month had probably been the toughest month of our respective lives. We would miss our friends who were killed, but we had to accept what happened and force ourselves to move on. The guys looked at me and at each other, with some saying, "Yeah," or nodding their heads.

I went on by telling the guys to keep talking to me and with each other to release their emotions about the bushmaster. I also reminded them that we would go back to the Ho Bo Woods someday. We needed to be ready to deal with it. Someone asked, "When are we getting some FNGs?"

I told the men that the CO had requested eight men, including a platoon leader, a medic and two NCOs. I said I would talk with the CO in the morning to see what was happening. "All right guys," I then said, "It's New Year's Eve. We need to pull guard tonight, but I want to pay tribute to the men we lost and celebrate a little before dark."

I reached into my backpack that was lying nearby and pulled out the fifth of Jim Beam. I reminded the guys it was the bottle that arrived for Lieutenant Foreman the day before. Rather than sending it back, I kept it to have a drink in honor of him and the other men we lost. For the first time in a while, I heard a cheer from the men and saw smiles on their faces when I handed the bottle of Jim Beam to Junior Houchens who was standing beside me. I said, "Hey, Houch, share it with everybody else."

"Oh sure, Sarge," he said, with a big smile on his face.

The men found cans of soda and poured out some of the soda and poured in a little whiskey. I soon had a Beam and Coke in my hand that someone had mixed for me. After a few minutes, I told the guys I wanted to make a toast. Everyone stopped talking and gathered together again.

I said, "Let's take a minute to pay our respects to the men we've lost. Hal Harris, Red, Haywood and Spivey, and the eight men who died on December 28th. Let's give them a moment of silence." We all stood in the middle of Venice East with our heads bowed. I then said, "Men, we miss each of you, and we'll never forget you. But we'll see you in heaven someday because we've all served our time in hell, Vietnam."

I had tears in my eyes as I raised my Beam and Coke and somberly said, "May they rest in peace." Every man raised his can of soda, with some of them giving their own brief tribute as we shared a drink in honor of our fallen comrades. It was a much sadder moment than I had anticipated. I took a minute to dry my eyes and clear my throat before I could talk to the men again.

We began sharing stories concerning the guys who died. Ed Leberski reminded us of the day Haywood came running back from the hill firing his M-16 with one hand like John Wayne. The guys chuckled, "Yeah, I remember."

Other guys talked about Whitey and smiled as they recalled his stories about living in the wide-open countryside of Oklahoma. We remembered Red as the happy-go-lucky guy from South Carolina and Chuck Merritt as the quiet guy who read his Bible nearly every day. I reminded the men that many of us should be thankful that Lieutenant Foreman had spotted that second land mine on December 17th.

It was good to see the guys smiling again as they talked about their fallen comrades. Although I had started the tribute on a somber note, it turned into the beginning of the healing process for us. We were letting the good memories concerning those men overcome the grief and sadness we felt during the past two days. Although we had repeatedly endured the tragedy of losing friends, the camaraderie between those of us who survived grew even stronger. Whatever happened to us, either individually or as a group, we would help each other overcome our losses and hopefully make it through that damned war alive.

It was also important for those of us who survived the night of December 28th to move on without letting it destroy us individually or as a platoon. The new men joining the Third Herd would be looking to us old timers not only to learn the routine of field duty; they'd be looking to us for emotional stability too. We had taken on a new burden.

Wop came up to me while I was sipping my Jim Beam and Coke and said he had been talking with some of the guys about having a memorial service and a twenty-one-gun salute.

"Great idea," I said, "I'll talk to the CO."

I enjoyed one of my Crooks cigars during the afternoon that quickly passed into evening while the fifteen guys in the Third Herd enjoyed the Jim Beam and toasted to an early Happy New Year. Hopefully 1970 would begin better than 1969 had ended.

The men grabbed some chow along the way, and when darkness neared we closed the front gate for the night. Most of the guys quietly settled into their bunkers when we began pulling one-hour guard shifts in the tower. I took advantage of being the ranking man in the platoon and didn't pull guard duty. I settled into my hammock for a good night's sleep. During the night the light of a flare lit up the sky and woke me up. Startled, I stepped out of my bunker thinking the men on guard had spotted something. I yelled to the men in the tower, "What's going on?"

Mike Myers leaned over the sandbag wall and said, "It's New Year's," and pointed toward Patton to the north. He fired a red flare over Venice East. I looked towards Patton and saw colored flares flying into the air in celebration of the New Year. Several other men had been awakened and had stepped out of the bunkers anticipating that something serious was happening. I told the guys everything was OK and said, "Happy New Year."

January 1, 1970 began as a sunny morning in South Vietnam. The rice paddies were dried up, and the local civilians were busy harvesting rice. The dry weather was a relief from the daily rains we had endured during the monsoon season, but then we had to endure the hot and humid afternoons.

Like the U. S. military had done on Thanksgiving and Christmas, a one-day truce was declared on New Year's Day. The men at Patton and the other patrol bases wouldn't be going out on RIFs or ambushes and could relax along with those of us at Venice East. I talked with Captain Dalton by radio later that day. He told me four new men would be arriving the following afternoon. I also asked about having a memorial service for our guys and the CO said he would work on it.

Although I knew the men could use a few days at Venice East to relax, I also knew the platoon needed to get back into the action before too long to help put the month of December in the back of everyone's mind. With four FNGs arriving, we would have nineteen men, which was as many as we had operated with on several occasions. But we needed a medic, and I hoped for a couple NCOs to help me out until a new platoon leader arrived. Just after two o'clock the following afternoon, the supply convoy from Cu Chi stopped by. I walked out to the road and waved at Jim Overbey sitting in the back of one of the deuce-and-a-halves. Jim said, "Hey, Hound Dog, here's four new guys for you." The four men walked toward me.

I said, "How are you, Jim?"

He replied, "I'm doing better; how's the platoon?"

"We're hanging in there; we'll make it," I said.

Some of the guys came out to help unload our supplies and also to say "hi" to Jim. After the convoy moved on toward Patton, I motioned for the new guys to gather around me. "Welcome to the Third Herd as we're called. I'm Sergeant Hogue." I flashed back for an instant and recalled that was similar to how Sergeant Brown had welcomed me to Venice East. "In case you haven't heard, we lost a dozen men a few nights ago, including our platoon leader. So, I'm acting platoon leader, platoon sergeant and most everything else."

I recognized one of the new men as Sergeant Richard Benson, whom I had met on Christmas Day in Cu Chi. I reached out to shake his hand and welcomed him to the platoon. I shook hands with three PFCs, Greg Kilgore, Greg Valdez and Norm Wilson, while they introduced themselves.

I briefly explained the purpose of Venice East and our responsibilities while we were there. I also told those men that the duty there was going to be the easiest duty they would see in the field. I then smiled and said, "So don't get used to it." I led the four new guys through the entrance and gathered the rest of the platoon for introductions. We re-arranged ourselves in the bunkers to make room for the new men. The bunkers at Venice East were big enough to accommodate everyone with no problem. The next day, two more men arrived. One was a medic, Bill Covington, who didn't carry a weapon because of religious beliefs.

He told the men, "You take care of me, and I'll take care of you." It was that simple.

The other man was another shake'n bake, Sergeant Warren Hansen. I sat down with Sergeants Benson and Hansen to divide the platoon into two squads, with a mix of old timers and FNGs in each squad. I assigned Sergeant Hansen as first squad leader, and Sergeant Benson as second squad leader.

Captain Dalton stopped by later that day and asked when we would be ready to move back to Patton. I thought we should move back in the morning. The CO also said he was planning an awards ceremony in a day or two, and that the chaplain was arranging a memorial service at the same time. He asked me to organize a firing squad and said I could deliver a eulogy if I wanted to.

"That would be great," I said, "I'd like to say a few words about those guys." As we stood together on the road, the CO said he would call on the radio and let us know when to be ready to move out. He also told me a new lieutenant should be arriving in a few days.

I smiled and said, "You can just promote me if you want to."

The CO chuckled and said, "I wish it were that easy, Hound Dog," and gave me a friendly smile before he climbed into his jeep. The next day a new platoon arrived to take charge of Venice East and the third platoon returned to Patton and settled into a group of bunkers along the southern perimeter.

When I talked with Captain Dalton later that afternoon, he wasn't planning to send us out on ambush that night, but he wanted us to go out on a RIF near Patton in the morning to break in the new guys. He also said the memorial service and awards ceremony was scheduled for two o'clock the following afternoon. I had thought about who I wanted to have in the firing squad, and one of them was Bill Casey. He had joined the Third Herd shortly after me and had been one of our RTOs until Captain Dalton asked him to be one of his RTOs in November. Casey had known the men who were killed and probably saved several lives by shooting the three sappers. He was the hero on the bushmaster and was being recommended for a Silver Star (the third highest military decoration) for his action.

When I found Casey and first told him about our New Year's tribute at Venice East and the fifth of Jim Beam we enjoyed, he smiled and said, "Boy, I wish I could have been there." I then asked Casey to be on the firing squad during the memorial service. He gladly accepted.

When I returned to our bunkers, I gathered the men and told the new guys to make sure their weapons were clean and asked Sergeants Benson and Hansen to make sure their squads would be ready for a short RIF in the morning. I then asked Mike Myers, Vic Ortega, Carlton Quick, Dave Hardy, David "Wop" DiBasio and Ed Leberski to stay with me. I told those men I wanted them to be in the firing squad during the memorial service the following afternoon. I told the guys that we should take a few minutes to practice.

I asked someone to find Bill Casey and have him come over to our bunkers. After Casey arrived, the guys each grabbed an M-16. I would be in charge of the firing squad and give the commands. The seven men lined up and I led them through the sequence of raising their weapons to "port arms" and then to their shoulder ready to fire. After a few practice runs, the men decided they were ready. We had all seen firing squads back in the world, and I had conducted hours of drill and ceremony during my training. But since arriving in Vietnam, we didn't have much need for military formalities. Hopefully we would do it right during the memorial service.

After I received a route for our RIF from Captain Dalton the following morning, I told Sergeants Benson and Hansen I wanted them to take charge. I would observe and take over if we ran into trouble. After the platoon walked along the path through the wire on the east side of Patton, Sergeant Hansen gave Bugsy a compass heading, and we moved out. I had taken Bugsy up on his offer to walk point. One of the new guys, Norm Wilson, walked second as our pace man and was given the distance to the first checkpoint. We walked in a single column with one man out thirty meters on each flank. Our route initially took us toward the grove of trees northeast of Patton, where the two VC had been shot out of the trees that past November. I told the new guys that although the area looked peaceful, they needed to be ready for anything at anytime, just in case.

We moved through the trees and found nothing. I let the two new NCOs keep track of our route and hopefully ensure that Bugsy and Wilson kept us on course as we continued on. We had walked one klick south from our second checkpoint when I sent the word forward for Bugsy to stop. I had the men circle up in a perimeter and I knelt down while motioning for Sergeant Hansen and Sergeant Benson and Bugsy and Norm Wilson to join me in the middle of our perimeter.

I said, "We're off course, guys." Quickly, Sergeants Hanson and Benson pulled out their maps, trying to pinpoint our location. Bugsy was sure he had been leading us on the correct compass heading. When I asked Wilson if he had been accurately counting his steps, he said, "Well, I think so."

"Well have you or not?" I was very familiar with the area around Patton and I knew where we were, but I was getting a little upset by not hearing a definite answer from Wilson. He reluctantly admitted that he might have miscounted his paces to the second checkpoint.

I laid my map on the ground to show the men what had happened. We had topographical maps that showed trails and roads, streams and rivers and identified the terrain as being rice paddies or trees or whatever it actually was. By comparing the countryside to the details on the map, I could determine where we were.

I pointed to my map and explained that we should have been moving to our third checkpoint between two clusters of trees 300 meters to our west. Wilson must have miscounted his paces to the second checkpoint and taken us too far east.

I showed Bugsy where I wanted us to backtrack so that we would end up back on course.

I stood up and said, "Bugsy, get us out of here."

"Yes sir," he said jokingly.

Before we moved out, I told Wilson I would talk with him when we got back to Patton. I had Ed Leberski walk second and count paces the rest of the way. I knew he wouldn't miscount. We finished the RIF by walking through rice paddies east of Venice East and then along the road back to the firebase.

I was taking off my gear when Norm Wilson walked by. I'm sure he hoped I wouldn't notice him, but I told him to follow me as I walked away from the bunkers for a private conversation. I said, "You know you could have gotten us in trouble out there today?"

"Yes, Sergeant."

"I know that was your first RIF, but all you had to do was to count your paces. Was that too much to ask?"

"No Sergeant."

I raised my voice and said, "Do you want to walk point so you don't have to count paces?

"Not really, Sergeant."

"The next time you count paces, you damn well better get it right. If you get the entire company lost, the CO will be on you a whole hell of a lot worse than I am. Understand?"

"Yes, Sergeant."

"If you ever have trouble counting your paces again, you stop the column and talk with me." I walked away leaving Wilson standing by himself.

A few minutes after one o'clock I quickly unhooked the gear from my pistol belt and clipped the belt around my waist. I told Dave Hardy I was going to the CP, and asked him to make sure the guys in the firing squad were standing by near the chopper pad at the aid station by 1:45. I would meet them over there. I grabbed my helmet and headed toward the command post.

The chaplain was talking with Captain Dalton when I walked into the CP area. I said hello to Chaplain Wideman and shook his hand. The chaplain told us he had arranged the memorial service to start with opening remarks by Captain Dalton. Chaplain Wideman would then conduct a brief service. Rick Shields, who had come out to Patton for the service, and I would each deliver a short eulogy, and then I would command the firing squad. The service would conclude with a bugler playing Taps.

The Chaplain had printed handouts with a picture of the Tomb of the Unknown Soldier at Arlington Cemetery on the front. Below the picture were these words:

"That we here highly resolve that these dead shall not have died in vain." Lincoln's Gettysburg Address 19 Nov 1863

Inside it stated the service was being held on January 5, 1970 at Firebase Patton. The names of Willard Spivey and Glenn Haywood and the eight men who were killed on December 28th, were listed along with the order of the service. The Chaplain would have copies distributed before hand. The awards ceremony would follow the memorial service.

The men in the firing squad were standing by when I arrived on the north side of the firebase. There was an open area adjacent to the chopper pad that provided plenty of room for the company to gather. The rest of the company had flown out early that morning for a RIF and had returned to Patton shortly after we did. The entire company soon gathered for the memorial service. I hadn't spent much time thinking about what I would say and didn't have any written notes prepared. Although delivering a eulogy would be a new and difficult experience for me, it was something I wanted to do.

An organ had been brought out for the service, and the organist played prior to the service. When two o'clock arrived, the firing squad stood in line along the north side of the area facing south. The remainder of the company gathered in platoon formations on the east side of the area facing west. First Sergeant Seavey called the company to attention, and Captain Dalton walked forward. We were given a "parade rest" command.

Captain Dalton began by saying, "Men, we're here today to pay our respects to ten members of Alpha Company, third platoon, who gave their lives for their country. I know the loss of these men has left feelings of sorrow and frustration, especially for you men in the third platoon. Unfortunately, their deaths and the deaths of thousands of other brave men are the tragic consequence of this conflict. We can only hope their deaths are not in vain. I share in the sadness for their loss. We all lost ten brave comrades, but many of you have also lost ten good friends. May those men rest in peace."

Chaplain Wideman continued the service by saying a prayer for our fallen comrades and for their families back in the world. He then read the 23rd Psalm: "The Lord is my shepherd, I shall not want ...".

The Chaplain then talked briefly about war. He addressed the death and tragedy inflicted by the fighting and how difficult it was to understand. He said, in summary, that God allowed us the free will to create the destructive tools of war, and if we choose to use those tools to battle our fellow man, we must endure the consequences, including the loss of good friends. Although we were grieving the loss of our comrades, we would become stronger men as we ultimately moved on from that tragedy as grateful survivors.

After the Chaplin concluded, we all joined in singing as the organist played the National Anthem, while two men presented the American and Army flags.

Rick Shields then stepped forward to deliver a brief eulogy, talking about some of the men he knew best and expressing his personal sorrow over losing good friends and brave comrades with whom he had served.

I then stepped forward and read the names of the ten men who were killed in December 1969:

> Second Lieutenant John Foreman
> Sergeant Robert Emery
> Specialist Forth Class Daniel Heiderich (Whitey)
> Private First Class Otis Carthage, Jr.
> Private First Class Roger Cox
> Private First Class Glennon Haywood
> Private First Class Charles Merritt
> Private First Class Willard Spivey
> Private First Class Terry Thornton
> Private First Class Allan Rader

I hesitated to clear my throat before I continued. It was one of the most somber moments of my life.

"These men were ten of the bravest men I have ever known. Glenn Haywood and Willard Spivey accepted the risks of being our point team while leading us into an area infested with booby traps and land mines on December 17th. Lieutenant Foreman saved several lives when he spotted a second land mine that same day. Whitey could have stayed behind when we left for the bushmaster because of a medical condition, but he willingly went with us. Bob Emery could have moved to the mortar platoon, but he chose to stay with his friends in the third platoon. And Terry Thornton had talked with me about re-upping to get out of field duty, but he never pursued it. Charles Merritt had a strong religious belief and read his Bible nearly every day. Three of those men joined the third platoon just days before they died. I barely knew them. Although other men will be assigned to the third platoon, these ten men will never truly be replaced. They were fellow soldiers and were our friends. These ten men are not with us here today, but they will remain in the hearts and minds of many of us forever. Although the families of these men are mourning their loss, I hope they will somehow find comfort in knowing their loved ones bravely made the ultimate sacrifice while fighting for their country."

My voice was quivering when I concluded, and I fought back tears as I walked back to the firing squad. I stood at attention to the right of the squad and faced down the line of seven men.

Chaplain Wideman returned and asked that we observe a moment of silence, and then he offered a benediction. The chaplain then turned toward me and nodded his head indicating we should proceed with firing the volleys.

I cleared my throat and said, "Squad, Atten-hut."

The squad came to attention, standing shoulder to shoulder with their rifles to their right sides. First Sergeant Seavey called the remainder of the company to attention and then gave the command, "Company, Present Arms," which was the command to salute. Each man in the company raised his right hand in a salute. I gave a "Port Arms" command and the squad raised their rifles and held them across their chests.

"Ready." The men raised their rifles to their shoulders with the barrels pointed in the air as they stepped forward with their left feet and turned sideways.

"Aim." The men aimed into the air to the south over Firebase Patton.

They stood ready for an instant, and I shouted, "Fire!"

The thunderous sound of seven M-16s simultaneously firing broke the silence of the moment and startled many of the men who were standing at attention.

The men in the squad kept their rifles pointed in the air, and I again shouted, "Fire!"

A second volley roared into the air.

And for the final time, I shouted, "Fire!"

The sound of the shots again rang out and echoed over the firebase.

I gave the "Port Arms" command and the men returned their rifles to across their chests. They stepped back with their left feet and again stood shoulder to shoulder.

I then gave the command, "Squad, Present Arms," which was the command to salute. The men in the squad held their rifles vertically in front of their chests with the barrels pointed straight up. I raised my right hand to salute.

The bugler in the distance played Taps, and again, tears formed in my eyes. After the bugler finished playing Taps, I cleared my throat and gave the command, "Order Arms," the command to lower the hand salute. The memorial service was over.

I gave the squad the unofficial command of, "OK guys, you can relax." We all breathed a sigh of relief. It went just as we had practiced. I told the guys thanks and shook hands and gave them pats on the back for a job well done. Our formal tribute and sad goodbye to our ten fallen comrades had been completed. Captain Dalton walked over and thanked us for doing a great job with the firing squad.

We took a few minutes to reorganize and then the awards ceremony began with Captain Dalton speaking briefly to the company. He said he was proud of the way we had performed during the bushmaster and again expressed his sorrow for the losses we had sustained. The CO then began presenting medals to 15 men who were lined up in front of the rest of the company. He worked his way along the line and presented each man his medal or medals. Rick Shields received a Silver Star for rescuing Lieutenant Fielding during the ambush that past November. Our Chieu Hoi, Hue, was awarded a Bronze Star for leading us back to Patrol Base Hunsley that same night.

When Captain Dalton reached me, one of his staff said, "For wounds received in action on December 17, 1969 in the Republic of Vietnam, Sergeant Richard F. Hogue is awarded the Purple Heart."

While Captain Dalton took the Purple Heart from the leather carrying case and pinned the medal on my fatigue shirt, he said, "Hound Dog, don't get any more of these."

"I'll try not to, sir." We exchanged salutes.

After the last man received his medal the company was dismissed. I took pictures of the guys in the Third Herd who received medals and hung out for a while talking with guys in the company.

261

The third platoon was assigned an ambush patrol that night. After getting off course during our RIF that day, I wasn't sure all of the new men were truly ready, but I also knew they wouldn't learn anything sitting inside their bunkers. None of us knew everything we should have when we went on our first RIF or first ambush. Every man had to learn on the job and hopefully survive through his mistakes. I told Sergeant Hansen his squad had ambush duty that night and gave him the location. Dave Hardy was in Hansen's squad, so I told Dave to keep an eye on Hansen and help with the ambush. Dave had pulled dozens of ambushes and he knew what to do out there.

The night passed with the ambush patrol not having any contact. While Sergeant Hansen and his squad stayed at Patton to catch up on some sleep, the rest of the Third Herd joined the company for a RIF the next morning that would take us northeast of Patton and west of the Saigon River. We were soon aboard choppers, with several new men headed for their first RIF in the boonies. We were going to another uninhabited area near the Ho Bo Woods.

We landed in an open area on high ground. The first platoon led the RIF, with the third platoon in the middle along with Captain Dalton and his CP group. The second platoon pulled up the rear. We encountered easy going through open countryside dotted with trees, bushes and hedgerows as we moved along our route. As the hot, dry morning progressed we found trails with footprints that definitely weren't made by GI boots. Although we hadn't seen any enemy troops, they had been moving through the area.

The sound of a single explosion suddenly came from the front of the columns. And then there was silence. We all kneeled down and kept a watchful eye out around us. I had been in the field long enough to know a single loud explosion was almost always a booby trap.

Tom Anderson, our RTO, was next to me listening to his radio. Tom confirmed my suspicions when he heard that the first platoon had hit a booby trap and there were two men down. I told Sergeant Benson to move his squad forward and help the first platoon set up a perimeter. We patiently sat in our perimeter for fifteen minutes, but surprisingly, there was no medevac. We usually had a pretty quick response from medevacs. I knew we were a long way from Cu Chi, but one should have arrived. I walked over to Lieutenant Cartwright, the first platoon leader, and asked, "What's up with the chopper?" He didn't know but said the CO was raising hell over the radio. Lieutenant Cartwright told me his point man and pace man had been peppered pretty badly with shrapnel. He said, "They'll make it if that damn chopper ever gets here."

A couple of minutes later someone popped smoke when they heard a chopper in the distance. The two wounded men were quickly loaded on board. We slowed our pace after the first platoon hit the booby trap. There were surely more in the area. The ground was dry, and there was plenty of vegetation for concealment making the landscape ripe for planting booby traps. Even if there weren't any NVA or VC in the immediate area, the booby trap they had left behind had nailed two GIs.

The afternoon got even hotter with almost no breeze to help cool us down. I could see by the expressions on the faces of some of the new guys that their butts were dragging while we continued on the RIF that would cover five more klicks (three miles). Those men reminded me of myself on my first RIF on a hot and dry afternoon that past August when I was dragging butt and sucking down water. I had plenty of water and shared it with a couple of the new guys who had emptied their canteens and needed it much more than I did. We completed the RIF without any further incidents and were picked up by a lift of choppers late that afternoon. While we flew back to Patton, I noticed the new guys enjoying the wind blowing on them through the open doors of the Hueys.

Although peace talks and initial American troop withdrawals commenced in 1969, 20,501 U.S. personnel were killed in South Vietnam from 1969 to 1973 when the last American troops left South Vietnam. Lieutenant Colonel William Nolde from Mount Pleasant, MI was the last American casualty of the Vietnam War. He was killed on January 27, 1973, eleven hours before the cease-fire took effect.

Memorial service firing squad at Fire Support Base Patton on January 5, 1970. Left to right - Sergeant Richard Hogue, Mike Myers, Vic Ortega, Carlton Quick, Bill Casey, Dave Hardy, David "Wop" DiBasio and Ed Leberski.

Chapter 17

The Ambush

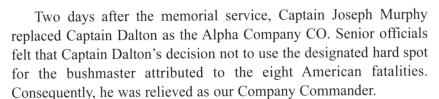

Two days after the memorial service, Captain Joseph Murphy replaced Captain Dalton as the Alpha Company CO. Senior officials felt that Captain Dalton's decision not to use the designated hard spot for the bushmaster attributed to the eight American fatalities. Consequently, he was relieved as our Company Commander.

We were operating out of Firebase Patton during the second week of January, when Captain Murphy brought Second Lieutenant David Phillips to our bunkers and introduced him as our new platoon leader. After Captain Murphy left I introduced Lieutenant Phillips to several men in the platoon then told him what we had been through during the past month. I pointed out the "old timers" as men he could rely on until the rest of the new men gained more experience. With our new 3-6 on board, we had twenty-two men in the Third Herd.

A short while later I heard yelling from the next bunker as though something serious had happened. I ran over and saw Carl Seals exiting from the bunker holding his blood-covered right hand.

I yelled, "Doc, grab you're bag!"

I then asked Carl what happened. He told me that Chester Sampson was throwing his knife at a beam and accidentally hit his hand. I turned and saw Sampson, one of the new guys, standing behind me. I pointed at him and said, "I'll have a talk with you later." Nearly all of us carried a knife, but this was the first time anyone had been injured by one. Carl was grimacing in pain when Doc Covington ran up and bandaged Carl's hand to control the bleeding. Doc then led him over to the medical aid station.

I immediately walked off with Sampson for a little ass chewing. I asked, "What the hell were you doing in there?"

"I threw my knife at a rafter and I hit Carl," Sampson guiltily said.

"You know, there are thousands of VC and NVA who are trying to kill us. We don't have to try to kill each other!" I was mad. I said, "Since Carl is one of our point men, maybe you'll have to take his place."

Sampson didn't say a word. He was really a good guy and had become one of our machine gunners. I actually didn't want to reassign him, but I also didn't want to let him off the hook for what he had done. Carl was later flown back to Cu Chi for X-rays. The knife had gone completely through his hand and might have broken a bone or severed a tendon.

Lieutenant Phillips and I later decided to leave Sampson as one of our gunners to avoid having to break in a new man. I gave Sampson extra details around the firebase and made sure he knew we had let him off pretty easy. A couple of days later we received word that the knife had severed a tendon in Carl's hand and he couldn't move his trigger finger. He was being evacuated back to the world for surgery. We never saw him again.

While we continued working out of Patton for several days, I spent time with the new guys telling them about my past six months in the field, and sharing some of my personal observations on the war. I had walked hundreds of miles through the rice paddies and woods of South Vietnam, flown about seventy-five air combat missions in choppers, saw many of my friends killed and wounded, slept in the rain, and literally fought for my life. And for what? Nothing had really been accomplished. When we suffered casualties, new troops arrived, and we would start all over again. It was a waste of lives and money. Additionally, we were risking our lives for the South Vietnamese people who didn't seem to give a damn one way or the other. In fact, many of them were making money from the war and wanted to see the war continue forever.

On January 23rd we were flown to a remote area near the Ho Bo Woods to join a mechanized unit at a hard spot, where our primary mission would be to pull nightly ambushes. The countryside was flat and covered with tall grass that had turned brown from lack of rain and thick vegetation much like I had seen before in the Ho Bo Woods. It was another desolate place, the kind the enemy liked to hide out in.

There was one armored tank to provide artillery fire and three APCs, each with a .50-caliber machine gun. Our three rifle platoons were spaced around the perimeter and assigned to foxholes with small sand bag walls in front. The mortar platoon and command post were set up near the center of the site.

During our first afternoon at the hard spot, Captain Murphy

assigned the third platoon an ambush site 500 meters south of the hard spot. Lieutenant Phillips and I both planned to go on the ambush. I would keep an eye on the new men and could take charge if necessary, if we had to pop the ambush.

They didn't fly out hot meals for us; therefore we each grabbed some dinner from a case of C-rations. As the sun was starting to set, Sergeant Benson's squad gathered their gear and walked through the perimeter wire along with Lieutenant Phillips, Doc Covington and me. I wasn't comfortable going out near the Ho Bo Woods with so many new men, but I also knew the only way those men would learn about pulling ambushes was to keep taking them out.

We easily found the ambush site and then moved to a holding position a short distance away and waited until it got a little darker. As darkness neared, I put my finger to my lips and looked around at the new guys to remind them to be as quiet as possible while we moved back to the site. I identified three positions, with two directly behind a hedgerow, giving us visibility along the trail and in the distance to the west, and as usual, the third position to cover the rear. Sergeant Benson and I each settled in at one of the two forward positions, and Lieutenant Phillips took the rear position.

It was completely dark, and with the ambush in place, we began our routine of having two men on guard at each position. I snuggled up in my poncho liner, put on mosquito repellant, pulled my mosquito net over my head, and hoped for some sleep before I took my first hour on guard.

Carlton Quick woke me up during the night, and whispered, "There's movement out there." I quickly sat up and Quick handed me the starlight scope. It was a clear night, and with the light from the stars and moon, I saw three people moving from left to right over 100 meters in front of us. They were too far away for us to ambush them, but I got on the radio to notify the CP and other ambush patrols that we had spotted three people to our west who were moving north.

Ten minutes later we heard several explosions in the distance. We soon heard over the radio that the first platoon popped their ambush on three NVA troops. Luckily, the first platoon sustained no casualties because claymores and hand grenades killed all three enemy troops without a firefight. The NVA had gotten by us, but the first platoon nailed them. The remainder of the night was uneventful and we safely returned to the hard spot the following morning.

We didn't go on a RIF that day, giving the men the freedom to write letters or clean their weapons, while others found a comfortable spot to catch up on their sleep. Because we didn't have enough water to spare for showers, we cleaned ourselves up as best we could with the available water. Some of the men had a small plastic pan they filled with water to wash with or shave. I normally pulled the liner out of my steel helmet, turned the helmet upside down and poured water in it to wash with or shave. I would set up the small mirror I carried, or hold it in my right hand while I shaved with my left. Except for the fact we were engaged in armed combat, serving in the field could have been described as an extended camping trip.

For the next three nights I alternated taking Sergeant Benson's or Sergeant Hansen's squad on an ambush and leaving the remaining platoon members to help guard the hard spot. We didn't spot any enemy movement during those ambushes, and for the most part, the new guys were catching on and fitting into the platoon with no major problems. Sergeant Benson was frustrated that the learning process seemed to be going slowly. I told him that he would learn something new every day he was in Vietnam.

Most of us old timers talked periodically about the men we had lost during the bushmaster a month earlier. Although it became easier to talk about what had happened, the pain of losing our good friends would never go away. Some of the new guys didn't understand what we were going through, but they would someday. I knew it would only be a matter of time before we would lose more friends.

On January 27th, we were told the hard spot would be abandoned on the first of February and we would return to Firebase Patton. During a conversation that afternoon with Lieutenant Phillips and Captain Murphy, we agreed I would stay with the platoon until another NCO was ready to take over my job. I was nearly the senior NCO in the company and hoped to find safer duty in the not too distant future. I told them that Sergeant Benson appeared to be the best NCO to replace me eventually. As an alternative, I suggested that Dave Hardy be promoted to serve as platoon sergeant. We didn't put a definite date on my reassignment, but the CO said he would get me out of field duty at some later point.

After eating another dinner of cold C-rations, I gathered my gear for what I hoped would be an uneventful ambush patrol. After we moved through the perimeter, Bugsy led us towards the ambush site through terrain covered with tall grass and scattered bushes, trees and hedgerows. We often had less than 100 meters of visibility in any direction once we left the immediate area around the hard spot. With that kind of concealment, it was easy for the enemy to move undetected. After we reached the ambush site we stopped for a minute while Lieutenant Phillips looked around, and then he asked me what I thought.

I said, "We can't set up here." It was a wide-open spot with no concealment or protection for us to set the ambush. The nights had been clear, and there had been a nearly full moon the past evening. Enemy troops could easily spot us if we set up there. I told Lieutenant Phillips I had seen a better site 100 meters back down the trail. We still had enough daylight if we hurried back and set up there.

Lieutenant Phillips agreed that we should find another site. I motioned to the men that we were turning around and told Bugsy to lead us back. I followed Bugsy and told him to stop when we arrived at the new site as the sun began setting. There were a few dirt mounds and bushes on the west side of the trail that we could use for concealment. It wasn't an ideal location, but it was too late to look elsewhere.

Lieutenant Phillips and I quickly designated positions for the men to settle into. I had originally planned to take the rear position, but for some reason I changed my mind and set up in the left forward position along the trail. Sergeant Benson set up in the right forward position while Lieutenant Phillips settled in the rear. I was with Bugsy, Greg Valdez and Greg Kilgore. When we were ready to set up our claymores, I told Bugsy and Kilgore, "Go ahead," while Valdez and I stood guard.

The two men walked out and placed their claymores facing the trail. When Bugsy stood up and began to walk back toward me, I started walking out to set up my claymore. I had taken only a couple of steps when I heard a seemingly muffled explosion. It was different from any other explosion I had heard in Vietnam. I immediately felt a terrific force and a blast of heat from the explosion, and in what seemed like slow motion, I fell backwards on the ground.

I lay on my back, dazed, not sure what had happened. But I knew something was seriously wrong. I felt the strangest feeling of both numbness and pain in my body. My ears were ringing, but I could hear other men screaming in pain and yelling, "Doc!"

I slowly sat up on my own in an effort to see what had happened to me. What I saw scared the hell out of me. My left thigh was slightly raised. All I could see was blood squirting out of my lower left leg with every beat of my pounding heart. My first frightening thought was, "I'm going to bleed to death."

I yelled, "Doc, get over here!"

I then looked up to the blue sky overhead and silently said, "Lord, don't let me die this way."

The first man to come to my aid was Greg Valdez. It was the first time he had seen anyone seriously wounded. Valdez knelt beside me staring at my leg and said, "Jesus Christ." Those weren't encouraging words for me. Valdez was frozen by what he saw.

I yelled, "Put something on my leg to stop the bleeding!"

Valdez opened the field dressing he was carrying and placed it over the gushing shrapnel wound in my leg. He then took the towel he had around his neck and tightly wrapped it around my left leg. I was relieved not to see any more blood squirting. I hoped and prayed that the bleeding could be controlled long enough to get me back to Cu Chi alive.

There was a lot of commotion and shouting voices around me. Men were screaming in pain and I heard Lieutenant Phillips yell, "One man at each position stand guard!"

"That's good, 3-6," I thought to myself.

While some men stood guard others helped Doc Covington attend to the wounded men. There had been only a single explosion and we weren't taking any enemy fire. I knew we had hit another booby trap and shrapnel had wounded several of us. One man continued to scream in pain as Doc Covington knelt beside me.

I tried to sit up but Doc put his hand on my shoulder and said, "Lie down, Hound Dog." Doc looked at my left leg and immediately pulled a large field dressing from his bag and tightly wrapped it around my leg.

I grabbed Doc's arm and asked, "Is the bleeding stopped?

Doc replied, "It's under control, you'll make it."

I breathed a sigh of relief. I then asked Doc, "Who's screaming?"

"It's Benson."

I rested my head on the ground and thought, "Damn, he just got here."

Doc gave Valdez another bandage to wrap around my right hand that had been hit with shrapnel and was covered with blood. I also told

Doc Covington my right foot hurt. Doc quickly checked my foot and said there were shrapnel holes in my boot, but it didn't look too bad. He wanted to leave it alone. I just nodded my head, indicating I understood.

I felt the sensation of pain, warmth and numbness in my left leg while I lay on the ground. I told myself, "It's gone." My right hand and right foot both hurt like hell, but I was more worried about staying alive long enough to get back to the 12th Evac in Cu Chi. Just before Doc moved on to check the other wounded men he asked if I wanted some morphine.

"Yeah, Doc," I said. I was feeling more pain than I had ever felt in my life.

Doc gave Greg Valdez a morphine tube and said, "Just stick it in his arm."

Morphine came in little disposable tubes (like a small tube of glue) with a needle on the end. You stuck the needle into someone and squeezed the tube. Valdez had never given anyone a morphine shot before.

I told him, "Go ahead, stick it in my arm."

Valdez stuck the needle into my upper left arm. I didn't feel anything with all of the other pain I was experiencing. Mike Myers kneeled beside me and handed me my glasses that he had found on the ground nearby. Surprisingly, they were still in one piece. Mike then put his hand on my shoulder and said, "Hang in there, Hound Dog. We'll get you out of here in a few minutes."

"I'm trying; but it hurts like hell, Mike."

I was awfully thirsty and I asked Mike for a drink of water. I knew we weren't supposed to give an injured man water, but he quickly grabbed his canteen and gave me a sip of water anyway. I said, "Thanks."

Mike told me it looked like Bugsy had tripped the booby trap a few feet to my right. The explosion must have blown shrapnel to the sides rather than straight up. Greg Kilgore and Norm Wilson had been peppered with shrapnel but were not too seriously injured. Bugsy and I had been more seriously wounded, and Sergeant Benson had been critically wounded in his left arm, left leg and abdomen. I continued to hear Benson's screams and moans of pain while we waited for a dustoff. The Third Herd was still recovering from the loss of half of our men a month earlier, but again, in a split second, five more of us were down.

271

Tom Anderson, our RTO, had called for a dustoff immediately after the booby trap detonated. I hoped and prayed it would be there soon. I was totally at the mercy of the good Lord. If the enemy attacked us, I was a goner. And if a dustoff didn't get there pretty soon I might be a goner anyway. I knew the bandages on my left leg wouldn't stop the bleeding forever.

To my great relief, I soon heard the most beautiful sound in the world – the distant sound of rotor blades chopping their way through the evening air. Someone popped smoke to identify our position, and I heard Anderson talking with the pilot on the radio to guide him into our location.

As the chopper neared, Lieutenant Phillips came over to me and said, "They don't have enough litters for everyone. Can you walk?"

If I hadn't been in so much pain, I would have laughed.

I said, "You're shitting me." He walked away without saying another word.

My initial fears of bleeding to death began to subside as the chopper neared. Although we were fifteen miles north of Cu Chi, the dustoff had arrived in what seemed to be only a matter of minutes after the booby trap detonated. But I wasn't out of there yet. They still had to get the chopper down, get us loaded aboard and get out of there before "Charlie" had a chance to ruin the rescue.

Mike Myers leaned over and put his arms around my head to protect me from the dirt and debris the chopper stirred up while it descended onto the trail in the front of our ambush site. Men ran to the chopper and pulled the litters off. A litter was placed on the ground beside me. Doc helped Mike and Valdez lift me on to the litter with Doc saying, "Be careful with his leg!"

I was quickly carried to the waiting dustoff and my litter was locked in place on the floor of the chopper. Three of the other wounded men were lying on litters loaded above and beside me. Norm Wilson was able to walk to the chopper with some help and sat on the floor. I lay on the litter with the noise of the chopper blades drowning out all other sounds.

I thought, "Let's get out of here."

The pilot revved the engine and slowly lifted the chopper off the ground. I looked over my shoulder and glanced out the open door and saw the remaining seven men starting to pack up all of the gear. Since the site had obviously been revealed to the enemy, they would have to get out of there. They could set up another ambush site, but with only seven men, they were vulnerable. I assumed they would try to move back to the hard spot. Ready or not, Lieutenant Phillips was fully in charge of the Third Herd.

A brief moment of sadness hit me as I lay on the litter. I might never see any of those men again. Guys I had fought with in the field and had fun with back at Cu Chi were quickly being left behind as the chopper roared through the evening skies over South Vietnam.

The medic on board checked on each of us while we flew along, making sure our bandages were secure and asking if we were OK for the moment. I told him my body hurt like hell, but there was nothing more he could do for me. I didn't hear any more screams from Richard Benson. I hoped he was still alive. I was grateful to have gotten off the ground and that we would be at the 12th Evac within minutes.

As we flew above the countryside, I thought about the thousands of wounded men in previous wars who died or suffered for days before being evacuated. I had helped carry several of my buddies to a waiting chopper after they were wounded, and most of them survived because of the prompt medical attention they received. I hoped that chopper would be the salvation for Sergeant Benson and the rest of us lying there, clinging to our lives.

The morphine didn't seem to be having much impact. My left leg started throbbing in pain and my right hand and foot continued to hurt terribly. But all of that was bearable. I knew I would soon be receiving medical attention from a host of doctors and nurses. Unless some new complication set in, I started to believe I was going to live.

I looked at the bandage on my right hand and noticed my watch was still attached to my wrist and was still running. It was 7:00 p.m.

I lifted my head and saw the outline of the perimeter bunkers as we neared Cu Chi. I could see a few dim lights as we flew overhead and neared the 12th Evac landing pad. I remembered my previous flight in a dustoff a month earlier. I had easily walked off the chopper after it landed at the hospital. Unfortunately, I wasn't going to be so fortunate the second time.

Nearly 8,000 American women served in Vietnam, most as military nurses. Several women were wounded and eight nurses died in Vietnam. One was killed by hostile fire. Army Lieutenant Sharon Lane died during an enemy rocket attack at Chu Lai on June 8, 1969.

Chapter 18

Doc, Save My Leg

When we touched down on the hospital landing pad, medical personnel rushed to the chopper and quickly carried us into the emergency room and placed us on examination tables that were aligned down the center of the room. Doctors and nurses immediately surrounded me and began cutting off my fatigues while they examined me to determine the location and the extent of my wounds. I felt a surge of pain and gritted my teeth when they cut the boot off my right foot. The medical staff also removed some of the bandages Doc Covington and Valdez had put on my wounds in the field. I couldn't see what they were doing with my legs, but one doctor was concentrating solely on my left leg to control the bleeding. I didn't ask him any questions. I hoped that by some miracle my leg could be saved.

One nurse asked my name, rank and service number as she began documenting my personal information and recording information the medical staff was telling her about my injuries. I heard doctors and nurses shouting orders and asking for help as a flurry of activity continued while they aided the five of us. Richard Benson periodically screamed in agony as another team of doctors and nurses attended to his serious injuries. I heard nothing from the other three wounded men as bustling activity continued in the emergency room. I endured surges of extreme pain while the medical staff continued to examine my injuries.

A nurse poked a needle into my left arm and quickly started an IV while another nurse put a new dressing on my right hand. After several minutes, most of the medical staff stepped away. I slowly lifted my head again to look at myself and realized I was completely naked. A nurse asked if I wanted a towel placed over me rather than being totally exposed. I told her I really didn't care. Lying there naked was the least of my concerns. She did lay a towel over my waist. I softly said, "Thanks."

Soon afterward a chaplain stopped by and asked if I would like him to say a prayer for me. I said, "Yes," whereupon he leaned over and said a brief prayer in my ear. I don't remember what he said, but it was comforting knowing he was praying for the five wounded men from the Third Herd.

A doctor walked to my side and introduced himself as Dr. Sullivan. He told me they would first take X-rays and then I would be taken into surgery. He also said my left leg was seriously damaged. Dr. Sullivan put his hand on my left shoulder and said, "I don't know if we can save it." I said, "I understand," and he walked away.

The doctor's words confirmed what I had feared from the moment I first saw blood gushing from my leg. I raised my head one more time, realizing that I wasn't just having a bad dream. I saw my left leg wrapped with dressing and gauze from my thigh to my ankle. My right foot looked like one huge bandage. I also moved the tips of my right fingers that were sticking out of another large bandage to make sure all five were still attached. They were.

Two medics soon wheeled me toward the X-ray room. I had to wait a few minutes because Richard Benson was given first priority among the five of us. Although I remained conscious while they took a series of X-rays, I was in a daze, only partially comprehending what was going on around me. I was then wheeled into the operating room and gently placed on an operating table. While the medical personnel scurried around, I struggled to remember what had happened during the past hour.

We were establishing an ambush site like I had done forty times before. Suddenly, an explosion threw me to the ground, and I was quickly fighting for my life. There would be no more firefights, no more booby traps and no more ambushes for me. From that night forward, my challenges would be much different than I had ever imagined, and might be as difficult, if not more so, than any of the challenges I had experienced during the past six months in Vietnam.

Dr. Sullivan walked up to the operating table and told me they were ready to administer the anesthetic. I reached up and touched him with my left hand and said, "Doc, save my leg." He said he would do the best he could. I began counting. "1, 2 ..." Everything went black.

When I first opened my eyes after the surgery I was so groggy I didn't comprehend anything that was going on around me. I heard muffled sounds of the medical personnel talking and moving around me and sensed them touching me periodically. I was in pain, but more so my whole body felt numb while I drifted in and out of consciousness. It was like I was in a dream and had no control over what was happening. Sometime later they wheeled me into a recovery ward and carefully moved me onto a bed. My left leg felt totally numb. I was too weak and groggy to lift my head to look and see if I had one leg or two. No one said much to me, and I wasn't alert enough to ask anyone about my leg. I spent the rest of the night sleeping most of the time but woke up periodically because of the severe pain and general discomfort.

When I woke up the following morning, I gradually began to feel a little more alert and also felt a lot more pain. I slowly sat up enough to glance down at the foot of my bed. I was stunned when I saw only my right foot sticking up from under the sheet. My left leg was gone. I didn't know where they had amputated it; I only saw that the sheet was lying flat where my left foot should have been. Although I had known there was little chance of saving my leg, I was still shocked to see that it truly was gone. I had often thought about being killed in Vietnam, but surprisingly, I hadn't thought about losing one of my legs.

A nurse stopped by to check on me and asked how I was doing. I told her I felt pretty lousy. She brought me some cereal and juice for breakfast, but I wasn't hungry. I just drank some juice.

A short while later another nurse walked up to my bed, followed by Dr. Sullivan. He explained that the bones, nerves and blood vessels in my left leg had been so severely damaged by shrapnel it was impossible to save my lower leg. My leg was amputated four inches below my knee. He showed me an X-ray of my left leg taken before I went into surgery. There was a three-inch section of bone missing below my knee. The bones had been completely shattered. Only a few bone chips were visible on the X-ray.

Dr. Sullivan went on to say that shrapnel had broken bones in my right foot and a bone in by right hand. He had also removed several pieces of shrapnel from my right hip. With all of the pain I had experienced elsewhere, I hadn't realized my hip had been injured. My right eardrum had also been broken by the concussion. Although I had sustained life-threatening injuries, he believed I should fully recover. The doctor concluded by telling me that I had lost a lot of blood. They had used three units of ringers lactate and two units of blood during surgery.

I wasn't alert enough to ask any questions. The news was so overwhelming it was all I could do to just comprehend what had happened to me. After Dr. Sullivan left, the nurse told me I would be leaving Vietnam in a couple of days and would be flown to Japan where I would stay for several days before I would be flown back to the world.

After the nurse left I took a moment to look at my mangled body. My left leg was gone below the knee. A huge dressing covered my knee and severed limb. My right foot was bandaged, and a splint wrapped with gauze extended up to my right knee. A large bandage was taped over my right hip. And there was a big dressing wrapped over my entire right hand, with only the tips of my fingers sticking out. Fortunately, I was left-handed.

Later that morning someone brought me a small bag with my personal belongings including my wallet, my watch and my glasses. I was happy to see my wallet again. I didn't have much money in it, but all of the addresses for my family and friends were in there. I hoped to write a few letters soon to let family and friends know more concerning what happened and how I was doing.

One of the nurses told me a telegram had been sent to my parents, but she didn't know how long it would take to be delivered. I wondered how Mom and Dad would take the news. At least I was alive. I knew whenever the telegram did reach my folks, the news would quickly spread all over town. I asked a nurse if I could have a sheet of paper and a pen to write a letter to my folks. I remembered my mother saying that, going by the date of my letters, she would receive them two or three days after I wrote them. I knew they would be anxious to hear from me personally. I wrote the letter as follows in shaky handwriting:

---

28 Jan

Hi

Well you probably heard what happened, don't worry. I am going to be all right. We hit a booby trap and five of us were hit. They had to take my left leg off below the knee. Besides that, I wasn't hit too bad. Now don't worry, I will be ok. I'm going to Japan tomorrow, I will be there awhile and then come home. They say I will walk OK again but will take a while. Now don't worry, I will be home safe soon.

Love Dick

Shortly after I had finished the letter to my folks, three men entered the ward. They were awarding Purple Hearts. Getting another Purple Heart had been the farthest thing from my mind. When the men reached my bed, a colonel asked my name to confirm they had the right man. Another man read the citation:

"The United States of America. To all who shall see these presents, greetings: This is to certify that the President of the United States of America has awarded the Purple Heart, first Oak Leaf Cluster (meaning second Purple Heart), established by General George Washington at Newburgh, New York, August 7, 1782, to: Sergeant Richard F. Hogue, United States Army for wounds received in action January 27, 1970, Republic of Vietnam. Given under my hand in the city of Washington this 28th day of January 1970."

The colonel handed me the citation and the Purple Heart medal in a blue leather-covered case. He shook my left hand and wished me well. The men then moved along to award Purple Hearts to several other men on the ward. With much less fanfare than was associated with my first Purple Heart, I was holding my second. My injury in December wasn't much more than a scratch. But when I was wounded on January 27th, I could have died. Upon reflection, my first Purple Heart was easily earned, but the second one definitely wasn't worth it.

In addition to the pain I felt, I was also very uncomfortable. I could only lie on my back. It was too painful to even try rolling to one side or the other. I was able to fall asleep periodically, and when I was awake, I watched the activity on the ward to pass the time. The ward was nothing more than a steel Quonset-hut type building with a row of hospital beds aligned along each side. Fortunately, it was air-conditioned.

Most of the other men on the ward also appeared to be seriously wounded. For the most part, we were a pretty quiet bunch. If the rest of the men felt like I did, I knew they weren't in a talkative mood. I tried to look around and see if any of the other guys from the Third Herd were on the ward, but I didn't recognize anyone.

To my surprise, I saw familiar faces a short while later. Vic Ortega, Dave Hardy, Ed Leberski, Mike Myers, Bill Casey and Wop were walking toward my bed along with Rick Shields and Jim Overbey. It was great to see those guys again. I shook their hands with my left hand while they gathered around my bed.

I smiled for the first time since I had been wounded. I summarized what Dr. Sullivan had told me. My left leg was amputated below the knee but the rest of my wounds should heal with no major problems. I talked about the past night with the guys who were on the ambush with me. Vic said after they loaded us on the medevac, they quickly packed up and slowly made it back to the hard spot in the darkness. Before those men were flown back to visit me that morning, the company had returned to the ambush site to be sure no gear had been left behind. It appeared the booby trap was a mortar round, or possibly a 105MM artillery shell. Either way, I was lucky to be alive.

I then asked the guys how they got back to Cu Chi. Bill Casey said he told Captain Murphy some of them wanted to come back to see me before I was evacuated, and the CO had a chopper flown out to bring them in. Seeing my friends one more time was a great boost to my morale. I couldn't remember any time in the past when they let men fly back to Cu Chi to see someone who had been seriously wounded. We normally just loaded men aboard a medevac and never saw them again.

I asked the guys what they knew about the four other guys who had been wounded. They thought everyone would be OK, except Richard Benson. Benson's left leg was amputated above his knee and his left arm was badly mangled. He was in critical condition after going into cardiac arrest three times during the past night and wasn't being allowed visitors.

Those men made me feel very special by coming back to visit me. After going through hours of hell the past night, flying those men in to see me was the best thing anyone could have done for me. Amazingly, I didn't feel the pain of my injuries while they were there.

The camaraderie and friendship that had developed among all of us was special. Although I knew I might never see most of those men again, I also knew I would never forget them. Each of those men said, in their own way, they were sorry I had been wounded and hated to see me leaving that way. Jim Overbey was pretty quiet that day. Seeing me lying in the hospital bed was difficult for him.

I shared a good-bye with a handshake or gentle hug with each of my friends before they left and we exchanged best wishes, knowing we were moving our separate ways to fight totally separate battles. I said, "You guys be careful out there without me. I'll keep in touch."

Dave Hardy said, "Let me know where you end up back in the world. I'll look you up someday."

Soon after the guys left, a nurse we called Maggie came by and asked if I was ready for a sponge bath. I said, "Sure."

A cute young nurse giving me a sponge bath, why not? After seeing some of my buddies, that would be my second treat for the day. I hadn't had a real shower in over a week and had some aged dirt and grime on me that hadn't been cleaned off during my surgery. I had noticed earlier in the day I was still naked under my sheet. I didn't know why and, frankly, didn't care.

Maggie started by washing my face and then she shaved me. I hadn't shaved for a couple of days and was in need of one, at least according to Army standards. Maggie then used the sponge to wash my arms, chest and back. She lifted the sheet at the foot of the bed and washed the upper part of my legs that weren't covered with dressings.

Maggie gave me a little smile after she finished my sponge bath and asked if I felt better. I said, "I sure do, thanks."

A short while later I had more visitors. Captain Branch, my former CO and Lieutenant Donaldson, my former platoon leader, stopped by. A few minutes later, second platoon leader Lieutenant Higginson came in followed by Chuck Gorman, our former RTO, and Ken Hungate, an RTO in the CP group. I didn't know where all of those guys had come from, but I was happy to see them. They were all naturally concerned about me and quietly listened while I explained my injuries and what I knew about my prognosis.

Lieutenant Higginson said he hated hearing about me being wounded so badly, but he could tell by the expression on my face that I was happy to be going home. I told those men that I never expected to end up like I was, but fortunately I wasn't lying in the morgue. I had to accept my fate and be thankful to be alive to talk about it. Those men stayed for a while and then we shared good-byes and best wishes.

I fell asleep later that afternoon and woke up when they served dinner. I still wasn't very hungry, but a few bites of food did hit the spot. After dinner I was told that unless complications arose, I would be flown to Saigon the next morning, and then on to Japan to continue my recovery. I had looked forward to leaving Vietnam almost from the first day I had arrived but I hadn't planned on leaving flat on my back. However, after seeing twelve of my friends killed in action, I knew I was still one of the lucky ones. The hours after being wounded had been the most traumatic hours of my life. Although physically, and possibly mentally, I would never be the same, I was anxious to leave Vietnam. My fighting days were over.

Lying in bed and sleeping whenever I chose was a huge contrast to the past six months. But nearly getting killed was an awfully hard way to get some bed rest. I awoke again later that night when most of the lights on the ward were turned off. It was quiet while the other men slept, but I stayed awake wondering what would happen to me and how losing my leg would impact the rest of my life. Maggie and another nurse were on duty, quietly talking and catching up on paper work. When Maggie saw me stirring, she walked over to see if I needed anything. I said I was fine, just concerned about my future.

Maggie pulled up a chair and began talking with me. It wasn't a nurse-to-patient conversation; rather, it was a young woman talking with a concerned GI. She asked me about myself and what I had been doing during my tour in Vietnam. I told Maggie I was from Iowa and briefly summarized my experiences stomping through rice paddies and the Ho Bo Woods and seeing twelve friends killed.

Maggie told me she had worked in the emergency room for the first few months of her tour, but enjoyed the less traumatic pace of work since she had moved to the recovery ward. She would be ending her tour that June and was looking forward to leaving Vietnam. Maggie said it was difficult watching all of us guys coming through the hospital with missing limbs or bodies otherwise maimed. Maggie asked me how I was dealing with losing my leg. I told her I had accepted what happened and was just glad to be alive.

"That's great," Maggie replied with a smile and then offered her insight into my future. She thought I would be in Japan for a week or two and then be flown back to the world. I would likely end up at Fitzsimons Army Hospital in Colorado, because it was the largest military hospital close to Iowa. Maggie said she might be traveling through Colorado in June and would try to stop by and visit me. I doubted she would ever look me up, but it was nice to hear her say so anyway.

Maggie went on to say I would be fitted with a prosthesis (artificial limb), and I would be able to walk with no major problems. She encouragingly told me I should be able to lead a nearly normal life. Maggie spent half an hour talking with me and then said she should check on other patients. I said, "Thanks for visiting with me, Maggie."

She leaned over and gave me a little kiss on my cheek.

After Maggie walked away I thought about our discussion. Her words relieved my concerns and made me feel more comfortable regarding my future. That conversation was the best medicine she could have given me. Maggie's words helped me get through the next few days and weeks of my slow recovery.

I fell asleep later, but continued to wake up periodically with severe pain or discomfort. I was also anxious about leaving the next morning and taking the first step on my road to recovery by moving on to Japan. There was a lot of uncertainty in front of me, but I anticipated it wouldn't be any worse than what I had experienced during the past day and a half.

I awoke the morning of January 29th to the sounds of the staff moving around the ward. The lights were on and the nurses were checking patients and dispensing medications while others served breakfast to those who were hungry. Maggie stopped by before she went off duty and gave me her best wishes. I thanked her for taking good care of me and said good-bye.

While I lay in bed that morning I wondered if my parents had received the Army's telegram, and if so, how they were dealing with it.

(The following happened in Schaller, IA on Thursday, January 29, 1970.)

It was a typical cold winter day in Iowa with a few inches of snow on the ground. Dad had left for work around 7:00 a.m. and would be out of town for the day delivering hybrid seed corn. Like most small towns, Schaller didn't have a Western Union telegraph office, but there was a telegraph machine at the Central Popcorn Company. When the office staff arrived on the morning of January 29th, the following telegram was there:

WESTERN UNION
TELEGRAM
W. P. MARSHALL, President

Paid from Washington D.C. Jan. 28, 1970   10:37 P.M.

Mr. & Mrs. Charles Hogue
Schaller, Iowa

Secretary of the Army has asked me to inform you that your son Sgt.
Richard F. Hogue was wounded in action in Vietnam on 27 Jan. 1970 by
fragments while establishing a night defensive position when a booby trap
detonated. He received traumatic amputation on the left leg below the knee
and wounds to the right hand, right foot and flank.

Please be assured that the best medical facilities and doctors have been
made available and every measure is being taken to aid him. He is
hospitalized in Vietnam. Address mail to him at the hospital mail section
APO San Francisco 96381. You will be provided progress reports and
kept informed of any significant change in his condition.

Kenneth Wickham, Major General USA

THE COMPANY WILL APPRECIATE SUGGESTIONS FROM ITS
PATRONS CONCERNING ITS SERVICE.

Everyone in the office knew my family and me. Jane Witte, who first saw the telegram, was shocked and she knew my parents would be terribly upset when they received the news. She took the telegram to Jim "Ham" Currie who worked in the office. They talked about how they should deliver the news because they assumed my mom would be home alone.

Ham was a member of our Presbyterian Church. He decided he would find our minister, Reverend Nusbaum, to go with him to deliver the telegram to my mother. Around ten o'clock that morning Ham Currie and Reverend Nusbaum stopped in front of our house and walked up to the door. When my mother answered the door she knew they were delivering bad news.

They knew Mom's first thought would be that I had been killed, therefore the first thing Ham said was, "He's alive."

They gave my mother the telegram and quietly stood with her while she read the shocking message. She started crying, partially in grief that I had been seriously wounded and partially in relief I was still alive. Although my parents knew I was facing combat in Vietnam, that telegram was naturally very disturbing.

Ham Currie called the plant where Dad worked and explained what had happened. They would try to contact him somewhere along his delivery route. Mom then called my sister Marilyn in Sioux City and gave her the news. My sister planned to drive to Schaller to be with Mom. Ham called his wife, Norma, who came to our house and stayed with my mother until my sister arrived.

Mom, with Norma's help, called my sister Jan and a few other relatives and friends to tell them the news concerning me. My granddad walked over to be with mom after she had called him. After many people around Schaller heard the news, they called, and some stopped by the house to see if there was anything they could do. My lifelong friend, Dennis Christiansen, had arrived home on leave from the Army a couple of days earlier. He immediately stopped by to see Mom after he heard that I had been wounded.

My sister Marilyn arrived early that afternoon. She later called Jan Griffin in Omaha to deliver the news that I had been wounded. Ironically, Jan had received a letter from me a day earlier saying that I was doing fine.

They hadn't been able to contact my dad during the day; he pulled up in his truck late that afternoon not knowing I had been wounded. When he walked into the house Mom immediately told him what had happened and handed Dad the telegram. Marilyn spent most of the evening with my parents and helped call more friends and relatives to give them the news.

The word of my being seriously wounded again brought the war close to Schaller and created more worries for the families of several hometown men who were still in Vietnam at the time. My parents spent the next couple of days worrying about me and waiting for more news regarding my condition. Fortunately, they had the support of many friends and family.

Back in Cu Chi during the early afternoon of January 29th, they prepared to move those of us who were stable enough to leave. A nurse helped me through the painful task of putting on a pair of blue hospital pajamas. Almost any movement hurt. I was then placed on a litter and taken from the ward to a waiting bus. We were then taken to the airfield and loaded onto a C-123 twin-engine propeller transport plane designed to carry litters on both sides of the main cabin. The men walked slowly while they carried us on board and then gently laid each litter onto the brackets that held the litters in place during the flight. They thoughtfully didn't want to create any more pain for our already aching bodies. Once we were secured on board, the engines roared as we rolled down a bumpy runway and lifted off the ground and turned south towards Saigon.

I had experienced many long days and nights trying to survive in the boonies during the past six months, and there were many times when I thought my tour in Vietnam would never end. But when we lifted off that afternoon I remembered my arrival in Cu Chi like it had been yesterday. My tour of duty was nearly finished. We flew over the rice paddies and hills below where other men were still exposed to firefights and booby traps. I wondered, "How many more men would lose their lives and limbs before the war was over?"

It was a short flight to Saigon thirty miles southeast of Cu Chi. The pilot made his approach and made a smooth landing at Tan Son Nhut airbase. I was carried from the plane and transported by bus a short way to a hospital holding ward where I would spend the night. I would fly on to Japan the next morning. I was beat and in pain after I was helped from the litter onto a bed. My whole body ached from the vibrations and bumps during the trip. I obviously had little endurance.

After I settled into my home for the night, a nurse came by to check on me. She gave me a shot of medication to ease my pain that was getting worse and also gave me a penicillin pill. All of us who had been seriously wounded were given penicillin for several days to combat infection from the rusty shrapnel, dirt and debris that had pelted our bodies. When they brought my dinner that evening, I nibbled on a few bites of mashed potatoes and corn but left most of it on the plate. I didn't feel like eating. Later they offered me the choice of a beer or soda. I normally wouldn't have passed up an offer of a beer, but I felt so bad a beer didn't sound good. I asked for a 7-Up and slowly sipped it through a straw.

For the first time since I had been wounded I was depressed. Physically, I felt lousy, and I felt completely alone. Bugsy and some of the other injured men from the Third Herd might have been somewhere on the ward, but I hadn't seen any of them during the day. All my other Army friends were back in Cu Chi or out in the field, and I was still a long way from my family and friends back in the world. Just as I had made an emotional transition when I left home that past summer, I had to make an emotional transition as I left Vietnam.

Although I was given medication that helped to relieve some of my pain, I actually felt worse that night at Tan Son Nhut than I had the previous night in Cu Chi. I was dead tired, but couldn't fall asleep. I couldn't find a comfortable position for long and nearly any movement was painful. And the wound in my right hip started to become, literally, a pain in the butt. If I happened to turn toward my right side, it hurt like hell. I took several short naps during that long and uncomfortable night.

The hustle and bustle started early the next morning as the hospital staff got us ready for our scheduled nine o'clock flight to Japan. I finally felt a little better. Much of the severe pain I suffered the past night had subsided, but it was still very painful to move any of my injured limbs. I was hungry enough to eat some of my breakfast along with taking my early morning dose of medication. And I was also surprisingly in better spirits knowing I was leaving Vietnam in an hour or so. That would lift anyone's spirits.

They again started the ritual of moving each of us onto a litter and loading us on a bus that carried us to a large Air Force C-141 transport plane. It took quite awhile to load us on board and to make sure dozens of us wounded GIs were secured for the trip to Japan.

After the four jet engines started to whine we were soon headed down the Ton Son Nhut runway and lifted off from South Vietnam. It was a remarkable feeling, knowing I no longer had to worry about serving in combat. During the past six months I had grown accustomed to being exposed to the hazards of war and accepted the consequences of serving as an infantryman, including the possibility of death. I was still amazed how most of us had accepted our combat duty. We got up every morning, put on our gear, grabbed our weapons and, in a fashion, went to work. With one big difference – we never knew if we would live through the day.

But that was all being left behind while the plane rose skyward, leaving Vietnam in the distance. Although I was leaving seriously injured, I felt as though the burden I had been carrying for the past six months was being lifted from my shoulders. After the plane leveled off, the nurses came around to check on each patient. I was doing fine. I settled into a reasonably comfortable position under the circumstances and finally went to sleep.

The six-hour flight to Japan was uneventful for me, although it was a challenge to pee into a little disposable urinal since I only had the use of one hand. I ate a little lunch and drank a small carton of milk, but for most of the flight I watched the nursing staff take care of the patients and dozed off now and then.

The pilot finally announced we were approaching Kadena Air Force Base at Yokohama, Japan. When they opened the large door on the rear of the plane I felt something I hadn't felt in a long time, cold air. I had expected it to be warm in Japan, similar to what it had been in Vietnam, but I had guessed wrong.

I was glad I had a blanket over me when they carried me from the plane that afternoon. It wasn't a freezing cold like I had often experienced back in Iowa, but it was cold enough to be a bit of a shock to my body until I was inside the warm bus. After another short ride, we were taken off the bus through the cold air again and into a large hospital. I was placed on a wheeled cart and rolled down a long corridor and into a ward that held a dozen men. After I was transferred into a bed, I put the small bag containing my wallet, shaving gear and a pen and paper I had been given before I left Vietnam on a little stand beside my bed. I was settled.

I looked around to check out my new home. There were windows behind a row of beds on each side of the ward with men lying in them, looking much like me, covered with huge white dressings. I saw several other men with limbs missing; two men had lost both of their legs. Everyone basically looked in relatively bad shape. I guessed that we had all been wounded in Vietnam and were recuperating until stable enough to be flown back to the world.

After crossing nearly 3,000 miles of ocean that day and being a little closer to the world I felt pretty good. It still hurt when I moved, but I didn't have constant pain like I had during my first couple of days and nights. After dinner I settled in and got a decent night's sleep. The next morning I encountered some of the new experiences associated with what I anticipated would be a long hospitalization. I had used a urinal several times the past couple of days but hadn't had a "BM." After breakfast it was time. A nurse knew it would be too difficult and too painful for me to move to a toilet. She handed me a bedpan and then pulled the curtain around my bed to give me a little privacy. I pulled myself up with my left arm using a bar that hung over the center of my bed. After some painful maneuvering, I finally scooted my butt onto the cold, metal pan. Getting on was tough, but getting off without creating a mess was an even greater trick. As the days passed, we laughed at each other when we called for a bedpan, knowing what a pain in the butt it was to use. I couldn't wait to be able to use a toilet again. Even those smelly out houses in Vietnam were better than using a bedpan.

My next experience was to be taken from my bed in a wheelchair to physical therapy. I thought after nearly being killed and losing one leg, I would be able to relax for a few days. But no, they wanted me to start exercising to help the healing process and prevent my muscles from degenerating too much. A therapist helped me lift small cloth bags filled with steel pellets with my arms and legs. My right foot didn't hurt too much when I lifted the weight with my leg, but it was painful when I lifted a pellet-filled bag with my right hand. I could lift my left thigh with little pain, but when I tried to bend my left knee, my stump, as I had learned to call it, hurt like hell.

After spending thirty minutes with the physical therapist, he wheeled me back to the ward. Later that morning a doctor told me I would be going into surgery the following morning to make sure all of the shrapnel and debris had been removed from my left leg and to further close the wound with stitches. I wasn't looking forward to another operation but I wasn't given a choice.

That afternoon a corporal came around and asked me if there was anyone I wanted to call back in the world. They would arrange for calls through the Military Affiliate Radio System (MARS). MARS would transmit a radio signal from Japan to a radio operator in the United States, who would contact our desired party by telephone to communicate with us. They would coordinate in advance with the calling party for a time to call and then bring a mobile phone to us at the designated time for our call. They normally made the calls during the mornings in Japan when it was the previous evening back in the world.

My folks were the first ones I wanted to call. I knew they would be relieved to talk with me and hear how I was doing. I also listed my sister Marilyn, girlfriend Jan, and college buddy Paul Alesch as people I would like to talk to. I was excited about being able to talk with my folks and others back home during the next few days.

I hadn't done much the past couple of days except travel, but the time had passed quickly. I kept wondering what the guys in the Third Herd were doing and how Lieutenant Phillips was adjusting without me. I hoped every man I knew in Vietnam would eventually make it safely home, but I also knew that was a long shot. Between December 17, 1969 and January 27,1970, the Third Herd lost twenty men. Ten were killed and ten others had been seriously wounded, including me.

A nurse woke me up early the next morning for my eight o'clock surgery. I'm not sure how long I was in surgery, but I woke up sometime later feeling groggy and my left leg ached. After an hour or so in the recovery room, I was taken back to my bed on the ward.

While I settled into my bed they tightened a harness around my left leg at my knee and attached a cable from the harness to a weight suspended from a pulley at the far end of my bed. The weight kept traction on the skin they had saved around my stump and would keep the skin from shrinking upwards. I was told they were able to save enough skin to form a flap over the end of my stump that would heal and become durable enough to hold up after I was walking on an artificial leg. That harness soon became another discomfort and further limited my movement.

Later that day I got some bad news. The practice for those who had amputations was to leave an area around the amputation open for several days to allow any infection to drain out. A nurse or corpsman would come around twice daily to change the dressing over that open wound. I had seen the staff changing the dressings on other men the previous day and listened to them moan and sometimes scream in agony when they removed the old dressing from their raw open wounds. I didn't realize I would be in store for that same treatment.

But I was told I was fortunate. I had only a relatively small opening near the end of my stump. Changing my dressing would be less painful than for those men who had nearly the entire end of their stumps open because doctors weren't able to save natural skin. Those men would require skin grafts from other parts of their body to cover their stumps.

Late that afternoon I experienced my first dressing change. After watching the other men, I knew it was an experience to prepare for. Before they started I put a washcloth in my mouth to prevent breaking a tooth when I gritted my teeth. I then grabbed the crossbar over the bed with my left hand and tightly held on for the oncoming pain. I almost felt sorry for the corpsmen and nurses who had to change our dressings. They knew how much pain they were inflicting, yet they knew it was something that had to be done.

The corpsmen unhooked the traction from my left leg and removed the harness. That felt great. He then started removing the heavy dressing covering my stump. I felt no pain at first. But when he removed the layers of gauze closer and closer to my open wound, I first felt some tingling and then a little pain, and then it hurt like hell! I gritted my teeth and quietly moaned while gripping the wooden bar with all my might during the excruciating pain while the final few layers of gauze were removed from the exposed tender nerves. They had moistened the dressing closest to the open wound with saline to make it easier to remove, but it still hurt terribly.

I breathed a sigh of relief when the corpsman said, "I'm finished."

Putting on the new dressing wasn't quite as bad as removing the old one. It hurt, but I knew the worst was over, until the next change. Enduring those dressing changes was definitely the worst pain I had ever felt in my life. They hurt much worse than any of the pain I endured when I was first wounded. After experiencing all of that pain with my first dressing change, I definitely felt sorry for those men with large open wounds on their stumps who literally screamed in agony during each dressing change. A nurse told me they would reduce the number of dressing changes in a few days and allow my stump to heal if there were no signs of infection.

During the morning of my third day in Japan a mobile telephone was wheeled near my bed. My parents had been reached. I had to say "over" at the end of each of my statements so the radio operator could switch the controls to bring in the other person from "the world" when they talked. Mom had a list of questions, "Could I sleep? Did I have my glasses? How was my hand? and How long would I be in Japan?"

We talked for several minutes, and I reassured her I was doing fine. I told her I would let her know when I would be leaving Japan and where I would be hospitalized in the United States. I then briefly talked with my dad. He mostly wished me the best and hoped I wasn't in too much pain. Our conversation was slow because each transmission took a few seconds to travel half way around the world through the airways. But it was great to talk with my folks again. I knew they also felt much better after hearing my voice.

With each passing day, I began to feel a little better and was able to do a few more exercises as I continued with physical therapy each morning. But it was still too painful to lie on my right side because of the wound on my hip. One afternoon my doctor cut off the large bandage that covered my right hand and removed the stitches that had closed two wounds between my fingers and several stitches below my right thumb. A corpsman then put a plaster cast on my hand that extended to just below my elbow because shrapnel had broken the bone at the base of my thumb.

The days in Japan were wearisome. I was confined to my bed with the traction attached to my left leg except when I went to PT. I spent a great deal of time writing to my family, Jan Griffin and many friends to make sure they knew I had been wounded and to let them know I was doing fine under the circumstances. When one of my calls back to the world was arranged, a phone was brought to my bed. I talked with my sister Marilyn and she sent her love and best wishes. Jan Griffin was glad to hear from me and she passed along the best wishes from the Wayne State gang. Paul Alesch said he had received my first Purple Heart and the Bronze Star I had sent to him a few weeks earlier. I had sent the medals to Paul rather than to my parents to avoid having to explain the events of December 17th to them.

One morning I woke up and felt the toes on my left foot itching. It was like a dream. I wanted to scratch them, except they weren't there. A nurse smiled when I told her about the sensations. They were phantom feelings caused by the nerves that formerly went down to my foot. Although they were severed, my brain sensed those nerves were sending feelings from my toes. She said I would continue to have those sensations and that the severed nerves would also cause periodic phantom pains in my stump for the rest of my life.

One afternoon I was surprised when Bugsy rolled up to my bed in a wheel chair. He had somehow tracked me down and came over for a visit. We smiled and shook hands. It was good to see a familiar face. He had been peppered with a lot of shrapnel, but it didn't hit anything vital. His doctor told him he would be flying back to the world in two days, but it would be a couple months before he could do much again.

I said, "Well, you got your Purple Heart."

"Yeah, I sure did," Bugsy said with a little smile. "That sure was a stupid wish." Bugsy shook his head as we both chuckled.

The only remembrance Bugsy had about the booby trap was walking back from the trail and being surrounded by a huge explosion that threw him to the ground. He hadn't found any of the other guys who had been wounded and didn't have any news about them. We wished each other well and shook hands before he wheeled back to his ward. I never saw Bugsy again.

Almost every day a few men on the ward left for the United States, and others moved into the vacated beds. Although I had left the war 3,000 miles behind me, seeing seriously wounded men arriving every day reminded me of the brutal battles that continued in Vietnam.

After several days of painful dressing changes on my left stump, my doctor said he believed the risk of infection was over. From then on they changed the dressing only once a day while the wound began to heal. With each passing day, movements became less painful and I was able to partially turn on my left side to sleep. Some days it felt like my butt was totally numb after lying on it all the time. Unfortunately, my left leg was still attached to that uncomfortable traction that was nearly enough to drive me crazy.

After eight days in Japan my doctor told me my injuries had stabilized enough to be shipped back to the world. My orders hadn't been finalized, but he believed I would be going to Fitzsimons Army Hospital in Aurora, Colorado, just like nurse Maggie told me. I was able to place a call to my folks the following morning and told them I would arrive in Colorado in a few days.

Two days later it was my turn to hit the road, so to speak, and catch my flight back to the world. I had been given two books and some stationery and a few letters that had caught up with me while I was in Japan. But all my personal possessions still easily fit into a little travel bag I was given for the flight. Once again I was placed on a litter and taken out in the cold for a bus ride to the airfield. I had never imagined flying back to the world lying on a litter, but it was a lot better than going home in a box.

After we lifted off the pilot told us we would fly to Alaska for a brief refueling stop and then fly to Scott AFB in Illinois. I would be flown on another plane to Colorado, my final destination. I read a book to pass the time and took a couple of naps during the flight to Elmendorf AFB near Anchorage. When they opened the door I could see it was dark outside, and it was very cold.

An hour later we began the last leg of the flight that would bring me back to the heart of the good old USA. While Vietnam got farther away with each passing hour, I continued to think about my friends in the Third Herd and the thousands of other men who were still fighting for their lives. Although I was seriously wounded, I would soon be safely back in the world. A month ago, the world seemed so far away. Gradually, Vietnam was becoming the far away place.

After a flight of nearly six hours we touched down at Scott AFB, Illinois. Scott was used as a central stop for many of us wounded GIs before being transported to our final destination. Again I was taken from the plane and transported to a hospital ward to await a flight to Colorado the following morning. When I finally settled into another bed late on the afternoon of February 12th, I actually felt pretty good, the best I had felt since being wounded. It was probably the combination of my wounds continuing to heal and the fact that I was back in the world, the United States of America.

That evening a nurse helped me slowly move from the bed and into a wheel chair, so that I could call my parents from a pay phone located in a hallway just outside the ward. It was difficult navigating the wheelchair with only one good arm, but I slowly maneuvered down the aisle in front of the row of beds and eventually made it to the phone.

When I reached Mom I said, "I'm back in the world."

"What?"

"I'm in the United States, near St. Louis." Mom finally understood.

I went on to tell Mom I would fly to Colorado in the morning. She said to call her when I arrived at Fitzsimons Hospital. She and Dad planned to drive from Iowa to visit me. Mom said Dennis Christiansen was still home on leave and was planning to come along to visit me and help Dad drive. I hung up the phone looking forward to seeing my parents and a good friend again.

The following morning was cold, but the sun was shining brightly as the jet lifted off carrying me to Colorado. I had never been to Colorado, but I got a glimpse of the snowcapped Rocky Mountains in the distance to the west before we touched down that morning at Buckley Air National Guard Base in Aurora, Colorado. I breathed a short sigh of relief when the plane rolled to a stop. My traveling days were over for a while. I was 700 miles west of Schaller, Iowa, but I finally had arrived at what would be my home for several months. I wondered what was in store for me in Colorado.

Approximately 300,000 Americans were wounded in Vietnam. 75,000 Americans were permanently disabled by their wounds. 5,283 suffered single limb amputations and 1,082 suffered multiple limb amputations.

Chapter 19

Fitz

It was a bus ride of about five miles to Fitzsimons Army Hospital in Aurora, Colorado, an eastern suburb of Denver. Six of us were wheeled into the large hospital on carts and lined up in a corridor while a clerk took the files we carried with us and checked us in. I was anxious to get settled in, but it was another one of those Army drills of "hurry up and wait." After almost an hour of waiting, the clerk returned, and I was taken to Ward 5-East, the men's orthopedic ward. I was wheeled down a long corridor and then we stopped by a bed in the middle of the large ward. With some help I slid from the litter onto the bed. I took my few worldly possessions from my little travel bag and put them in the bed stand to the left of my bed. Traveling light sure made it easy to unpack.

Ward 5-East was divided into several sections, with twelve men in two rows of beds in each section. Again I saw men with missing limbs and others with dressings covering their multiple injuries received in Vietnam. The man in the bed directly across from me slid off his bed into a wheel chair and rolled over to say hello. He had no option but to use a wheel chair, because both of his legs were missing.

"Hi, I'm Gale Bertrand."

I reached out with my left hand and shook his hand.

"I'm Dick Hogue."

Gale told me he had lost his legs when two enemy hand grenades exploded almost at his feet. He was lucky to be alive. Gale briefly explained how things functioned around the ward and introduced me to a couple of men who were in other beds nearby. A young nurse then stopped by to take my vital signs and check my injuries and dressings. She said a doctor would visit me the next morning.

I then asked the nurse if I could make a phone call. She brought a phone and connected it to a phone jack near my bed to call my folks. It was early afternoon on February 13th. My mother had been anxiously awaiting my call and was happy to hear I was safely in

Colorado. Mom, Dad and Dennis would start out during the early morning hours on Saturday and arrive in Colorado that afternoon.

I also called Jan in Omaha. It was great to hear her voice again. She was also glad I had finally made it back to the States and was anxious to see me. I told Jan my parents were driving out that weekend, but I recommended she not rush out to see me until I was feeling better and could leave the hospital. I asked her to call some of my Wayne State buddies to let them know where I was.

Later that afternoon a corpsman brought a wheel chair to my bed that was designed for patients who only had the use of their left arm. Most wheel chairs had a metal ring attached to each wheel to turn them. But with my right hand in a cast, I couldn't grip the metal ring on the right wheel very well. That wheel chair had the normal metal ring for the left wheel, but it also had a second ring adjacent to it attached to an axle that ran to the right wheel. I was shown how to grasp the two metal rings with my left hand to turn both wheels. After I slid into the chair I wheeled around the ward, and after a few zigzags I was finally able to go where I wanted most of the time. I used that time to check out Ward 5-East. I found the restroom at the rear of the ward with running hot and cold water and real flush toilets.

"Welcome back to the world," I thought.

Near the front of the ward was the nurses' station and patient treatment rooms. Along the main corridor leading into the ward were private rooms occupied by officers and higher-ranking enlisted men. Rank had its privileges, even in a military hospital. There was also a balcony we could go out onto when the weather was nice to get some fresh air and see the mountains to the west. President Eisenhower had spent time on that balcony after he suffered a heart attack while in Colorado and was hospitalized at Fitzsimons in 1955.

Most of the terminology I had learned up to that point in my Army career was associated with the infantry and combat duty in Vietnam. But for the past couple of weeks I had learned new terminology associated with hospitals and medical care. I had learned I had a "BK" (below the knee) amputation. An "AK" was no longer an enemy rifle, but was an "above the knee" amputation. Accordingly, I was a BK amputee. The men and women who assisted the doctors and nurses weren't called "medics," they were "corpsmen." They didn't serve meals in a "mess hall," the hospital had a "dining hall." The medical term for what remained of my left leg was "residual limb," but it was normally called a "stump." And I quickly learned that Fitzsimons Army Hospital was simply called "Fitz." The list of new terminology grew every day for a while.

That evening I wrote a few short letters to friends letting them know where I was. I was then reminded of another reality of the world back home. I had to pay postage. After a relatively good night's sleep, I woke on Saturday morning when they delivered breakfast. I hadn't paid too much attention to the food while I was in Japan, mainly because I often wasn't hungry. But I was regaining an appetite. The meals at Fitz tasted pretty good, a heck of a lot better than C-rations.

After breakfast a corpsman brought me a pan of warm water to wash up and shave. I had just finished shaving when a man stopped by my bed and introduced himself as Dr. Marti, an Army captain, who would be my doctor. He asked a few questions while he looked at my medical records and then took a few minutes to check my injuries to make sure I was being properly cared for. He said a cast would be put on my right foot in a couple days after he reviewed my X-rays. He would also develop a long-term treatment plan for me after he had an opportunity to examine me further. After my right foot and right hand healed, he could also determine the extent of any muscle and nerve damage and whether it could be corrected by surgery.

I then asked Dr. Marti how long he thought my recovery would take. He said it would be at least six months. He explained it would be a few months before I could be fitted with a prosthesis and that I wouldn't be discharged until the medical staff had done everything they could for me and I could walk again.

When I looked at myself I knew I had a long way to go before I would be anywhere close to normal. But as bad as it looked, I had been lucky. Gale Bertrand was one of several double amputees on the ward. He had an AK and BK amputation. One man had lost one leg and one arm, and another man had lost one arm, one leg and his testicles. Several of the patients moved around in wheel chairs while others were confined to bed.

I wondered how some of the men on 5-East were dealing with the emotional impact of their gruesome physical wounds. Although most of the men appeared to be in relatively good spirits, I wasn't sure if I would have a very positive outlook if I were lying in bed with both of my legs gone, or an arm missing. It looked like most of us on 5-East would have to endure extensive rehabilitation before we would be discharged. Each of us would also have to deal with the emotional impact of serious injuries, in addition to our traumatic combat experiences in Vietnam.

While I waited for my folks after lunch, I wrote a letter to Rick Shields and Dave Hardy in Vietnam, telling them I was in Colorado. I asked them to keep in touch and let me know how things were going with the Third Herd. It was a strange feeling to be back on the opposite side of the world from those two men who had been such a big part of my life for the past six months.

Around three o'clock that afternoon, I looked up and saw a nurse leading my parents and Dennis toward my bed. I smiled and raised my broken right hand to wave at them. Mom almost ran to my bed and gave me a big hug while tears filled her eyes. I reached out with my left hand to shake my dad's hand while he greeted me with a big smile. I didn't notice at the time, but Mom later told me my dad cried when he first saw me. She said it was the first time she had seen him cry. Fortunately, they were tears of joy. Dennis stood at the foot of my bed while my folks hugged me.

He then moved closer and said, "Hey, guy, glad you made it back." We shook hands and shared a hug.

I didn't realize how much I had missed my parents until I saw them that day. Vietnam slipped a little farther to the back of my mind. My mother sat down in a chair next to my bed, but Dad wanted to stand for a while. He had been sitting for nearly 700 miles.

I was bombarded with questions concerning how I was feeling, the extent of each of my injuries and what they had been doing to treat me. My parents were obviously most concerned about the loss of my left leg. I told them I would ultimately be fitted with an artificial leg, and would walk again. I was fortunate to still have my knee making it easier to walk with a prosthesis than someone with an AK amputation.

Dennis was on leave before reporting for duty in Belgium. I was glad he took some of his precious leave days to come out and visit me. His twin brother Dean was still doing fine at Fort Ord, California. Dean was actually sitting on the plane headed for Vietnam that past July when they cancelled the flight. Everyone on board was reassigned elsewhere.

While we talked, Mom pulled out a plastic bag of homemade

chocolate chip cookies and handed them to me. I quickly took a couple and gobbled them down. She also had several cards people had given her to deliver. I opened those cards and enjoyed reading the get-well wishes. My mom said the phone had nearly rung off the wall the past two weeks with people calling to share their concerns and asking about my progress.

After talking with Dennis and my parents into the evening hours, they spent the night at a Holiday Inn outside the main gate to Fitz, and returned to see me early Sunday morning. My parents were naturally happy to see me, but were shocked when I told them some of the "realities" of my duty in Vietnam that I hadn't previously shared with them. They were even more thankful I was alive after learning twelve men in my platoon were killed while I was there.

Mom and Dad felt much better after seeing I wasn't suffering extreme pain and learning I should be able to lead a fairly normal life. Late Sunday afternoon I slid off my bed and wheeled myself down the corridor to the elevator where I shared hugs and good-byes with my parents and Dennis. They planned to drive to Fort Morgan, Colorado, seventy-five miles east of Denver, and spend the night with our former high school coach, Bob Keenan, and his wife, Barb. They would drive back to Schaller on Monday. The elevator door slowly closed. I was on my own again. I wheeled myself back down the corridor toward my bed.

The following week Dr. Marti examined me and put a walking cast on my right foot. He also removed the stitches from the wound in my right hip that would leave a nasty looking six-inch scar for the rest of my life. I then started a twice-a-day PT regimen designed to maintain my existing strength.

I soon learned my way around the hospital, which was on a two-mile-square Army post. The main hospital building was eight stories tall and had a post office and a small PX on the first floor. Fitz was one of the largest military hospitals in the country and provided medical care for several hundred men who had been wounded in Vietnam, in addition to caring for active duty and retired military personnel and their families. There was also a larger PX, Commissary (grocery store), movie theater, NCO and Officer's Clubs, bowling alley and administrative offices and maintenance facilities located in other buildings on the post.

I soon got to know several of the men on the ward and spent time with them shooting the bull or playing cards. The man in the bed to my right was Don Chilson. He and his twin brother had both been drafted, and his brother Ron had been sent to Vietnam. Because it was the Army's policy not to allow brothers to serve simultaneously in Vietnam, Don was stationed at Fort Riley, Kansas. Ironically, he broke his hip when he accidentally fell from a bridge. His brother Ron had survived his tour in Vietnam to that point without a scratch.

I also met Rodney Wunschel who was from Ida Grove, Iowa, twenty miles southwest of Schaller. We learned we both knew a few people from each other's hometown, and quickly developed an "Iowa" connection. An exploding B-40 rocket had seriously wounded Rodney in June 1969, and forced the amputation of his left arm above his elbow.

One evening shortly after I arrived at Fitz, two girls visited Don Chilson. While the girls were visiting, I boldly wheeled over to Don's bed and said hello. One of the girls was his cousin Vicki McKee. She hadn't visited Don before that evening, but said she would stop by again and gladly drive us off-post when we were able, since none of us had a car. Most of us on 5-East were in the early stages of recovery and weren't allowed to leave the hospital until our doctor determined we were well enough to do so. But eventually, we would receive our doctor's blessing to go off-post during the evenings or weekends.

During my first few weeks at Fitz I received a couple of hundred cards and letters. I returned to my bed on several days to find a big stack of mail lying on it. Some of the other patients were amazed.

"Where are all of those cards coming from?" Gale Bertrand asked one day. He then laughed and said, "There can't be that many people out there who like you."

I received cards or letters from what seemed like nearly every family that lived in or around Schaller. I also heard from relatives I hadn't seen in years and college friends I had nearly forgotten. I appreciated everyone's expressions of concern and their best wishes for my recovery. Like Gale had joked with me, I didn't realize there were so many people who cared about my welfare. I also received several letters from guys in the Third Herd and opened them with hesitation; hoping for good news, but also knowing the news could be bad. Fortunately, all the men I had left behind in the Third Herd were still alive and well. A couple of the guys mentioned that Lieutenant Fielding had recovered from his injuries received that past November, and had voluntarily returned to Vietnam. He was serving as the first platoon leader in Alpha Company.

I continued to encounter new events during my first month at Fitz. When the cast on my right hand was removed they discovered two problems. The shrapnel had severed nerves in my hand and left numbness in my ring finger and little finger, and the underside of my right thumb was completely numb. I felt no pain when they poked my thumb with a needle. Dr. Marti said the nerves would partially heal and I would regain some feeling; however, that would take years.

The more serious problem was that I had no movement or control of the tip of my right thumb. When I tried to grip something, the tip of my right thumb would bend backwards. Dr. Marti believed shrapnel had injured or severed the tendon leading to the thumb. I worked with a physical therapist daily for two weeks hoping to regain movement. When I tried to move my thumb I felt the tendon move in my wrist but the tip of my right thumb didn't budge. Finally Dr. Marti was certain the tendon leading to the tip of my right thumb had been completely severed. It would have to be repaired surgically.

Around the first of March Dr. Marti also ordered a pylon to be placed on my left leg. A pylon was a plaster cast molded over my left stump and continued six inches above my knee. Built into the plaster was a connecting device that enabled them to attach a metal pipe with an artificial foot on the far end. With the pylon, I could start walking to rebuild strength in both legs.

When the plaster dried, a pipe was cut to the proper length and a shoe was put on the foot. I was anxious to try walking again. But that was difficult. I still had the cast on my right leg, and the pylon didn't allow any flexibility in my left knee. After a couple of days walking in the parallel bars, I graduated to walking with metal crutches. It was slow progress, but each day I became more proficient.

One evening in early March I received a call from Allen Schwab. He had made it safely back from Vietnam that January and was stationed at Fort Carson, Colorado near Colorado Springs. His parents were coming out the following weekend, and he offered to drive up to Fitz and take me to his home that same weekend. When Allen and his wife Vicki arrived that Friday, we greeted each other with hugs, happy and thankful to be together again. Vicki and Allen proudly showed me their six-month-old son, Gary. Dr. Marti granted me a weekend pass, and Allen drove us to Colorado Springs.

Allen's parents arrived later that afternoon and greeted me with smiles and a hug. It was great being with old friends again to help put my experiences in Vietnam behind me. Allen and I didn't talk much about Vietnam. We enjoyed a relaxing time with his family and left conversations concerning Vietnam for another time. Allen was hoping to get an early discharge from the Army and start his final semester of college that summer.

Although I certainly wasn't happy about losing my left leg, being around other men who had similar and often more traumatic injuries, helped me with my emotional recovery. Periodically sharing "war stories" about our tours in Vietnam and telling each other how we were injured kept many of us from feeling self-pity or becoming emotionally destroyed. All I had to do was remember my twelve friends in the Third Herd who died to realize how fortunate I really was.

During the second week of March, I was transferred from 5-East to the outlying Ward 502. Ward 502 (or just 502 as we called it) was a two-story World War II era building 100 meters west of the main hospital. It housed over sixty patients. As a patient's medical condition improved, he was transferred to 502, to free up bed space on 5-East for the new patients who arrived daily. Eventually each man completed his rehabilitation, and was discharged from Fitz, and normally was medically retired from the service.

During that same time period, the cast on my right leg was removed, making it much easier for me to walk. The shrapnel wounds had left a large scar across the top of my right foot and other scars around my ankle. I could move all of my toes, but the shrapnel had severed nerves leaving most of the topside of my foot totally numb. Although the numbness felt strange, it didn't affect my ability to walk. Within a few days I was actually walking without crutches. Although it was far from walking normally, I felt like I had been given newfound freedom.

While our injuries healed and we became more mobile, many of us patients pursued our liberty again. Don Chilson's cousin Vicki drove Don, Gale, Rodney and me to the mountains west of Denver one Saturday. I was amazed by the beauty and vastness of the Rocky Mountains and clear blue skies. It was great to have Vicki to help us get out and about, because getting around wasn't an easy task. Guys were either in a wheel chair or using crutches and moving pretty slowly. Although for most of us it was a challenge just getting into and out of a car, getting out into the world again was a great emotional boost for all of us.

I was scheduled for surgery on my right hand the third week of March. Dr. Marti said tendons acted like a rubber band when severed, and the tendon had retracted into my arm. A hand specialist would assist him to make an incision on my right thumb and wrist until he found my severed tendon. They would then pull the tendon back and attach it to my thumb or, if necessary, take a section of an unused tendon from my forearm and graft it onto the severed tendon and reconnect it to the tip of my thumb.

I was transferred back to 5-East, and on March 17th, I was wheeled into the operating room for my third surgery in less than two months. I awoke in the recovery room feeling lousy, with my right hand in pain. I slowly regained my senses and returned to 5-East later that afternoon. My hand then started to throb and hurt like hell. I tried to sleep that evening but the pain kept waking me up. The following morning Dr. Marti stopped by to see me.

I said, "Hey, my hand hurt like hell last night. What did you do to me?"

Dr. Marti then told me they had to graft in an unused tendon to attach to my thumb. A large dressing around my hand and forearm held a splint in place. He said everything went well and I should regain movement in my right thumb.

After a couple of days the pain and discomfort subsided and I was back to my two-a-day PT visits. A week after the surgery on my hand, the stitches were removed, and Dr. Marti explained the scars from the incisions made during the surgery. One incision went from the tip of my thumb down to my wrist looking for the severed tendon. They didn't find it. A second incision was made from the base of my hand going three inches up the underside of my arm until they found the retracted severed tendon. Three little incisions across my forearm were made to remove an unused tendon, which was then attached to my severed tendon and finally reconnected to the tip of my thumb using a thin wire. The end of that wire protruded through my thumbnail. It seemed pretty amazing to me. A plaster cast was placed on my hand and forearm to keep my thumb immobile for the next month.

I had been talking with Jan Griffin about once a week after arriving at Fitz. She was planning to fly to Denver and visit me over Easter weekend, which was the last weekend of March. When I asked Dr. Marti for a weekend pass he asked me if I had been home yet. I told him no. Rather than giving me a weekend pass, he gave me two weeks' leave, starting March 27th. He asked me to see him Friday morning so that he could check my hand before I left.

I called Jan and told her to cancel her plans to come to Colorado. I then called my parents and told them to get ready; their son was finally coming home. I would spend Friday night in Omaha and drive with Jan to Schaller on Saturday. I made plane reservations on a United flight leaving Denver at three o'clock Friday afternoon. I also called Paul Alesch and told him to plan a party because I was arriving in Omaha around five o'clock Friday evening.

After completing my physical therapy Friday morning, I began looking for Dr. Marti. It was after noon when I finally saw him returning to his office. He checked my thumb to make sure I had good circulation and then wanted to remove the little piece of wire that was protruding from my thumbnail. He found a pair of tweezers, and like doctors normally say, he said, "This will just hurt a little bit."

I smiled and said, "Yeah, right, Doc."

He clamped onto the wire with the tweezers and pulled the wire out through my thumbnail. Surprisingly, it did hurt only a little bit. I had learned to walk fairly comfortably with the aid of my pylon and I normally walked without crutches. But Dr. Marti recommended I take my crutches just in case I had any problems while I was on leave.

I quickly cleaned up and changed from my hospital pajamas into civilian clothes that I had purchased at the PX. We were no longer required to wear our military uniforms when we traveled. When I walked to the nurses' station to check out, the place was a zoo. It took forever for a corpsman to record my leave.

It was almost two o'clock when I walked to the main floor that afternoon. I had called a cab and there was supposed to be one waiting by the main entrance to take me to the airport. There was no cab in site. About ten minutes later a corpsman who worked in physical therapy saw me waiting and he offered me a ride.

The corpsman dropped me off by the United entrance and I walked as fast as I could to the ticket counter. The ticket agent requested an electric cart when she saw my crutches, because I only had a few minutes to catch my flight. I was soon whisking down the long concourse toward the gate.

However, when I arrived at the gate the plane was being pushed away from the terminal. "Damn," I said, "I missed the plane."

Fortunately, there must have been a compassionate staff working that day. They returned the plane to the gate allowing me to board. Within a few minutes we lifted off into the skies over Colorado and turned east toward Omaha.

After a one-hour flight, the plane stopped at the gate in Omaha, I maneuvered to the front of the plane and stayed to the side of the walkway to allow other passengers to pass by while I slowly walked into the terminal. I smiled when I saw Jan waving at me. We greeted each other with a kiss and long hug.

She said, "Welcome home, Dick. You look great."

I smiled and said, "I do? I'm being held together with plaster."

I showed Jan the cast on my right hand and I told her about the pylon on my left leg. I explained what I had been going through at Fitz as we walked out to her car and while Jan drove us across town to Paul and Jane's apartment where some of the Wayne State gang was waiting for me. I anxiously walked to the apartment door and heard the noise from my friends inside.

I didn't knock, I opened the door and yelled, "You guys can't have a party without me!"

The cheers went up, and I was mobbed with hugs and kisses and handshakes. Naturally, Paul and Jane Alesch were there, Dick and Sheila Thompsen, Larry and Cheryl Dolish, and Dennis Pederson and his girlfriend Cindy were there too. I was soon laughing and chatting with the old gang and answering their long list of questions. Everyone was interested in how I was able to walk and was astonished when I showed them the pipe attached to the pylon.

A short while later Paul asked for everyone's attention. Paul went on, "Sergeant Hogue, for wounds received in action I present you the Purple Heart. For bravery in action I present you a Bronze Star."

I had forgotten about the two medals I had sent to Paul for safekeeping in January. The gang gathered around to see the medals and then quietly listened while I described the events of December 17th when the land mine killed Willard Spivey and then Glenn Haywood dying on Christmas Eve.

Jan and I enjoyed the evening together while I soaked in the pleasure of seeing her and my good friends. Only a few months earlier, I had wondered whether I would ever see them again. After experiencing some of the lowest emotional times of my life in Vietnam, I was beginning to experience some high points. I shared good-byes with the gang late that night and spent the night with Jan in the apartment she shared with two other girls.

Jan and I slept in Saturday morning and then we headed toward Schaller shortly after noon. I sat behind the wheel of Jan's Chevy II and drove a car for the first time in eight months. When I drove over the little rise on the south edge of Schaller and saw the familiar rows of houses, I felt an unbelievable sensation of happiness. I almost cried joyful tears as I drove into town that afternoon.

I stopped in front of my parents' house and saw my sister Jan who had just arrived home from college. She welcomed me with a big hug. Mom and Dad walked from the house and greeted all of us with big smiles on their faces. They remembered my being confined to a wheel chair when they visited me at Fitz six weeks earlier and were amazed to see me walking toward them.

Just before we sat down for supper that evening, Dwain Bloyer, a friend I had grown up with, called. He and his wife Sharon were home for the weekend and he asked if I was able to come over to see them. I told Dwain I would be there later that evening.

Dwain and Sharon greeted me with hugs and smiles when Jan and I walked into Dwain's parents' house. A short while later the front door opened and Marlys and Kenny Kroese rushed in. Marlys smothered me with a big hug followed by a hug from Kenny.

Other friends stopped by during the evening when they tracked me down as the word spread around town that I was home. Everyone was amazed to see me walking. After six long months in Vietnam and two months in the hospital, it was wonderful being with Jan again and relaxing with old friends while I answered many questions regarding my time in Vietnam.

After spending Sunday with my family and me, Jan returned to Omaha. During the following week, I continued receiving warm greetings from people while I ventured around Schaller each day, or when well-wishers stopped by our house to see me. It was as though I was a long-lost hero who had finally come home. On Monday evening during my second week at home, I went out with my old buddy John McDonough, and Ron Holstein who had been in Vietnam in 1966. We went to Carl and Dorothy Borger's place, a little bar and restaurant in Galva, another small town seven miles west of Schaller.

I got up during the evening and went to the restroom. When I took a step to leave the restroom I heard a "cracking" sound from my pylon. I stopped and shifted my weight to my right leg until I could determine what was wrong. I leaned down and could feel the pipe connection to the pylon was loose. When I moved it, the pipe came off in my hand.

I yelled, "Help!"

Carl, John and Ron rushed through the door. They were all stunned as I stood there on my right leg while holding the pipe in my left hand. After John and Ron helped me back to a barstool I looked at the pipe and saw the connection attaching the pipe to the pylon had broken. Everyone got a good laugh about my leg falling off in the restroom. John and Ron helped me into the house later that night and I slept on the living room couch.

The following morning Dad took the pipe and broken connection downtown to Glenn Woodke's Machine Shop. Glenn couldn't salvage the connection but used a torch and brazed another adaptor to the pipe that worked out well. I was again happily back on my "two" feet. I stopped by that afternoon to thank Glenn for fixing my broken leg.

He laughed while he told me that he had fixed almost everything over the years, but it was the first time he ever welded someone's leg back together. Glenn was a member of the VFW's Hup-Tu Squad. He asked me if I could attend their annual steak dinner the following Sunday evening as their special guest. I gladly accepted his invitation.

I also made a trip to Omaha near the end of my second week of leave to see Jan and to enjoy more time with some of the Wayne State gang. Jan had graduated from nursing school and was working at a hospital in Omaha. Although we both enjoyed being together, I had been gone for most of the past two years and would be in Colorado for several more months. We both acknowledged it was difficult trying to maintain a long-distance relationship, but we agreed to keep in touch with each other, and would see what happened after I was discharged from the hospital. We were both comfortable with letting our casual relationship continue with no commitments and no restrictions. Jan and I shared a hug and kiss when I left to return to Schaller Friday morning to spend my final weekend of leave.

Sunday morning Dad's brother Hallie and his wife Marie drove up from Des Moines to see me. Hallie had been drafted during World War II and was called back again to serve during the Korean Conflict. We chuckled while I told him that I thought one tour of duty in the Army was all I planned to give them.

After church I enjoyed another delicious dinner with my family. I had lost weight after I was wounded, but had regained a few of those pounds eating Mom's home cooking. I shared pleasant good-byes with everyone when they left that afternoon, nothing like the sad good-byes we shared when I left for Vietnam.

That evening the members of the Hup Tu Squad and their wives warmly greeted me when I arrived at the VFW Hall. After enjoying a great steak dinner I used a slide projector to show the group some of my pictures from Vietnam, while many of the men recounted some of their own experiences when they were in the service many years earlier. I enjoyed describing the event or men in each picture, but it was difficult when pictures of Whitey, Bob Emery or the other men who had been killed popped up on the screen and I explained how each of those men had been killed. Although I answered lots of questions, many of those men and women quietly watched and listened as I described the grim realities of the war in Vietnam.

That evening was a very special and emotional time for me, as I repeatedly listened to expressions of thankfulness that I had made it home alive and received sincere gratitude for serving in Vietnam. I gave everyone my heartfelt thanks for honoring me as their guest and I received their best wishes when I left the VFW Hall that night.

Monday morning, April 13th, I drove with my folks to Sioux City to catch a noon Ozark Air Lines flight to Denver. As we gained altitude and turned west toward Colorado, I lay back in my seat and thought about how great it had been to be home the past two weeks. I had never received so much attention in my life. I was truly thankful to have been from the small town of Schaller, Iowa, which had so many loving and caring people. The war in Vietnam was unpopular with some Americans. A few GIs were welcomed home by people spitting on them or yelling obscenities. I couldn't imagine how fellow Americans could be so cruel to men who were just doing what Uncle Sam asked them to do – serve their country.

After I checked back in at Fitz I found Dr. Marti. He had a good laugh when I told him the connection on the pylon broke, and my dad took it to Woodke's Machine Shop to get it fixed.

Shortly after I returned from leave I received a letter from Rick Shields in Vietnam. He was doing fine, but he had bad news. Rick wrote, "On April 1 (1970) Lieutenant Fielding was killed instantly by a booby trap."

I couldn't believe it. I read Rick's words again. That gung-ho son-of-a-gun had voluntarily returned to Vietnam after his wounds healed, and it cost him his life. Sadly, it must have been his destiny. He had arrived back in country a few days before I was evacuated, but I didn't see him. I unexpectedly had to deal with losing another friend in Vietnam. Ironically, Lieutenant Fielding had been a patient at Fitz after he was wounded that past November.

Rick said the rest of the guys in the Third Herd were doing fine, and he also enclosed a picture that made me laugh but also nearly made me cry. It was a picture of me stark naked, taking a shower with water flowing from the rusty bucket in the middle of the little grove of trees that past November. Rick said he found the picture when going through Terry Thornton's personal gear after he was killed on December 28th. Rick obviously didn't think Terry's family would appreciate a naked picture of the old Hound Dog. I chuckled to myself as I looked at that picture and wondered why he had taken it, unbeknownst to me. But then I sadly thought about Terry being killed one month later.

After the cast was removed from my right hand during the first week of May, Dr. Marti asked me to move the tip of my thumb. It moved! It felt stiff, and there was a little pain, but I could move it. I continued physical therapy for several weeks and regained partial movement of my right thumb without pain. Although I would have permanent limited flexibility of my thumb, my right hand looked normal except for the scars.

The following week Dr. Marti had my pylon removed to examine a deep scar on the front of my stump. Dr. Marti believed the scar would be problematic when I was fitted for my prosthesis. He determined that a "revision" was required to cut out the deep scar and re-close the wound to leave a smoother scar. He would simply revise the shape of my stump; therefore, the procedure was called a revision.

Without the pylon I couldn't walk. I either moved around on crutches or rolled around in a wheel chair. It was a little disappointing to lose my mobility, but I accepted it as part of my recovery. I knew it wouldn't be forever, and I also reminded myself I was still one of the lucky ones. The double amputees, like my friend Gale Bertrand, faced more difficult challenges than I did.

Now and then one of the men who had lost one leg would fall when he got up from bed. Simply from habit, he would try to take a step with that missing leg and fall to the floor. Just like phantom pains gave us the sensation that our missing limbs were there, when those men were still half asleep, they sometimes forgot they had lost a leg. Unfortunately, those men were quickly brought back to reality as they were lying in pain after their stump hit the floor.

There was one advantage to not having a cast on my right arm and the pylon on my left stump: I could finally easily take a shower. It was nearly impossible to take a shower with both the pylon and the cast. I washed myself with a washcloth as best I could. After my cast was removed from my arm, I would sometimes put a plastic bag over the pylon and wrap tape tightly around my leg to keep it dry while I took a shower. But now, without the pylon and the cast, showers were much easier. Except I had to take a shower while standing on one leg; something I would have to do for the rest of my life.

Early on the morning of May 12th, I was prepared for surgery. After I was wheeled into the operating room and a nurse readied a tourniquet around my left thigh, Dr. Marti walked to my side and asked the anesthesiologist to put me to sleep. I slowly woke up in the recovery room with pain in my left leg. That was my fourth surgery since I had been wounded and I hoped it would be my last. That afternoon I was back in my bed on 5-East.

Don Chilson had told his cousin, Vicki McKee, I was having surgery. She visited me the evening after my surgery. I had gotten to know Vicki when she had taken a group of us out a couple times. While she visited me that night, I asked her if she would like to go out sometime. She said, "Yes," and gave me her phone number. I told her I would call her when I was able to get up and around again.

There were no complications to my surgery and I was transferred back to 502 a couple of days later. Most of the men I had originally met while on 5-East were gradually being transferred to 502. Don

Chilson's cast had been removed from his hip, and he was allowed to walk with crutches. Gale Bertrand faced a skin graft on his AK amputation, but he had been sent to 502 until they performed the surgery. My fellow Iowan, Rodney Wunschel and other newfound friends eventually joined me as fellow patients on 502 while they continued their recovery.

Each ward at Fitz had a ward master, whose job it was to keep the patients in line, so to speak. They usually held the rank of E-7s, Sergeants First Class, and they enforced the rules of living on the ward, made sure that we didn't let our hair get too shaggy, and they also dealt with administrative matters involving the patients. The ward master on 502 was Sergeant First Class David Alderson. He was a big, bald-headed guy with a gruff personality. If he didn't like something, he yelled at us. Although Sergeant Alderson had a gruff exterior he was a good guy once you got to know him.

While the ward master was the enforcer, like Top was in Vietnam, most of the doctors were young captains or majors who were more interested in practicing medicine than following military protocol. They didn't ask us to call them "sir" and didn't expect a salute when we met them outdoors. In fact, the doctors were sometimes the ones getting in trouble for wearing their hair too long or not following the Army's rules.

Although my first few weeks in the hospital had been somewhat agonizing and often monotonous, my life at Fitz eventually became relatively comfortable and was far different from life in the "real" Army. Although we all had suffered traumatic injuries, we enjoyed a relatively "soft" military life while we continued on our respective roads to recovery. Each weekday morning in 502 started with a 7:30 roll call. We were then left pretty much on our own, but were expected to stay on the hospital grounds during the day to attend our daily PT sessions and any appointments with doctors or other hospital staff. We wore dark blue military hospital pajamas while we were on post to identify us as patients. Those blue pajamas weren't too attractive, but they gave us certain benefits, like not having to pay to see a movie at the post theater and going directly to the front of the line when we went to the main dining hall. We could check out after four o'clock each weekday afternoon and could stay out all night as long as we were at roll call the following morning. On weekends we could check out from Friday afternoon until 7:30 Monday morning.

I called Vicki McKee during the first week in June and asked her for a date. I didn't have a car, but she was more than willing to pick me up. We went to the drive-in theater near Fitz on our first date. One weekend shortly thereafter Vicki and I visited her parents, Glen and Thelma, at their Rocky Mountain home in Estes Park, Colorado. Glen had served as a Navy Seabee during World War II. Although Glen cussed when he criticized President Nixon and Congress for the way they handled the war in Vietnam, he had a lot of respect for us guys who fought over there. Although we were a generation apart, I felt an immediate camaraderie with Glen as a fellow veteran.

As time passed, Vicki often joined me and Don, Gale, Rodney and others when we went out on evenings or during the weekends. One of our favorite outings was going to Central City, an old mining town in the mountains thirty miles west of Denver, that was mostly gift shops, restaurants and bars. Our favorite place was the "Gilded Garter," a honky-tonk bar with a band playing lively "old-time" songs the crowd could sing along with. We always drew lots of attention when we arrived with some men in wheel chairs or others on crutches with a missing leg. We appreciated the sincerity of many strangers who generously bought us a round of drinks when they learned we had been wounded in Vietnam.

The Army also took us on "outings" periodically. We went to the horse race track one afternoon, and Don, Rodney and I pooled our money and actually came out ahead. We also went to Mile High Stadium and watched the Denver Zephyrs, a minor league baseball team. One night the American Legion post in Coal Creek Canyon (northwest of Denver) invited us as their guests for a steak dinner.

I also enjoyed visits from several people from Schaller when they stopped by to see me during their vacations in Colorado. In mid-June, my sister Marilyn and her husband Gary and two year old son Tim came out to see me, and I enjoyed camping with them in the mountains west of Denver. My former high school coach Bob Keenan and his wife Barb invited me to spend a weekend with them in Fort Morgan, Colorado later that summer.

Having friends and relatives make a special effort to visit me always lifted my spirits, and being able to get away from the hospital with them helped me to realize that I would be able to continue with a near normal life despite my injuries. I began to look forward with anticipation to my eventual discharge from the hospital and moving on with my life.

After the surgery on my stump, I had to wait six weeks while they reduced its size by keeping an elastic wrap tightly bound around it. Forcing my stump to shrink before I was fitted for my prosthesis would minimize further shrinkage after I began to walk. If my stump shrank too much later on, my prosthesis wouldn't fit properly and I would require a new one. Although my stump would continue to slowly shrink for years, my first prosthesis would cost the Army approximately $1,000. They wanted to get as much "life" out of it as they could before I would need a new one. I watched some of the other guys begin to walk with their "new leg(s)," while I patiently waited for my stump to shrink so that I too could start walking again.

One day near the end of June, I picked up an Army Times Magazine that was lying in a stack of magazines in a little recreation area on 502. The Army Times listed the names of men recently killed in Vietnam in each edition. I often checked those lists, knowing I still had many friends serving there, but hoping not to see a name I recognized. I scanned down the list and read "William A. Branch, Capt., June 6, 1970."

I was stunned and read the name again. It was Captain Branch, my former company commander. He had visited me in the hospital in Cu Chi, and I could clearly remember him walking out with Lieutenant Donaldson and turning to wave good-bye to me. He was a great guy. Sadly, he was gone. I sat there for a few minutes and quietly mourned the loss of yet another comrade. I wondered how many more friends I might lose before they all ended their tours in Vietnam.

A couple of days later a sergeant in a Class-A army uniform walked toward my bed and said, "Hey, Hound Dog."

The nickname "Hound Dog" hadn't caught on around Fitz, and therefore I was surprised to hear someone calling me by that name. In amazement I realized it was Dave Hardy from the Third Herd. We both smiled and shared a handshake and hug.

On his way home to Wisconsin, he had stopped in Denver to see his brother and wanted to see me too. Dave fortunately had completed his tour in Vietnam without being wounded. Although it was great to see one of the Third Herd again, we solemnly talked for a moment regarding Captain Branch being killed. Dave said the chopper Captain Branch was riding on was shot down, and the Captain and another man were killed. Dave also told me that no one in the Third Herd had been killed after I left, but Rick Shields had been sent back to the field and was shot in the leg a second time. Maybe that was why I hadn't heard from Rick in a while.

I felt a special bond with Dave Hardy. He had been a great help to me during my first few weeks in the field and ultimately became a good friend. The comradeship that existed between us in Vietnam continued after Dave's brother drove us to his house in Denver, and Dave and I talked and relaxed that afternoon. Dave said after I left Vietnam, they stopped rotating men from the field to the rear because there weren't enough replacement troops arriving in country. Dave and most of the men who were in the Third Herd when I left had to stay in the field.

Dave and I went out that night and we ended up at a little bar called the Lemon Tree with some of the guys from Fitz. Dave and I shared a few war stories, and everyone laughed when Dave talked about the first time I jumped out of a Huey and fell on my face. Dave later stood up, put his hand on my shoulder and said, "And Sergeant Hogue was the best platoon sergeant we ever had," and raised his glass to toast me. I laughed and said, "Sit down, Hardy. You've had too much to drink."

It was great to see Dave Hardy again. We shared a farewell when he left for Wisconsin the following morning, and we vowed to keep in touch with each other.

On the first of July, Dr. Marti told me it was time to be fitted for my new leg. The Army contracted with private prosthetic firms called "limb shops" to make the new arms and legs for the patients at Fitz. I was sent to Kliber Limb Shop on East 17th street near downtown Denver. The first step in making my prosthesis was to take a plaster mold of my stump. Al Kliber pressed on the plaster as it dried to form a mold exactly the shape of my stump. The mold would be used to build a socket at the top of the prosthesis for my stump to comfortably fit into. Al also took measurements of my stump, measured my height and the approximate distance from the end of my stump to the floor and began constructing my new tailor-made leg.

A couple of days later I returned after Al had made my socket out of a hard plastic material that was temporarily set into a small block of wood. A pipe was attached to the block, with a series of adjustment bolts used to make refinements and alignments to design my permanent prosthesis. On the far end of the pipe was an artificial foot. It was a weird looking contraption.

Al gave me a heavy wool sock that I easily pulled over my stump to provide a cushion between it and the hard socket, and to make a snug fit. A thick foam pad was molded to fit into the bottom of the socket to provide additional comfort and support. I stood up and slipped my stump into the socket while standing between parallel bars. I slowly shifted my weight to my left leg. It hurt like hell.

I said, "I can't walk on this thing?"

Al said, "Don't worry, it'll feel better in time."

A small harness slipped over my knee and was held in place with a strap that wrapped around my leg to hold the socket on. I slowly took a few painful steps holding onto the parallel bars. When I identified the pressure points in the socket that caused pain, Al sanded down those areas to relieve the discomfort and more evenly distribute my weight. I continued to walk between the parallel bars for nearly an hour, and Al made adjustments to lengthen or shorten the pipe and adjust the alignment of the foot to eventually give me a comfortable stride.

A few days later my new leg was ready. The block of wood and pipe had been replaced by a solid piece of willow wood that had been contoured similar to the size of my right leg. Willow wood was used because it had the best combination of strength and weight for artificial legs. Oak would be strong but was too heavy. Pine would be lightweight but was too weak. The willow wood was covered with a cloth material which was then coated with a flesh-toned liquid plastic. It didn't quite look like the real thing, but I took it. I slipped into the leg and walked between the parallel bars. After Al sanded down a couple of pressure points in the socket, my new leg gradually became comfortable.

I wasn't able to put all of my weight on my left leg, not so much because of the pain, but because it felt like my left knee would collapse. Al said that would disappear as I regained more strength in my thigh. After a few final adjustments, I was happily on my way back to Fitz with my new leg, knowing it would be a while before I would be strolling down the sidewalks again.

During the next few days the physical therapists worked with me while I walked between parallel bars, and then graduated to walking with crutches. The PT staff showed me how to navigate up and down stairs and helped me walk along inclines and declines, which wasn't easy. Although the artificial foot had some flexibility, there was no ankle movement. Walking on anything other than a flat surface was a challenge. I worked diligently and progressed each day, gaining confidence in my ability to walk again. I still could only comfortably take a few steps without crutches, but I was happy. I was walking and wasn't too far from being on my own.

Mom called during the first week of July and asked if I could come home for Pop Corn Days. The Chamber of Commerce wanted me to be the Grand Marshal in the Saturday morning parade. I said, "Sure, if that's what they want to do."

Mom also said Dad had bought me a 1964 Pontiac. I would fly back home and then drive my car back to Fitz. I flew to Sioux City on Thursday, July 16th and spent the night with my sister Marilyn and her husband Gary. Mom drove to Sioux City Friday morning and I drove with her back to Schaller early that afternoon.

One of the first things I did when I got home was check out my car. It was a light blue four-door full-sized Pontiac and it was in great shape. The second thing I did was to find my Class-A uniform to wear during the parade. I had purchased the colorful ribbons that represented the medals I had been awarded and attached them to my uniform. When I left for Vietnam I had only been awarded the National Defense Service Ribbon – it was awarded to everyone who joined the service. However, after six months in Vietnam I had three rows of ribbons representing my two Purple Hearts, Bronze Star, two Army Commendation Medals, three Air Medals, Vietnam Campaign and Service Medals and a Good Conduct medal. I also pinned on my silver and blue Combat Infantryman's Badge above the rows of brightly colored ribbons. I was ready to proudly lead the parade.

My sister Jan was again home from college for the summer. I gave her a hug when she came home later that afternoon. After bringing my parents and sister up-to-date on my recovery, I took a spin around town in my new car and then stopped downtown.

I walked along Main Street using my crutches and was greeted with smiles, hugs and handshakes by almost everyone I saw. I soon became the main attraction as people walked up to welcome me home, happy to see me doing so well. When I later walked into the VFW Hall, I received cheers from a host of friends and soon had a cold beer in my hand thanks to someone's generosity. I answered a host of questions about my recovery and enjoyed more homecoming welcomes from everyone there.

Early that evening, I moved on to Marlys and Kenny Kroese's house where I knew a party was in progress. I was immediately greeted with more hugs and handshakes as I walked into their house. Marlys rushed in from the back yard and welcomed me with a big hug. She then said, "Follow me, I have a surprise for you."

When we reached the back yard, Marlys pointed and said, "Look who's here."

It was Allen Schwab. I heard he had gotten an early out from the Army, but hadn't seen him since I had visited him in Colorado Springs. We shook hands, and I shared a group hug with Allen and his wife Vicki. We talked about our past two years in the Army and our respective tours in Vietnam, but mostly we were happy to have survived and talked about how glad we were to be moving on.

Later that evening, Allen was looking for a partner to play yard darts. He yelled, "Hey, Hogue, get rid of those crutches and come out here and play."

With some encouragement, I left my crutches on the ground and cautiously walked out on the lawn and began playing. I was a little unsure of myself at first, and thought for sure I was going down a couple times. Playing yard darts with Allen and standing on my own two feet was a tremendous confidence builder and another literal step forward in my recovery.

I was up bright and early on Saturday morning to shave and shower and then put on my Army uniform. I hadn't worn that uniform in almost a year, but it fit fine. I walked outside and saw a red convertible waiting for me on the street in front of our house.

Each year the Chamber of Commerce selected an individual or sometimes a married couple as the Grand Marshal(s) to lead the Pop Corn Day parade. Vietnam had been on the minds of many people around Schaller, with about twenty men from the community having served or still serving there. They wanted to give me a special welcome home by honoring me as the Grand Marshal.

I sat on the back of the convertible as we drove to the start of the parade route, where I saw the Hup-Tu Squad. Glenn Woodke, my old leg repairman came up and shook my hand.

Ron Holstein and his brother Bob, David Siebricht, Bill Winkler and Bill Currie, guys I had known all of my life and who had served in Vietnam, walked over to say hello and shake my hand. It was wonderful seeing those men again and briefly sharing our newfound camaraderie as Vietnam veterans. Promptly at ten o'clock, the Hup-Tu Squad led the parade, with Glenn Woodke calling the cadence, "Hup, Two, Three, Four," to keep the men in step while they carried their rifles and the American flag that ruffled in the breeze.

I followed the squad in the convertible, riding along the parade route waving and smiling to the crowd of people who waved back at me. I felt a sense of pride I had never felt before while listening to the applause and cheers from those watching the parade. I felt the tremendous sense of caring and love that hundreds of people were expressing to me as I passed by.

One year earlier I said good-bye to my family and friends during the Pop Corn Day weekend when I left for Vietnam. But during a beautiful sunny morning on July 18, 1970, I received an unbelievable hero's welcome home from those same people. Honoring me as the Grand Marshal was the greatest tribute I could have received from my life-long friends. I was the happiest and most grateful person in Schaller, Iowa. I was truly thankful to have survived my tour of duty as an infantryman in Vietnam and to be able to return to the peaceful and friendly surroundings I had known all my life.

Although I was moving on with a positive perspective about myself, I also knew my life had changed forever, because

"For those who have fought for it, life has a meaning others will never know."

➤ First Lieutenant Craig Fielding was from Salt Lake City, UT. Craig was my platoon leader who was wounded on November 6, 1969, while we were on an ambush in the Ho Bo Woods. He was evacuated to the United States and recovered from his injuries at Fitzsimons Army Medical Center. Lieutenant Fielding voluntarily returned to Vietnam on January 21, 1970, to again serve as an infantry platoon leader. On April 1, 1970, Lieutenant Fielding was killed by an exploding booby trap. He was twenty years old. Craig is buried in Wasatch Lawn Memorial Park, Salt Lake City, Utah.

➤ Captain William Branch was from Fitzgerald, GA. Captain Branch was my Company Commander during the late summer and fall of 1969. He was killed when the helicopter he was riding in was shot down on June 6, 1970, ten days prior to the end of his tour. He was twenty-eight years old. Other members of Alpha Company and I have been in touch with his daughter Jennifer, who was two years old when her father died. William is buried in Fort Benning, Georgia. To view pictures of William Branch visit:

www.members.aol.com/JD2813/Dad.html
(type site address exactly as shown)

You may also visit the web site for Sons and Daughters in Touch (www.sdit.org), established by children of those killed in Vietnam.

➤ Fighting for their lives in Vietnam took a tremendous emotional toll on many men. Some of those men returned to the world feeling bitter, hateful or withdrawn. Rodney Wunschel, my friend and fellow patient at Fitzsimons Army Hospital, committed suicide in 1991 after the Desert Storm conflict erupted. He was forty-two years old. His mother later told me Rodney never accepted the physical and emotional trauma he endured in Vietnam. The Desert Storm conflict created a flashback he couldn't endure. Rodney hanged himself. He left a wife and one stepchild.

The Vietnam War cost the American taxpayers an estimated $155 billion. Over 1,900 Americans remain missing in action in Vietnam.

A night out from Fitzsimons Army Hospital.
Left to right - Dick Hogue, Don Chilson and Rodney Wunschel.

Epilogue

Thank You To Family, Friends and Comrades

Although the Vietnam conflict was controversial and protested by some, the people in my hometown of Schaller, Iowa, welcomed those of us who served in Vietnam with open arms when we returned. To my family and friends who wished me well and extended their thoughts and prayers for me while I served in Vietnam and to everyone who welcomed me home with hugs, kisses and handshakes, I thank you from the bottom of my heart. You helped make that difficult time of my life much more bearable and provided me with fond memories.

I thank the citizens of Schaller, Iowa, who greeted me as a hero and honored me as the Grand Marshal in the 1970 Pop Corn Day parade. I also thank the members of the Schaller Post 4704, Veterans of Foreign Wars who honored me and paid my first year's membership.

To my comrades who fought beside me in Vietnam and who shared words of encouragement after I was wounded I say, "Thank you." I will remember you men forever. And to my fellow patients at Fitz, I thank you for your encouragement and friendship as we endured the long months of recovery and rehabilitation.

1970 to 2003

I was discharged from Fitz on August 28, 1970, and spent the next month visiting Rick Shields, Dean Christiansen and other friends in California and Nevada. I was medically retired from the United States Army on October 6, 1970.

I stayed in Schaller for several months working as a bookkeeper for the Pyle Truck Line and Schaller Fertilizer Company. I thoroughly enjoyed that time with my parents while I renewed many friendships and joined in welcome home celebrations when other friends safely returned from Vietnam. I returned to Colorado in May 1971 to begin a career of service with the federal government.

In February 1972, Vicki McKee and I were married. In December 1979, our son Benjamin was born. Vicki and I divorced in 1982. In

1986, I married Marilyn McMechen, who had two sons, Monte and David. Marilyn and I both retired in 1999, after thirty years of federal employment. Today we live in Morrison, Colorado, and enjoy time with our children and grandchildren. We both work part time when we choose to and like to camp and golf when we can.

I served as a volunteer and reserve firefighter for twelve years including one year as the Fire Chief with the Cunningham Fire Department in Colorado. I am a life member of the Disabled American Veterans and a Past Commander of Chapter 21 in Aurora, Colorado. I am also a life member of the Veterans of Foreign Wars, Vietnam Veterans of America, Combat Infantryman's Association and Military Order of the Purple Heart.

My father died in December 2000, at the age of 92. My mother still lives in Schaller, Iowa. My sisters Marilyn and Jan are both married and are teachers in Iowa. My draftee buddy Allen Schwab lives in Michigan. My friends Dean and Dennis Christiansen and Marlys and Kenny Kroese still live in Iowa. Former girlfriend Jan Griffin is married and is a registered nurse in Washington State. The old Wayne State gang is spread around the country, and all are doing fine. We now talk about our kids and grandkids and the "good old days."

Most of my friends from Fitz moved on to lead active and productive lives. Gale Bertrand owns a cabinetry business in Nebraska. Don Chilson is an engineer in Texas.

I have contacted many of my former comrades and found that most of them are doing fine. They still remember me as Hound Dog.

o Richard Benson, sergeant, wounded on January 27, 1970, underwent medical care for three years, involving twenty-five surgeries to treat his multiple injuries. He was a Congressional aide for twenty years and is currently retired in Connecticut.

o Bill Casey, RTO, is a semi-retired Realtor in South Carolina.

o Steve Donaldson, third platoon leader, retired from the Army as a Lieutenant Colonel in 1990 and lives in Virginia.

o Chuck Gorman, RTO, is a retired teacher in Nebraska.

o David Hardy, rifleman, retired from a bakery firm and lives in Wisconsin.

o Kevin Higginson, second platoon leader, is a retired New York State police officer.

o Junior Houchens, rifleman, is a car salesman in Kentucky.

o Larry "Doc" Jackson retired from the Navy and lives in California.

o Ed Leberski, rifleman, is an electrician in Pennsylvania.

o Sidney "Doc" Morrison, company medic, is a teacher in California.

o Mike Myers, rifleman, has struggled with the loss of his good friend Bob Emery in December 1969. He is an office machine technician in Idaho.

o Vic Ortega, rifleman, is a carpenter in Rhode Island.

o Jim Overbey, sergeant, lives in Kentucky; however, he suffers from Post Traumatic Stress Disorder that continues to diminish his quality of life.

o Dave Phillips, third platoon leader, retired from AT&T and lives in Indiana.

o Bob Ryken, the RTO seriously wounded on December 28, 1969, struggled for many years dealing with his tour in Vietnam. He now works for the Department of Veteran's Affairs in California.

o Carl Seals, rifleman, is a truck driver in Oregon.

o Rick Shields, sergeant, is a police officer in California.

o Mertis "Doc" Snyder, third platoon medic wounded on December 28, 1969, is a truck driver in Pennsylvania.

o Michael Stark, assistant gunner and gunner, works for a telephone company in Wisconsin.

Four former members of the Third Herd have passed away since safely returning from Vietnam:

o Dennis Schultz. RTO, died in 1982 (cause unknown).

o Carlton Quick, rifleman, died of a heart attack in Griffin, Georgia, in 1983.

o John "Bugsy" Bergen, rifleman, died in 1983, (cause unknown).

o Robert Draughn, rifleman, died in 1993 (cause unknown).

Epilogue

To gain further information regarding the men in Alpha Company and to view additional pictures please visit the following web site:
www.i-kirk.info/2nd14th/2nd14th.html
I thank Kirk Ramsey, former member of Alpha Company, for maintaining that site.

I have used my experience in Vietnam, not as an excuse for failure, but as a learning experience to grow and progress through my life. I was proud to honorably serve my country as a member of the armed forces, and I hold my head high when I say, "I'm a Vietnam veteran."

I fought for my life in Vietnam and endured the tragedy of seeing comrades die in what became a futile military effort. However, I believe the greatest tragedy of the Vietnam War was that our country allowed nearly three million young men and nearly 8,000 women to serve in a politically manipulated conflict that we weren't allowed to win. The tragic lessons of Vietnam should never be forgotten. We should all pray that America will never let those events be repeated.

GOD BLESS AMERICA

Richard F. Hogue

Bibliography

The following books were a source of reference in writing *We Were The Third Herd.*

The Vietnam Experience, Boston Publishing Company, 1982, fifteen volume series detailing the Vietnam War.

The Illustrated History of the Vietnam War, Chris McNab and Andy Wiest, Thunder Bay Press, 2000, an illustrated history of the Vietnam War.

The Vietnam War Almanac, Harry G. Summers Jr., Presidio Press, 1999, analysis and reference source for the Vietnam War.

One More Mission, Oliver L. North and David Roth, Zondervan Publishing House/Harper Collins 1993, assessment of American involvement in the Vietnam War.

Dirty Little Secrets of the Vietnam War, James F. Dunnigan and Albert A. Nofi, Thomas Dunne Books, 1999, military information you're not supposed to know.

The ARMY, Army Historical Foundation, Hugh Lauter Levin Associates, Inc., 2001, history of the Army.

United States Military Almanac, Walt Lang, Salamander Books Limited, 1998, a chronological compendium of over 200 years of American history.

Schaller Centennial, History Book Committee, 1983, history of Schaller, Iowa.

Other information was obtained from numerous Internet sites regarding general military information, the 25th Infantry Division, Vietnam and the Vietnam War.

Richlyn Publishing Order Form

To order copies of *"We Were The Third Herd"* copy this form and complete the following information:

*Number of Copies	Price	Total	
_____	$17.95**	$ _____	**Colorado residents add 4.2% sales tax.
Shipping and Handling:	$ _____	$ _____	

1 Book $2.95
2-3 Books $3.95
4-5 Books $5.95

Total Amount: $ _____

(Enclose check or money order for the total amount payable to Richlyn Publishing.)

* For large orders, please email for pricing: richlyn2@msn.com
You may order from our web site at www.richlynpublishing.com

NAME: _____

ADDRESS: _____

CITY: _____ STATE/ZIP: _____

PHONE: _____

Email: _____

Mail to: Richlyn Publishing
P.O. 621893
Littleton, CO 80162-1893

Orders will be shipped by regular mail book rate within 10 business days of receipt of order.

Books make excellent gifts that can last forever.